LA CROSSE PUBLIC LIBRARY
LA CROSSE, WISCONSIN

CONQUER THE COST/SERVICE COMPROMISE

A Five-Step Program to Improve Performance and Reduce costs

CONQUER THE COST/SERVICE COMPROMISE

A Five-Step Program to Improve Performance and Reduce Costs

Rupert Booth

IRWIN
Professional Publishing
Chicago • Bogotá • Boston • Buenos Aires • Caracas
London • Madrid • Mexico City • Sydney • Toronto

To my mother and father,
Pauline and John,
who appreciated the value of their children
before counting their cost.

© Rupert J. Booth, 1995

All rights reserved. No part of this publication may be reproduced, stored in a retrieval system, or transmitted, in any form or by any means, electronic, mechanical, photocopying, recording, or otherwise, without the prior written permission of the publisher.

Originally published as *Control Your Overheads: A Practical Programme to Improve Performance and Reduce Costs* by Pitman Publishing, a division of Longman U.K. Ltd., copyright 1994.

This edition of *Conquer the Cost/Service Compromise: A Five-Step Program to Improve Performance and Reduce Costs* is published by arrangement with Pitman Publishing, London.

Senior sponsoring editor:	Amy Hollands-Gaber
Project editor:	Ethel Shiell
Production manager:	Pat Frederickson
Compositor:	PanTek Arts
Typeface:	10/12 Palatino
Printer:	**Quebecor–Kingsport**

Library of Congress Cataloging-in-Publication Data

Booth, Rupert.
  Conquer the cost/service compromise: a five-step program to improve performance and reduce costs / Rupert Booth.
    p.   cm.
  Originally published: London: Pitman Pub., 1992.
  Includes bibliographical references and index.
  ISBN 0-7863-0210-0
  1. Cost control. 2. Industrial productivity. I. Title.
HD47.3.B66 1995
658.15' 52 — dc20   94–3722

Printed in the United States of America
1 2 3 4 5 6 7 8 9 0 Q-K 1 0 9 8 7 6 5 4

Preface

Our objective is to create an organization that can deliver higher customer service at lower cost as opposed to merely seeking a compromise between customer service and cost.

The ability to design and control organizational support structures is now one of the key competencies for major corporations. These support structures are not only a burgeoning cost but their performance is also crucial to satisfying customers through quality and timeliness. Control is no longer simply concerned with monitoring departmental budgets, but involves:

- Putting in place a support structure which will benefit the organization by optimizing the processes which add value to its products and services.
- Identifying the activities undertaken, measuring their value and their cost, and relating these activities to the outputs of the organization.
- Obtaining improvements, both individually and as part of a continuous process, which depends on the right information and attitudes being present in the organization.

These benefits can be obtained through the five-step program defined in this book. The program is not prescriptive, requiring every component to be carried out, but is generic, reflecting many years' experience, in management consultancy, of specifying and implementing programs to control overhead functions. While engaged in this work, it became apparent that that many of the individual programs followed a common theme, and in the words of the source, which is quoted liberally later in the book, that "All is vanity . . . There is no new thing under the sun." On this basis it seemed possible to define a generic program.

Every book gives a view from the perspective of the author. In this case, the author is typically engaged for a short time to undertake a project during which there are a number of "deliverables." This has had several influences on the program given in this book:

- The deliverables for each step of the program are highlighted.
- There is an assumption that to control overheads requires an initial program to *bring them under control*; in other words, specific action is required, rather than gradual adjustment.
- There is an emphasis on fact, not judgment, so that potentially controversial conclusions can be objectively justified.

The array of objective techniques described is very broad, taking a view far wider than is typical when considering overhead control. In particular there is an unusual emphasis on:
- Relating the support structure to the business strategy of the organization's customers.
- Establishing the requirements of the customers of the organization, with examples given of specialist techniques such as conjoint analysis and Quality Function Deployment.
- Simultaneously considering the operational and the information technology issues of overhead control to avoid the common tendency to develop these aspects independently.
- Describing the principles of procurement as a prelude to discussing outsourcing.

On the other hand, little room has been found for some traditional topics, e.g., budgetary control. The primary reason is that since the traditional aspects of administrative control are usually in place, even in situations where the support activities are not under control, there is no need to include them within the program; also, there are so many texts on these subjects, repetition would be futile.

It needs emphasizing that hardly any of the techniques contained within this book are new. There has, however, been a deliberate transfer of expertise from:
- Product design to process design. Product design has well-developed techniques to ensure the designs are relevant to customer needs, their costs are justified by the value attached to them, and the consequences of failure are understood. These techniques are equally applicable to process design;
- Manufacturing to service industry. Manufacturing industry has established methods for improving its operations, which have already been deployed in the area of repetitive clerical operations. Now, as manufacturing operations become more complex and flexible, new techniques (some of which contradict the old) have been developed. These new techniques are especially relevant to the control of overheads.

Finally, and most importantly, I want to thank some of the many people with whom I have worked and who have shared their expertise with me. In particular Mike Fradette and Ken Parekh introduced me to the concepts of activity-based management techniques and a structured interview methodology that has influenced the "Activity Analysis" step; Mark Musgrave worked with me on developing many of the concepts of the cross-allocation of costs between products and customers and Pearse Reynolds introduced me to the concept of challenge groups; thanks also to Peter Bould, Jaysari Chaudhuri, Andy Jasnos, and Douglas Tuttle, who provided advice on the final text. Similar comments apply to many others within the group who are too numerous to name and to many managers within client companies whom I would like to mention but for maintaining the anonymity of the case studies (whose details have also been altered for this purpose). The case studies are drawn primarily from the utility and manufacturing sectors from around the world. The case studies follow the chapters describing the five-step program but do not just relate to that chapter alone.

Needless to say, any errors are my own responsibility.

Rupert Booth

Contents

Chapter One
RESPONDING TO CHANGE   1

A Changing World, 1
Technology, 5
Responses, 7
The Five-Step Approach, 12

Chapter Two
EXTERNAL REVIEW   24

Introduction, 24
Business Direction, 27
Strategy Development, 32
Business Segmentation, 37
Critical Success Factors, 39
Customer Requirements, 44
Processes, 49
Benchmarking, 57
Information Requirements, 65
Sensitivity Analysis, 75
Benchmarking Case Study, 75

Chapter Three
ACTIVITY ANALYSIS   83

Introduction, 83
The Scope of the Organization, 91
The Cost Base, 94
The Activity Map, 103
The Activity Costs, 106
Attributes and Drivers, 108
Linking Activities to Processes, 112
Tracing Costs to Cost Objects, 118

Segment Profitability, 123
Information Assessment, 125
IT Support Tools, 130
Life-Cycle Costing Case Study, 132

Chapter Four
RADICAL CHANGE 138

Introduction, 138
Assessing Priorities, 140
Process Improvement, 141
Attributes and Drivers, 151
Cost and Service Levels, 153
Process Lead-Time Reduction, 156
Process Quality, 161
Segment Rationalization, 165
Information Systems and Technologies, 167
Organizational Structure, 176
Preparing for Implementation, 180
Customer and Product Profitability Case Study, 182

Chapter Five
FOCUSED CHANGE 187

Introduction, 187
Examination of Effectiveness, 190
Efficiency Improvements, 195
Economy, 203
Market Approach to Service Provision, 212
Information Systems and Technology, 219
Preparing for Implementation, 221
Organizational Efficiency Case Study, 222

Chapter Six
SUSTAINABLE IMPROVEMENT 229

Introduction, 229
Project Management, 230
Organizational Culture, 236
Performance Measures, 243

Management Information Systems, 249
Total Quality, 253
Organizational Change Case Study, 258

Epilogue
THE THREE LAWS OF HOLES   265

References   266
Index   268

Chapter One

Responding to Change

What profit hath a man of all his labour he taketh under the sun?

ECCLESIASTES 1:3

A CHANGING WORLD

Oversupply of the Markets

For the first half of this century, there was a shortage of consumer and durable goods. In this situation, the emphasis was on production. Companies were organized so as to maximize production efficiency, and to survive a company had to have an efficient production facility relative to the competitors in its market.

In this environment the voice of the customer was not generally heard. This is perhaps epitomized by Henry Ford's comment "Any color, so long as it's black." This view is ridiculed today, but at the time it was a sound summary of the market conditions: consumers hungry for goods and grateful (usually) for what they got. At the time, the view was that those involved in the manufacture of products needed to be insulated from the customers' demands. Today this is heresy, but then it made sense: Customers change priorities, and this lowers production efficiency.

The situation has now changed. Consumers are offered a vast supply of alternative goods, but there is a limit to the amount they can consume. As a result, there are three effects:

- The original exporting nations (e.g., the United States and the United Kingdom) have come under intense competition as the new manufacturing nations (e.g., Japan) have increased their export drives, after having satisfied their own domestic markets.
- Consumers no longer view a product as a commodity. They seek differentiation of the product from similar products, which gives rise to complexity.
- Consumers seek good service; manufacturers of products have to acknowledge that they do operate, to some extent, in a similar way to a service industry. In terms of Maslow's hierarchy, consumers

FIGURE 1-1
Pressure for Change

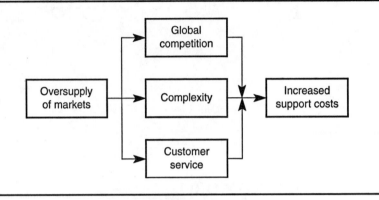

now have their physiological and security needs satisfied and are seeking the less tangible belonging and esteem needs, which are met more by service than specification.

These three effects, namely global competition, complexity and customer service, and their consequence of increased support costs are discussed below and illustrated in Figure 1-1

Global Competition

The advent of global competition is one of the main reasons for the new interest in organizational control. In the past, when markets were localized, a company only had to be as competitive as those in the locale. If a potential competitor with a better way of doing things existed elsewhere, it did not present a challenge.

This has now changed. Obviously if a company is choosing to export into a foreign market, it must be competitive in terms of cost, quality, and timeliness, compared to its rivals in that country. It is equally true for a domestic concern; while it may not have international aspirations, its customers will receive the attentions of foreign companies that do. In these circumstances, only "world-class" performance will suffice.

If all this seems too depressing, there is a positive side. Not only are there threats from overseas, there are also opportunities. If a company can attain world-class performance, its rewards will be on a global scale.

Complexity

Increased competition alone, however, would not have led to the renewed interest in the control of support activities. If companies were similar to those which prevailed during the Industrial Revolution, the emphasis would be on minimizing the cost of materials and blue-collar employees. At that time, companies offered a relatively small range of products, with long product life cycles. This had two effects:

- Administrative demands on companies were not great and therefore the administrative activities were relatively easy to control.
- Support costs were therefore not the predominant portion of cost and therefore the issue of their efficiency of operation or economy of the resources consumed was not a major issue.

The situation is now completely changed. Complexity has now permeated all levels of the business, including:

- *Markets and customers*. Different customers and markets have different requirements, in terms of buyer behavior, packaging, and distribution. Supporting this diversity within the company is costly and places large demands on the control systems of the company.
- *Products*. To differentiate themselves from competitors or to avoid focusing on particular markets and competing on price alone, the product portfolio of most companies is broadening. This obviously leads to an increase in complexity in the design and manufacturing areas, but this is only part of the infliction. Wide product variety imposes demands on forecasting, scheduling, purchasing, inventory holding, and, of course, general management time.
- *Operations*. Capital investment has greatly reduced the number of operators who are directly involved in producing a product or service but in parallel there has been a proliferation of support activities, ranging from maintenance to sophisticated scheduling. The control of an array of support activities is more demanding than a few manually intensive operations with large numbers of people doing the same thing.

In fact, this growth in complexity has progressed to the point where it must be reversed. An important part of the proposed approach to controlling support activities is the identification of the underlying reasons for complexity, namely the products and customers which cause it to happen. This is then carried forward to the quantification of the costs through activity-based costing so that a rational view can be taken on whether the revenue from a particular product or customer justifies its support; in parallel with this, opportunities for reducing complexity through reorganization often present themselves.

A further means of reducing complexity is to define the organization's business and, from this definition, understand its key competencies. The organization then concentrates on these competencies alone and contracts out the peripheral activities. In this way, the management avoids being swamped by complexity and can focus on the processes which really matter.

Customer Service

The production of a product or a service can no longer proceed protected from the demands of its recipients. As a consequence of having to increase the quality of service delivered for the various markets and customers, we see additional demands on the overhead functions from:

- More complex scheduling of operations to provide flexibility.
- The introduction of new dimensions, other than cost, to customer satisfaction, namely time and quality.

The first of these points follows the removal of the barriers between the customer and the company's operations. All other things being equal, an increase in flexibility leads to an increase in the need for support functions, though in response to this there is now a drive to rearrange the operations of organizations to make them inherently more flexible, often through the reduction of inventory and lead times.

The second point is both an opportunity and a problem. If customers are no longer simply interested in obtaining the lowest price, it is possible for the company to obtain higher prices through the provision of superior quality or delivery times. Nonetheless, competing on these additional parameters requires changes to systems and performance measures. It can also lead to a growth in administrative functions.

Increased Support Costs

Most support functions involve skilled white-collar tasks, which are usually difficult to define and consequently are difficult to measure. They require developed skills; as a result, the human resource is expensive.

The trend in productivity improvement in this area has not been encouraging. The most optimistic research has suggested that white-collar productivity can increase at a rate of perhaps 2 percent per year, though this compares unfavorably with an average blue-collar rate of increase of some 4 percent per year. However, much of the 2 percent productivity improvement is concentrated in the more mundane clerical tasks and not in the higher-skill functions. Furthermore, the disappointing increases in productivity have occurred despite large investments in information technology.

One reason for the inability of traditional approaches to deliver improvements in the skilled white-collar areas is that departments and even individuals have multiple roles. This makes pinning down what people actually do, let alone measuring and improving it, very difficult. For this reason, there is a new interest in "activity-based management" techniques which seek to closely define the activities of an organization prior to their improvement. One of these is activity-based costing, which has received particular prominence.

We now discuss the special impact of advances in technology on organizations.

TECHNOLOGY

Impact on Organizations

For administrative functions the relevant technology is, of course, information technology. The technology can appear to be a blessing; in a competitive environment, if the technology is not properly managed, the organization will be at risk from better-equipped competitors.

Advances in technology can provide incremental benefits, which arise from doing the same work more efficiently. More radically, they allow an entirely new approach to a current task or even make a task feasible, where it was formerly impossible.

Traditionally, information technology has been used to eliminate clerical work from tasks, thereby reducing staff costs, or for computation and analysis. However, when combined with advances in communication, new opportunities present themselves:

- *Better scheduling and monitoring.* It now becomes possible to plan and track the position of an item in far closer detail, perhaps through a factory or a distribution network.
- *Removal of "middle-men."* High-quality communication can remove entire stages of a process, threatening those who have created brokerage positions.
- *Reduction of lead time.* In the past, the transmission of information was time-consuming, especially over large distances. Transmission time need no longer be a major obstacle to transacting business.
- *Artificial intelligence.* This is the most recent opportunity offered by information technology, in the form of knowledge-based systems and neural networks. Information systems have always been used for the storage of data, but the drawing of inferences from these data in ambiguous circumstances is a new facility, which allows the dissemination of expertise throughout the organization.

These factors are leading to greater integration of an organization, as information is captured at one point and on one occasion and is accessible to all, no matter where they are located. Given the waste and lack of coordination associated with poor and inconsistent management information, the potential rewards are large, even if they have been elusive in the past. Some of these past failures have been due to faulty implementation, which has led to the full potential of the system not being realized. In other cases, the failure has been due to the installation of technology on top of an imperfect organizational system. To deal with the last point, the proposed program considers the organizational and information technology issues in tandem.

Shortened Product Life Cycles

Product life-cycles are shortening, as a result of:

- New product technologies superseding the old and bringing with them greater rates of innovation; for example, the displacement of the electromechanical technologies by electronic technologies, which evolve at a higher rate.
- The application of information technology to the design and development processes of traditional technologies; for example, the shortening of the product life cycles in the automotive industries.

Whatever the causes, the most immediate challenge of shortening product life cycles is to keep up. Failure to do so can be enormously costly. There is a shrinking period for which a product is viable and in a position to recoup its development expenditure. Any delay in development, therefore, has an increasingly serious effect on reducing this period, perhaps even to the point where development expenditure is never recovered.

Secondly, there is the challenge of operating the business under the new conditions. Generally, it is more difficult to ensure quality when operating under time pressure, and in many cases the previous way of operation may be untenable. In addition, shortened product life cycles usually lead to increased variety and complexity.

Shorter life cycles also have cultural consequences. They give rise to a need for increased learning and for the organization to be more adaptable.

Added-Value Crisis

The major shift in the economics of world trade is felt but often not understood in the industrialized nations. For most of this century, they were in the comfortable position of being able to buy raw materials at low prices from the undeveloped nations and add value during the remainder of the supply chain. Now, the undeveloped nations are developing and adding processing ability to produce finished goods and obtain the added value themselves. They are able to do this through advances in technology. For example, the advent of numerically controlled machines has rendered irrelevant their previous dearth of manual craft skills.

Table 1-1 shows the resultant impact on the traditional industrialized nations, in terms of the decline in added value as a proportion of gross domestic product (GDP).

TABLE 1–1
Added Value as Proportion of GDP

	1960	1971	1979	1983	1985	*Change*
France	29.1	28.5	27.0	25.2	25.4	–13%
Germany	40.3	37.0	33.8	31.3	32.3	–20%
Italy	28.6	27.4	30.6	27.1	26.2	–9%
Japan	33.9	35.2	29.3	29.1	29.8	–12%
United Kingdom	32.1	28.5	25.8	21.6	22.6	–29%
United States	28.3	24.9	23.0	20.6	20.4	–30%

Source: OECD

All nations have suffered a decline in added value as a proportion of GDP. The decline for the United Kingdom and the United States is particularly severe, perhaps as a result of their disdain for manufacturing and their belief in the "service economy": It is generally manufacturing which provides high added-value employment, and nations with a strong manufacturing sector, such as Germany and Japan, have retained a high added-value as a proportion of GDP.

RESPONSES

Overview

The impression that will have emerged from the previous section is that the world is getting to be a more complicated and competitive place. Previously, organizations were relatively simple; certainly, they may have employed large numbers of people, but these people were engaged on simple tasks that were easy to measure. Furthermore, it seemed that the demand for goods was insatiable; customers counted themselves lucky to own the products and were not too demanding in their expectations of customer service.

By contrast, today companies have to offer a wider variety of products to customers who are willing to go elsewhere if they are not satisfied, and there is no shortage of competitors to offer an alternative. As if this were not enough, the internal operations of the company are far more difficult to define. A smaller number of more expensive people carry out a variety of tasks that are difficult to monitor.

Given this shift, it is not surprising there has been a major drive to understand support functions and to bring them under control. For example, successful companies do not place a high premium on the tight cost control of direct labor; instead they raise productivity through superior design of products and services and in their use of support functions to add value.

To respond to these changes, companies must change. This is occurring on four fronts:

- *New analysis tools*, to allow the more complex overhead structures to be understood.
- *Better costing and performance measurement systems*, to ensure the new complex organizations work in unison to satisfy the customer and take full advantage of the improvement in information technology.
- *Cultural change*, to maximize responsiveness and ensure the better information systems allow delegation of responsibility to the lowest possible level to avoid needless checking and authorization.
- *Outsourcing*, to delegate nonstrategic skills out of the organization altogether to allow managers to focus on the essentials.

These four factors are sequential. The new analysis tools guide the design of the new information systems, which in turn allow changes to the way people assume responsibilities. This can be coupled with a willingness to forgo formal control and rely on trading relationships. To bring these changes about requires traditionally separate disciplines, such as marketing, activity-based costing, information technology, and human resource skills, to be combined. We now discuss the four areas listed above.

Analysis Tools

The roots of the difficulty in managing organizations are, first, a lack of understanding on how the administrative structure relates to a customer's need and, second, the inability to relate resource input to individual activities and outputs. These points are major weaknesses of the traditional control method: the annual budget. Much of a departmental manager's time is spent in the ritual of making "bids" for budgeted expenditure from the bottom, defending attempts to trim the budget imposed from the top, and finally explaining "variances" from the budget, many of which are outside his or her control.

The blindfolds in this game of blind man's bluff, which is generally performed with more panache in the public than the private sector, are impenetrable. The bid for expenditure is based on the need to maintain or increase the expenditure of a department; the function of a single department has little relevance to a customer, and therefore the value of the expenditure cannot be easily evaluated. For the same reason, when the corporate core seeks to reduce expenditure to a sustainable level, it has no mechanism for considering the relative priority of various areas and consequently applies across-the-board cuts or is swayed by personal advocacy. Finally, the inability to relate resource input to output, or even individual activities, frustrates the ability to monitor efficiency.

Much of the remainder of this book is concerned with describing a coordinated set of analysis tools to overcome these shortcomings.

Costing and Performance Measurement Systems

"You get what you measure" is a familiar adage. This should be encouraging, since it suggests that the control of the organization can be reduced to the selection of an appropriate set of performance measures, though of course life is not so simple. The reverse side of the coin is that the wrong set of measures causes havoc. Before considering the changes required to the existing information systems, it may be worthwhile to take stock of their most common problems.

The most benign problem is the simple absence of the information necessary to make decisions. In these cases, the manager cannot employ the rational approach to decision making and uses his intuition. He may often comment on the need for sound judgment or preface assertions with "I believe" or "In my opinion." Phrases such as these are sure signs of a lack of knowledge; no one says, "I believe two plus two equals four." The lack of management information in some organizations can appear bizarre to an outsider; for example, product rationalization exercises are carried out without access to product profitability information, price negotiations are carried out without access to customer profitability information, and budgets are set without reference to activity levels. Those on the inside are supported in the belief of their own judgment, though of course good judgment must be based on fact.

A further common problem is inconsistent information or information presented in an inconvenient form. The symptoms are a proliferation of inefficient and inconsistent PC spreadsheet and database applications, usually supported by manual rekeying of information. Such a situation arises when the information needs of the managers have not been assessed, and they therefore have to resort to developing their own systems. The solution is to determine the information requirements in a systematic way and invest in the technology to support coherent systems; for example, data links between the corporate systems and managers' PCs are a relatively simple way of encouraging consistency of data and avoiding manual reentry of data.

The final and the most common shortcoming in most cost and performance measurement systems is the inappropriate use of proxies. The organization as a whole will have a set of top-level targets on which the senior management measure their success; for example, return on capital and market share. These, however, cannot be used directly to measure middle management, so a different set of parameters is used; examples might include machine utilization, proportion of on-time deliveries, or budget variances. Two problems can arise from this substitution:

- The subsidiary performance targets are incompatible with top-level targets, with the result that the actions of middle management are incompatible with the aspirations of top management.
- The subsidiary performance targets are incompatible with themselves, with the result that the middle managers of the organization are not working together.

Reform of the cost and performance measurement systems begins with adopting a process perspective. Once the organization and its component activities have been related to the business processes that support customers' needs, it is then possible to define a set of process performance measures that work in unison to meet those needs; in some cases the measures will simply be the customer's eventual requirement broken down into small parts and applied to individual activities.

Furthermore, it is now possible to start defining the major decisions that have to be taken within a process for it to operate well and consequently to define the information requirements of the managers and operators. This definition of the information requirements is the first step in defining the information strategies needed to support the business process.

The cost and information systems are therefore constructed to support the processes, and their component activities, which satisfy the customer. This is in contrast to many of the existing systems that were developed to serve the organizational structure; often the boundaries of these information systems coincide with the organizational boundaries, and the performance parameters themselves are related to a narrow definition of departmental performance rather than measuring the performance which the customer experiences.

Cultural Change

It is worth bearing in mind that most of the overhead function "walks on two legs." No matter how impressive the analysis or the systems, if the employees have the wrong attitudes or are prevented from using their ability, very little will improve. In bringing about an organization where the right attitudes prevail, there are two salient principles.

The first is that the organization should be framed so as to meet the need of the customer as opposed to any functional specialization. Most problems within organizations occur at the interfaces between subdivisions. It is at these interfaces that the responsibility for actions is most ambiguous, and there is often a discontinuity between information systems. Enhancing customer service therefore requires minimizing the number of interfaces that must be crossed to satisfy a customer demand and designing a "pipeline" into which a customer demand is input and from which emerges a satisfied customer requirement.

This distinction is often expressed as a contrast between the organization represented by the internal functional hierarchy and the organization represented by the processes which traverse the organization and satisfy the customers' requirements. Moving from a functional form to a process form may seem simple in principle, but it does have a profound impact on the strengths and weaknesses of an organization and the career progression of staff:

- Functional structures encourage functional excellence, whether in accounting research, or manufacturing. Process structures encourage coordination between disciplines;
- Employees who succeed in functional organizations are those who master their chosen specialty. On the contrary, employees who prosper in a process environment are multidisciplinary and can appreciate the operation of the overall process.

A change from a functional to a process view is therefore likely to be controversial if the implications are fully understood.

The second salient principle is to push responsibility down to the lowest possible level within an organization and allow all within the organization to use their initiative to the greatest possible extent. This is in contrast to practice earlier in this century where tasks were subdivided into small components, to the point where individuals did not have a view of how their work fit into the overall picture and did not have any latitude to exercise initiative. This earlier system chose to maximize efficiency and reduce variation by very close definition of the task and the removal of individual discretion. This was appropriate to the era of mass production but creates difficulty where it is necessary to provide flexibility and deal with complexity.

Allowing staff to use their initiative permits them to respond flexibly to a more uncertain environment while minimizing additional overhead costs. In the last step of the program, we discuss the difference between "crisp" and "fuzzy" structures and where each type is most appropriate. At this stage, we simply note that the increase in complexity faced by support functions makes it less practical to use staff in a highly directed fashion and more practical to permit discretion. This trend has coincided with advances in technology which have made it possible for staff to have greater access to information, thereby increasing the potential for decisions being made at a lower level within the organization.

There are also substantial cost and lead-time savings to be obtained in avoiding the continual checking and approval of decisions taken at lower levels in the organization. Here again, technology can assist by use of artificial intelligence techniques to provide expert, on-line assistance for all employees.

We now discuss the growing trend of delegating tasks and responsibility out of, as opposed to down, the organization

Outsourcing Options

"Outsourcing" refers to the subcontracting of substantial parts of support processes. There is nothing new about subcontracting itself: there has always been a possibility of gain if the factors for subcontracting, for example, access to economies of scale in a specialized subcontractor, exceed the factors against, such as the additional cost of managing a new supplier. Subcontracting on this local level will continue to be an option.

What is new is the willingness to subcontract whole branches of activity, as long as they are not considered strategic to the business. The logic behind this move is that organizations cannot be good at everything. They should therefore focus on being good at what is essential for their success and allow other organizations to handle the rest. Often, the major advantage of such a move is that the attention of the senior management is no longer cluttered with the minutiae of administration, and therefore they can concentrate on matters of genuine importance.

The move to outsourcing has major implications for the shape and culture of the company. The company will tend to consist of a core of key employees, who call upon the services of outside companies. In some cases, the outsiders are not companies but simply freelancers, who are not viewed as being genuinely part of the organization.

The risks and benefits are therefore apparent. Management attention is more focused, but there is a risk of loss of control over quality as the organization becomes dependent on those it does not care for and who do not care for it.

THE FIVE-STEP APPROACH

Project Focus

It is possible to consider the task of creating new information for the control of support activities as either a specific project or as part of the ongoing tasks of a designated department. There are several advantages in creating a formal project, which include the following:

- Projects have an end. Therefore, there is an expectation that the improvement will be delivered by a specific date, rather than begin to appear gradually. This generally improves the probability of delivery.

- High-level backing can be given. The work will require the time and cooperation of many people, which may not be granted if the project has not been given conspicuous backing within the organization.
- Wide involvement becomes possible. A project team can be formed by drawing from across the organization. This ensures both ownership of the results and a wide contribution to the input.

Continuous Improvement

If a project approach is adopted, a natural question is whether it is intended to deliver a single improvement or to be part of a process of continuous improvement. The answer is that these two objectives are not mutually exclusive.

Where there has been an absence of information to control an organization effectively, it is natural that there is latent potential for saving; usually it is the knowledge that this latent saving exists that is both the motivation and the justification for carrying out the program. The justification is necessary, since the provision of better information is not without its cost, and there has to be a belief that the project will be financially viable. The latent saving represents a single improvement.

During the initial project, sound information on which to base decisions will have been produced. A natural consequence of better information, especially that which bridges departmental boundaries and focuses on the processes that serve customers, is that those who base decisions on the information will start to think and act in a different way. There is no better vehicle for cultural change than new information. Managers and employees adapt very rapidly to the performance criteria on which they are measured, and act accordingly.

The Program

One approach for a book on controlling overheads would be to set down the major principles, grouped by technical area; readers would then apply these principles to their own situation. The disadvantage to this approach is that even after reading all the text to gain a rounded view, a major hurdle would exist, namely to apply the understanding of the principles of overhead control to the planning of a set of tasks to achieve it. It is this translation from concept to practice which is usually the greatest difficulty in the application of knowledge.

To avoid this problem, the approach put forward in this book has been arranged into a sequence of steps in a program. In this way, the description of the concepts has been directly linked to their implementation. Five steps have been identified; at each step, we identify the objectives of the phase, the deliverables, and the major issues. We then describe in detail the tasks which need to be carried out and the tools to be used.

FIGURE 1–2 *Five-Step Program*

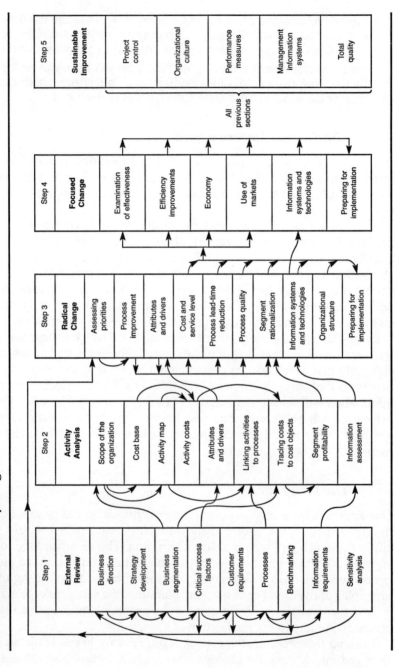

The program is a generic one, formed from the experience of numerous projects carried out in the public and private sectors. Not every task in the program needs to be executed, but the general approach is surprisingly universal. It is equally relevant whether the project seeks short-term or long-term benefits. It applies both to projects which have simple cost reduction as their objective and to those which have wider ambitions for a major performance improvement.

We now describe the five steps and logic behind their sequence. The program is illustrated in Figure 1–2, which also shows the main flows of information between the steps.

Outline of Steps

The five subsequent chapters describe the approach in detail. Each chapter details one step:

- *Step 1, External Review.* In bringing overheads under control, it is essential to consider the value of activities as well as their cost. An activity's value cannot be considered in isolation: Its value derives from its relevance to the business strategy and from its part in a business process, which in turn exists to satisfy a customer requirement. Therefore, the first step is to understand the fundamentals of why an overhead exists and the broad business processes which deliver satisfaction to customers.
- *Step 2, Internal Analysis.* Once the external assessment is complete, the next stage is to understand in close detail the activities which take place within the organization. Conventionally, organizations measure and describe themselves in terms of departments, but this description needs to be extended to obtaining an understanding of the actual activities that are undertaken. Acquiring an activity-based view of the corporation is absolutely necessary for the rational control of support activities.
- *Step 3, Radical Change.* Following from an understanding of the external demands on an organization and its internal activities, there will emerge options for comprehensive changes in the way whole processes are structured and the portfolio of products and services which is offered. These options need to be explored to identify benefits that accrue from a major alteration in the overhead structure.
- *Step 4, Focused Change.* Not all available improvements will involve widespread change. Once the overall shape of the organization has been determined, there will remain many opportunities for making gains in value for money through incremental improvements in effectiveness, efficiency, and economy within particular parts of the organization or through the use of markets.

- *Step 5, Sustainable Improvement.* Project planning is undertaken to prepare for implementation. Barriers to effective implementation are also considered; for example, poor corporate culture or inappropriate performance measures.

While these steps form a natural sequence, there are different possibilities of ordering the program, which are discussed in the next section.

Sequence of Steps

In bringing organizations under control, one possible sequence is to define the objectives of the organization, its customers, their requirements, and the business processes which must be provided to support these requirements. From this fundamental definition of the purpose of the organization, the component activities are defined and the level of resources set, and finally an organization structure is put in place.

A less radical approach is to begin with the present organization, make improvements in the existing arrangements and, after these have been achieved, to question whether a more radical approach is then required.

The first approach has the advantage of being the more logical and of having the potential to generate far greater savings, since there is not the danger of being heavily influenced by previous practice. The approach does, however, involve a greater degree of abstraction than the second approach. As a result, the project team has a more difficult task in conveying its ideas to the managers of the existing organization; in the extreme this can lead to a rejection of the proposals on the grounds they are "too theoretical," though it would be more accurate to describe them as "too unfamiliar."

The second approach would appear to the organization as more down-to-earth. Familiar language and departmental structures will be examined and improvements proposed. Furthermore, since the proposals for change will be less radical, they will be capable of implementation more quickly. The big drawback is that only incremental improvements will be forthcoming, and any major gains that may have been possible through changing the basic principles of operation will go undiscovered.

The five-step methodology, taken in its natural order, tends more to the first method, though it seeks the best of both worlds. Immediately after taking the global view in the first step, the second step involves a thorough review and costing of the organization's activities, before any proposals for change are made. Early on in the project, therefore, the project team will have acquired a great deal of information on the current

The Five-Step Approach

organization, and this will help ensure that any radical proposals are made with a full understanding of the current activities and their impact on the organization.

When proposals for change are made, Step 3, Radical Change, should precede Step 4, Focused Change, because some of the more radical ideas generated may make some potential local changes irrelevant. However, if a more limited exercise is appropriate to the reader's own organization, the initial work could lead from Step 2 to Step 4.

Alternatively, Step 3 and Step 4 could proceed simultaneously. This has the advantage of providing evidence of some early benefits to justify belief in the project. The simultaneous operation of the two steps reduces the chance that any local improvements generated will be incompatible with the more radical proposals. The drawback is that the organization now would have two independent initiatives taking place at the same time, and there would be room for confusion and overload of the organization's management as a result.

The different sequences are summarized in Figure 1–3.

FIGURE 1–3
Alternative Program Sequences

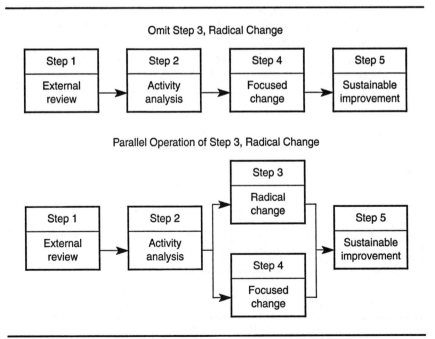

Program Timing

The program usually involves about four months of intensive effort before the start of implementation. This period would be sufficient to analyze an organization of several thousand employees and represents a natural balance between ensuring sufficient time for digesting the information and the risk of a loss of momentum. A typical program phasing is shown in the bar chart in Figure 1–4; however, there can be wide variation from this typical case. Below, we discuss the assumptions underlying the bar chart:

- *Step 1, External Review.* If the appropriate corporate strategy and market research work is in place, the external review can be completed very rapidly—in a week or two—since the only task is the collation of information. If the basic information does not exist in a usable form, it will need to be collected. There is a case for this being undertaken before the launching of the full project team, since both the corporate strategy and the market research would involve lengthy analysis, and the project team would have little to do while the information was being gathered.

- *Step 2, Activity Analysis.* This is a highly intensive part of the program, during which most of the information needed to make subsequent improvements is gathered. The key to success is to gather detailed information across the breadth of the organization and to relate it to an activity framework. The time taken can vary with the size of the organization, though a duration of four to six weeks can be expected.

- *Step 3, Radical Change.* This is the first creative stage in the program, where the external and internal views are brought together to identify where major improvements can be made. The idea generation

FIGURE 1–4
Program Timing

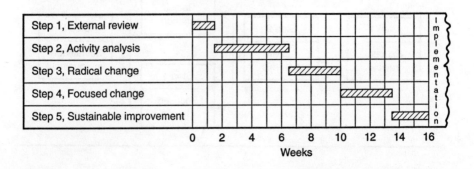

and consultation phase is likely to take three to four weeks, before the more promising ideas are developed to the point where they can be taken over by task forces responsible for implementation.
- *Step 4, Focused Change.* The ideas for improvement generated in this step will be smaller in scope but more numerous. Developing the ideas and obtaining consensus with the departmental managers of the practicality of the changes is likely to take three to four weeks.
- *Step 5, Sustainable Improvement.* This step involves defining the structures and systems to monitor the changes. The project team must hand over the project to the company's management. This may take two to three weeks before the team can be dissolved. The implementation follows and, depending on the changes proposed, may take months or years.

The largest effort is expended in Step 2 because this is the phase in which the organization is analyzed in detail. Thoroughness at this stage ensures proposed savings and benefits are realistic.

Sponsorship

A project to bring support structures under control is best led from outside the finance function. Since the finance function is the source of most of the current quantitative information, it may appear to be the natural choice for leadership of the program. There are, however, disadvantages and it is often better to choose a sponsor from the marketing or operations area of the organization, for the following reasons:

- There is likely to be dissatisfaction with the current information provided by the finance function, and this is less likely to translate into doubt over the proposed project if the sponsor is from elsewhere.
- The finance function is often viewed as the corporate police, and if the project is run from this function it could be misinterpreted as an attempt to collect more information with which to criticize operational employees.
- More use is likely to be made of the information by marketing and operational managers if it is viewed as their own, and this is more likely to occur if the project is led by the operational managers themselves.

However, regardless of who leads the project, the project team needs to be drawn widely, and include both operational and finance staff.

Project Team

We now consider the complement of skills that need to be present in the team for it to function well. A further dimension is the role each member prefers to play in a team. Readers interested in this topic should refer to the "Organizational Culture" section of Chapter 6.

A broad mix of skills is essential. Most of the ideas for improvement will arise because, possibly for the first time, there has been an in-depth review of all the functions of the organization simultaneously. For the review to retain credibility the project team needs to be well versed in the major functions. This will always include the marketing function and operations.

The other necessary skill is a familiarity with the accounting systems. Not only will there be a need to manipulate a large quantity of accounting information, but the results of the work will need to be fully credible with competing interests within the organization, and the accounting systems are usually viewed as the statement of record.

Therefore the minimum complement of skills is marketing, operations, and accounting. This is consistent with the minimum recommended size of a project team, namely three including the project leader. Larger organizations require larger teams, though in the author's experience, a team of more than six can become unwieldy, and it may be advisable to subdivide the work. After the project and during implementation, the number of employees involved in creating change may grow considerably.

It is also a great advantage if a senior person within the team can come from outside the organization. Many of the issues that need to be addressed will have a history within the company, and the presence of an outsider on the team can reassure the managers that even-handed treatment will be applied.

Impetus for Change

For the implementation phase to succeed, after the program itself has concluded, there has to be an overriding pressure to act. Sometimes this is the desire to exploit a new opportunity; more commonly, it is a reaction to pressure to change and improve.

Without this impetus, there is a danger that the implementation will falter, regardless of the quality of the analysis. Usually there are losers as well as winners in any change, and the determination of the former may exceed that of the latter. Even if there are no serious disadvantages to any party in the proposed change, sheer inertia and preference for the familiar can obstruct any serious improvement.

Therefore, during the program, an assessment has to be made of whether the managers consider the need for change to be paramount. If this is not the case, there must be an initiative to persuade them otherwise.

Hostile Environment

The question arises as to whether the program can be made to operate in a hostile environment. The answer is that it can work, but the scale of the improvements is likely to be far smaller. Many of the improvements come about from suggestions from within the organization itself. If managers hold back or operate according to hidden agendas, fewer benefits will arise. However, if the objectives are mainly concerned with cost reduction, it is possible to achieve them in the teeth of opposition.

It must be stressed that this is far from ideal, so a great effort needs to be made at the start of the project to win over the management of the company and convince them that their long-term interest is best served by cooperating.

Ancillary Structures

If the project team works in isolation within the organization, it will fail. Four types of structure need to be created during the project, the first two at the start of the project and the final two towards the end. The two groups to be created at the start are:

- *A control structure.* The manager of the project team needs to report either to the chief executive personally or to the board of directors. The senior level is necessary because of the significance of the changes which will be produced.
- *A steering group.* The middle management of the organization needs to be kept informed of progress, and the project team needs an independent view on the direction it is taking. These needs are best met through a steering group, meeting perhaps every two to three weeks during the project. The steering group is made up of middle managers from the major functions within the company.

While the project team will be soon become immersed in their own work and, if all goes well, become a cohesive unit, the overall success of the project depends on the receptivity of the organization. A good reception depends on the two groups defined above being confident of the worth of the project. The implication for the project manager is clear: There is a need to resist the temptation to become totally involved in the details of the project and devote time to building confidence in the project within the organization.

The two groups to be created towards the end of the project are:

- *Task forces.* The advantages of the intensive project approach have already been highlighted. The drawback is that, after the project has

finished, the team is dispersed, and there are no lasting benefits. The key to a successful transition is to set up groups dedicated to carrying forward specific initiatives. The task forces are formed by managers who are affected by, and can affect, the proposed transition.
- A *monitoring authority*. There is a need to monitor both the performance of the task forces as they implement the widespread changes and that of the departmental managers as they manage the changes within their own area. Ideally, this monitoring authority is the chief executive.

It is generally far more difficult to successfully implement change than to identify the opportunities and to develop the necessary project plans. Implementation requires a far wider participation, and there will inevitably be some who prefer the status quo and resist change.

A summary of the relations between the project team and the ancillary structures is shown in Figure 1–5.

Relation to Business Process Reengineering

This program for controlling overheads has not been termed a business process reengineering approach, though it may serve as one. "Business process reengineering" is a widely used term and, as is usual in these situations, it is used to mean different things. However, there are three common themes to the approach, namely the need to change:

- The entire organization significantly. The environmental changes described earlier are so significant that for most companies a small or incremental response is not an option. The major changes that are required will affect all functions of the company and lead to a radically different way of doing business, sweeping away the previous methods which were the result of gradual evolution as opposed to optimal design.

FIGURE 1–5
Ancillary Structures

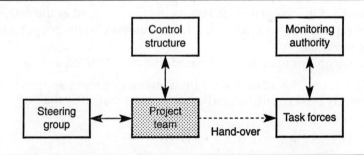

- Functional hierarchies. Existing hierarchies have evolved into functional departments that encourage functional excellence but which do not work well together in meeting customers' requirements; in particular, they incur excess cost, are too slow, and create quality problems by creating interdepartmental interfaces.
- Fragmented staff roles. Roles have become specialized, with the result that staff are only responsible for a small part of a global task. This can result in loss of accountability for a finished task, deskilling of work, the need for highly complex scheduling systems, and the use of sequential working patterns, which create further interfaces.

The five-step program tackles all of these issues. Whether the program is used to effect business process reengineering depends entirely on the reader: The more radical the change contemplated in Step 3, the more the result will tend to business process reengineering.

For those already following a prescribed business process reengineering methodology, the techniques given in this program should be useful. In particular:

- The program transfers many of the techniques proven in product design to process design and thereby helps avoid the "Now a miracle happens" step that is characteristic of many reengineering methodologies.
- The activity-analysis methods outlined in Step 2 relate the abstract top-level processes to the real organization. This relation can be a severe problem in business process reengineering.

In conclusion, full compatibility with business process reengineering is assured, though the five-step program covers only the preparation for implementation, as opposed to implementation itself.

Chapter Two

External Review

Cast thy bread upon the waters: for thou shalt find it after many days.

ECCLESIASTES 11:1

INTRODUCTION

Objectives

The overall objective of Step 1, External Review, is to look outside the organization and confirm the viability of its objectives and strategies. We begin by clarifying the objectives of the organization, hopefully drawing upon previous business strategy, and expressing the objectives as a set of targets. Once the target markets and products have been clarified, the next objective is to define the customers, channels, and products of the company. The critical success factors, upon which the ability of the organization to fulfill its objectives depends, are then defined and quantified, as far as possible, into the level of performance customers require in these areas.

The business processes which are to deliver the required performance are identified and a search made for examples of best practice in these business processes, often referred to as benchmarks. The decisions which have to be made within the processes are examined and these lead to a top-down review of the information needs and the information systems and technologies available on the market which can assist in decision support.

Finally the sensitivity of decisions to changes in the business or technology is examined to understand the possible impact on the external review.

Deliverables

In meeting the objectives given above, the project team will have carried out the tasks shown in Figure 2–1 and described in subsequent sections. These tasks will generate the following information, which will be used in subsequent steps:

Introduction

FIGURE 2–1
Step 1. External Review

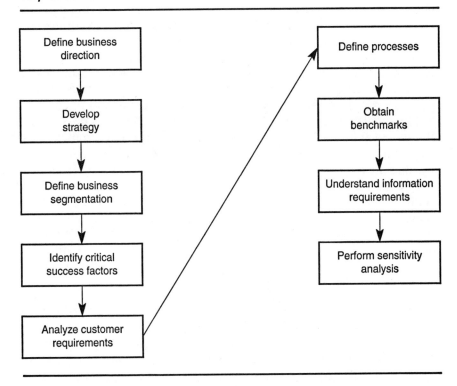

- A business direction.
- Confirmation of a business strategy.
- The business segments, in terms of customers' groups, products (or services), and distribution channels.
- A statement of the business's critical success factors.
- An analysis of customer requirements.
- A set of core business processes.
- Benchmarks showing the level of performance expected in the processes.
- The information required to support the decisions to be taken within the process.
- An assessment of the effects of possible changes in business and technology.

Issues

The first part of the external review draws upon information that should have been produced by a strategic planning exercise, namely a statement of business objectives and targets, a segmentation of the business, and a statement of the critical success factors. In practice, this may not have been carried out sufficiently thoroughly prior to the start of the project; correcting any shortfall will make heavy demands on the senior management within the organization.

Analyzing customer requirements obviously requires some contact with these customers, both through market research and through discussions with major customers. This is essential, even if there is some reluctance to provide access to customers. The statement of customer requirements should be as detailed and as quantitative as possible, but the practical limitations have to be recognized; if no preliminary work has been done in this area, the team will have to settle for a brief statement of the major factors, deduced from a few interviews.

The identification of the major processes is done in conjunction with senior management, either individually or as a group. The object is to name the processes and delineate their boundaries. The collection of benchmarking information would need the involvement of senior management, both to agree on the form of the exercise and to enter into agreement with the benchmarking partners. However, if this has not been begun before the start of the program, it is unlikely that completing the exercise in the available time will be practical.

The identification of the major decision-making areas and their information requirements follows. It might be thought that considering the information requirements of the company before even learning of its detailed activities in Step 2, Internal Analysis, is premature. There are, however, four advantages of obtaining an early top-down view:

- The practicality of the proposed definition of processes can be confirmed. By examining the necessary decisions to support the processes and their information needs, any ambiguity or overlap will be exposed.
- The project team can form an assessment of the information that is ideally required independently of current practice.
- For many processes, there are systems commercially available to provide support. These systems provide a view on outside best practice and are a source of ideas with which to challenge the current views of the organization.
- The state of relevant information technologies can be understood. These could have a dramatic effect on the design of the processes, and awareness of these developments may change the emphasis of the internal analysis.

For example, a process may benefit from the use of forecasting. Currently, the company may make little use of forecasting, and in the absence of this information, the advantages are not understood. If the external review showed that trends in technology were permitting better and cheaper forecasting, perhaps through the use of knowledge-based systems, forecasting would be an issue to be explored during the internal analysis. At this stage, however, we are only seeking an overview; the detailed analysis of information requirements is to be carried out in Step 2.

Finally, we need to ensure that any proposed organizational or systems solution is relatively robust to future changes in either the firm or its environment; we therefore include a brief sensitivity analysis.

BUSINESS DIRECTION

Terminology

We now discuss the steps involved in setting objectives. The steps used are mission, goals, and finally the objectives themselves. These terms are commonly used, often with different meanings. For our purposes, we adopt the definition given in *Power in and around Organisations* (Mintzberg, 1983) namely:

- The mission of a company is its basic purpose, its reason for existence. It gives long-term guidance and is usually not quantitative.
- Goals are the broad criteria against which the company judges its decisions. The goals are the principles which guide the organization.
- Objectives of the company are derived from the goals but in a form that is quantifiable and measurable.

We then conclude with a discussion on the use of targets.

The Mission

A new emphasis is being placed on corporate mission. This is a reaction to the situation which developed in the 60s and 70s, where a remote corporate planning function would make investment and divestment decisions without reference to the managers responsible for the operating businesses. The result was frequently a collection of businesses with little in common and led by management who had very diverse objectives.

This situation is tolerable if the subsidiaries are intended to be self-contained and are viewed simply as capital investments, intended to produce a rate return. At some level in the organization, however, either at the top of the company or at each of its self-contained subsidiaries, there has to be a sense of common purpose and understanding. Without one, it will not be possible to run the organization as a coherent unit. It is insufficient, for example, for the chief executive to rely on written directives because, while a written directive may not be overtly disobeyed, it can usually be circumvented. For this reason, it is necessary to create a common mission for the organization; of course some individuals will still pursue their personal aims, but at least this will be more evident when the corporate mission is properly clarified.

Where a mission only exists informally, or does not exist at all, it is necessary to articulate one. The chief executive will normally have views on the future of the company. These are the natural starting point. Missions vary dramatically according to personal and corporate circumstances and may encompass:

- *Sustainability*. This is common among leaders of substantial corporations in mature industries. The desire is to preserve the substance of the corporation. This set of values is also common among the middle management of large companies, where the primary concern is for career development and security. While this mission may be appear comparatively modest, in practice it appears to almost be unobtainable. To illustrate, the top 10 companies in the world today differ considerably from those of 50 years ago, the duration of a working career. The implication is that simply "being there" is a futile mission.
- *Preeminence*. Many companies pay lip service to this mission, but it is less prevalent than claimed because it requires a deferment of reward to allow investment for the future. For a company seeking to be preeminent, this will take time. This is incompatible with aiming a short-term view, whereby profits are made and distributed. There are two implications:

    Generally, economies which permit a longer-term view to be taken are more successful. For example, the Japanese and German economies, where companies are disciplined by long-term relations with banks, are more successful than those economies disciplined by the stock market, such as the United States and the United Kingdom.

    Specifically, the level of expenditure on corporate development will differ radically between a company which is genuinely seeking preeminence and is therefore deferring reward, and one which reacts to short-term financial pressures. We will return to this topic when we discuss the subject of targets.

- *Financial performance*. This is a very common mission for a public company; it does not relate to physical or operational characteristics, rather to financial proxies. These proxies are usually concerned with the short term and may include profitability, dividend payment, earnings per share or return on capital employed. Unfortunately, a mission of financial performance is inadequate for all business other than holding companies. The mission does not provide a sense of direction; a minimum financial performance is better thought of as a constraint.

Once the chief executive has articulated his own perception of the organization's mission, it can then be discussed among the managers and staff until agreement is reached. Eventually, it should be announced, so all in the company are aware of it. Before this is done it needs to be developed into sets of goals and objectives, to confirm that it is attainable.

Goals

The goals of the company will depend upon a company's mission; for example, if the mission of the company is preeminence, the goals will differ from a company seeking sustainability. In specifying the goals, it is necessary that if all the goals are satisfied then the mission of the company will have been achieved.

Goals can be qualitative and remain useful. The purpose of the goals is to provide a sense of direction by acting as criteria against which to make decisions. As long as there is sufficient clarity of the goals to indicate whether a particular decision will move the company nearer the goals or further away, this is sufficient. For example, a goal may be "To provide the most advanced product portfolio available in the world"; this will provide guidance on whether it is necessary to undertake a particular development program.

Objectives

Clear goals are necessary to give direction to the company, but they are not sufficient because they are typically too abstract. The next step is therefore to translate the goals into a series of objectives, which are more specific than goals. In drawing up a set of objectives, it is essential to ensure that:

- They are framed such that if all the objectives have been met, then the goals will have been attained;
- They are achievable. If this is inconsistent with the previous condition, the goals of the organization need to be refined, since they too will be unattainable;
- They are measurable and quantifiable. If this is not the case, it will not be clear whether an objective has been met or not.

If the business objectives have not been refined to this degree, this needs to be done prior to the start of the exercise. For public sector organizations this will involve a process of self-examination of what the organization can best achieve given the needs of its prospective clients and the facilities offered by other agencies. For the private sector, the emphasis is on seeking a viable competitive position. This is not a trivial task; for those starting from scratch, this topic could easily be the subject of a separate book. However, in the next section we provide a brief overview of the factors to be considered in defining a set of objectives for a private sector organization, to allow the reader to check the thoroughness of the process by which the organization's objectives have been derived and to make enhancements wherever possible.

Before this, we conclude the discussion on objectives by considering target-setting, which ensures a gradual progression towards their attainment.

Targets

The targets given to the managers of the organization are usually a major influence on their actions. Furthermore, the nature of some common targets can impede corporate development. Problems seldom arise with nonfinancial targets directly derived from the objectives of the company, since the objectives are closely linked to the company's mission and goals. The problems usually arise when financial proxies are used to measure performance, as opposed to measuring physical parameters directly. Financial targets are of three types:

- Liquidity targets, which aim to ensure there is sufficient cash in the business for it to continue in the *short term*. Adequate cash levels is the major short-term concern of any organization;
- Profitability targets, which address the *medium-term* requirement for sufficient profit to fund future developments;
- Investment targets, which measure the degree to which the money invested in the company, by either shareholders or lenders, is providing an adequate *long-term* return.

The liquidity targets can influence the pace at which market or product development can take place; however, there is not usually a tension between the short-term liquidity targets and corporate development itself.

The profitability targets fall into two categories. The first category recognizes the value of products and services to a customer and seeks to balance cost against revenue; examples include:

- *Profit, earnings per share, or dividend payment*. This is the most common situation for a profit center or for a company where the owners have expectations of sufficient earnings to guarantee a dividend payment. This provides a sharp short-term pressure to increase revenue or, where this is not possible, to reduce costs.
- *Added value*. This measure is common in retail operations, where the merit of the operations is taken as the value added to the inputs expressed as a proportion of revenue. It has far wider relevance, both to nations and companies: The rate at which value is added by an activity determines the rate of remuneration that is available to those engaged in it.

The second category considers cost alone; for example, annual cost. This particularly applies to cost centers within private organizations and to public organizations where revenue is difficult to identify. A variation on this is cost per unit of output which seeks to place a target on operational efficiency.

The first category clearly leads to a better future; however, unfortunately the regressive second category is the more common! A very typical situation occurs when the directors of a company realize halfway through the year that they will not achieve planned earnings or be able to pay planned dividends and search for a means to make substantial reductions to the cost base, often with new product development being high on the list. The assumption is that, for the relevant time span, revenue cannot be improved upon, and therefore the only course is to cut costs by a specified amount. However, a warning needs to be sounded against placing primacy on revenue and volume indiscriminately. To illustrate, assume a company operates at a 10 percent net margin, and all costs are variable:

- A 10 percent reduction in costs will increase profit by 90 percent (from 10 percent of revenue to 19 percent);
- A 10 percent increase in volume, assuming constant prices, will increase profit by 10 percent;
- A 10 percent increase in volume, obtained by a 10 percent decrease in prices, will lead to a 100 percent reduction in profit (i.e., remove it entirely).

The moral is that increased revenue should come about through increased added value, as opposed to a simple volume increase, especially if obtained through a price reduction.

The long-term financial performance targets seek to capture the efficiency with which capital is utilized, which is often measured by:

- *Return on capital.* This is the most common measure, though is criticized for discouraging capital investment by penalizing investment in both the numerator (profit is lessened by depreciation) and the denominator (the capital employed rises).
- *Residual income.* This is the operating profit, net of capital charges. This encourages investment where the increase in profit from an investment is sufficient to counteract the capital charge.
- *Value of the firm.* Theoretically, this target should equate to the present value of future earnings and be independent of the policy on the distribution of earnings; though, certainly for minority shareholders, share price and hence the value of their holding is dependent on dividend policy. Practically, however, a firm can be valued differently according to the purposes the purchaser wishes to make of it.

Although the first two targets consider long-term performance, their weakness is that they measure the firm at the present moment. Both of these "long-term" measures can still be improved by cost-cutting and divestment, which will nonetheless damage the long-term performance. The third target should avoid this and rise if the rate of return on an internal investment is in excess of the current cost of capital; however, it is difficult to measure in the absence of a sale. Share price is not a surrogate (except for small minority shareholders), since share prices reflect the current price for small quantities of shares as opposed to the company as a whole.

It is essential that the framework of corporate targets is understood and, if necessary, developed by the project team. The time-scales associated with the targets are also crucial. Targets requiring savings and improvements to occur in the near future place a far greater pressure on the project team to deliver hard proposals, since there is no intervening period for local management to develop the ideas. The short time-scales can be a two-edged sword, particularly where cost reduction is involved. On the one hand, the short time available to deliver provides impetus to provide real results, but on the other it can destroy any prospect of cooperation within the company if managers feel their interests will suffer as a result of the exercise.

Often managers within the organization are keen to acknowledge savings in the distant future but not in the present; this should not be encouraged. A saving or an improvement achieved early is far more useful than one achieved later. This is not only the case because the net present value of the cash flows is greater, but, more to the point, savings and improvements which are projected to occur in the distant future usually do not happen. There will often be an intervening reorganization or staff change which will destroy accountability for achieving the improvements.

Finally, when the project is announced to the organization, the announcement should link the project to the attainment of specific corporate objectives and targets. In this way, the management can place the project in the context of the business plans which the organization is working to achieve.

We now consider a process which can develop these objectives and targets, if this is required.

STRATEGY DEVELOPMENT

Defining Competitive Position

The starting point for determining a viable competitive position is defining the market the company intends to operate in. Even the step of actually identifying the market can be difficult, with the danger that the company defines its market in the narrow terms of the product being offered (i.e., the means to an end), while customers take a wider view, including the use of radically different means to obtain their desired end. Sometimes this broader view of competitive alternatives can be used by the company itself; for example, ferry operators facing competition from a high-speed rail link seeking to position their service as the first stage in the holiday experience, as opposed to simple transportation.

Once the market itself has been defined, the next step is to clarify its structure. One accepted format for this analysis has been provided in *Competitive Strategy* (Porter, 1980), which described industry as influenced by five sets of forces:

- The power of suppliers, bargaining for the highest prices for the factors of production.
- The power of customers, attempting to minimize the costs of goods and services produced.
- The threat from new entrants to the industry.
- The threat from substitutes for the products and services.
- The pressure that exists from the intensity with which the members of an industry compete.

Overlaying this analysis of competitive forces is the operation of the regulatory and legal structure and less formal social pressures, which can sometimes be the dominant short-term influence on an industry, whether through manipulation of tariff barriers, employee legislation, antimonopoly actions, environmental legislation, or simply disdain for certain types of goods.

These factors affect the conditions of supply and demand within the industry and ultimately determine the rates of return on capital that are possible. Using these factors, a "snapshot" can be taken, and from this projections made of the following:

- Change in the size of the demand from the markets in which the company operates, both as a result of changes in the actions of buyers and the economic cycle.
- Productive capacity capable of supplying to the market, including the effect of new competitors or substitute products.
- Opportunities and threats presented by takeovers, particularly through integration and the removal of intermediaries.
- Implications of new technology. Part of this will be concerned with the appearance of more advanced or substitute products or advances in information technology.

The preceding analysis is concerned with the external environment. To complete the exercise, it is useful to consider the internal strengths and weaknesses of the organization. This entails considering the stock of

FIGURE 2-2
SWOT Analysis

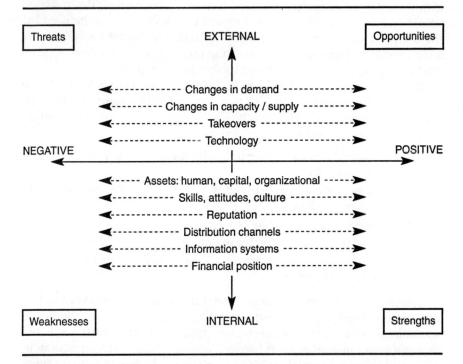

human, capital and organizational assets the organization possesses, and those assets it is lacking. The scope of this assessment is as wide as the organization itself, but as a minimum would include key skills, staff attitudes and culture, presence and reputation in markets, distribution channels, information systems, and financial position.

All this analysis can then be summarized in the form of a Strengths/Weaknesses/Opportunities/Threats (SWOT) analysis, shown in Figure 2-2, to provide an understanding of how the organization stands in its environment. From this analysis and an appreciation of the constraints of the organization, a business strategy can be developed which will either meet the business objectives or lead to their modification.

The strategy has to be confirmed at the highest level within the organization, and gaining agreement can be difficult. Ideally, the organization will have already carried out a strategic planning exercise, and any changes needed will simply be an amplification of detail. Once the strategy is in place, it can be cascaded down into sets of plans, and then into specific actions required for its deployment. First, however, we discuss the impact of information systems and technology.

Impact of Information Systems and Technology

One tenet of the proposed program is that the organizational issues should be considered in tandem with the information issues for the effective design of overhead structures. This is opposed to the typical arrangement where they are considered separately.

The consideration of the information issues begins at the very start of the program, namely the clarification of the business objectives. The impact of information systems and technology on the competitive position of the company can be assessed using Porter's five-force model as a basis. This was explored in "Using IS/IT to Gain Competitive Advantage" (Peppard, 1993). If this format is employed, the issues can be summarized as follows:

- *Suppliers.* Information technology enables a wider and more rapid evaluation to be made of alternative suppliers. Once a supplier is selected, it permits a tighter integration of both the design and operating functions by increasing the volume and speed of information transfer, thereby enabling new alliances to operate.
- *Customers.* The investment in electronic links can be a double-edged sword; it also has the effect of "locking in" customers to their suppliers. Therefore, it can be an advantage for a company to approach its customers and offer to invest in electronic data interchange so as to increase the switching costs and impede effective competition.
- *New entrants.* If a company wishes to deter new entrants to the market, raising the expectations of customers in terms of cost, time, and quality through a large investment in information systems and technology can be a means of achieving this.
- *Substitute products.* The ability of information technology to accelerate the design process increases the risk of substitute products appearing. Conversely, the investment in computer-aided design facilities allows a company the option of entering other markets.
- *Competitive rivalry.* Greater access to information and the ability to make a greater number of contacts increase the rivalry which may exist within a given market.

Information technology and systems affect all the influences on competitive position. It is therefore necessary to consider them when formulating strategy.

A further advantage of considering information strategy at this early stage is that it encourages the project team to consider both the systems and the technology as a vehicle for radical change and a source of advantage. By searching for potential uses for information systems and technology at this stage, the chance of genuinely radical ideas emerging for the better control of the overhead structure is increased.

Information Systems and Technology Strategy

We have outlined how information systems and technology can influence corporate strategy. In fact, this area of the business is deserving of a strategy in its own right. Any business strategy which seeks to maximize the strengths and opportunities will require a concomitant information strategy to ensure that the systems and technologies will be in place to deliver the expected benefits and that the resultant costs are affordable. Failure to do so will risk:

- either create a business strategy that does not exploit the full range of opportunities because those related to the use of information were not identified.
- or make unrealistic assumptions on the availability of systems and technologies because of lack of corporate resources.

Over time, the emphasis of information systems and technology strategy has changed:

- It seeks to retain flexibility rather than optimize functionality. In the past, functionality used to depend on ensuring sufficient power was available to process data; then, as hardware costs declined in significance compared to the cost of writing software, the main concern was to choose a platform (i.e., combination of hardware and operating system) which had a sufficient range of application packages (i.e., programs) to meet the needs of the business. Now the objective is to ensure that the proposed strategy is sufficiently flexible to take advantage of the continuous stream of innovations that become available, while protecting the previous investment. Paradoxically, flexibility is retained through adherence to standards, since they allow access to new products and suppliers which meet them. While this may appear straightforward, one wag has observed "The nice thing about standards is that there are so many to choose from."
- It has a far broader scope, encompassing voice and image as well as data, and communication and inference as well as processing and storage.
- It aims to facilitate the system's growth by allowing users to make additions to meet their needs, as opposed to centrally directing the development of the system. This is assisted by the use of client/server architectures, which are discussed later.

Furthermore, there is a greater emphasis on computer security, as systems need to be guarded against sophisticated attack. The definition of an information systems and technology strategy is the background against which any proposals for change need to be made. This strategy is formulated in Step 3, Radical Change, after the existing systems have been analyzed in the previous step.

BUSINESS SEGMENTATION

Principles

Dividing the business into segments is essential for proper control of support activities, with the exception of homogeneous companies. If this is not done, information on parts of the business with different characteristics will be mixed, and the quality of the information will be impaired.

Since the basic purpose of the project is to control support activities by obtaining the information necessary for rational decision making, the usefulness of the whole exercise depends on finding the right basis for division. The information produced during the project will be aggregated into these segments to support major decisions; not only must the segments form sensible groupings, but it is also important to avoid being swamped by detail by the use of too fine a level of subdivisions.

The first step in the segmentation is to identify the major groupings which are relevant to the external view of the business, often in terms of:

- *Markets and customers*. Where there are a few large customers, these are also identified individually; smaller customers are grouped into market segments.
- *Distribution channels*. If the same markets and customers use different distribution channels, these need to be identified. In cases when a given customer or market uses only one distribution channel, these segments fuse into those defining markets and customers.
- *Products or services*. The broad product and service ranges need to be identified.

This identification should not be difficult because these parameters were defined in the statement of business objectives. The aim should be to restrict the number of segments to no more than 30. If there are far more than this, the procedure for tracing costs to the segments becomes too complex, and the resultant information becomes too detailed to be useful.

We now outline the factors which need to be considered when defining the segments.

Markets and Customers

In aggregating customers and markets, the intention is to group together different types of customer, according to:

- Any special activities or demands which they impose on the support structure; for example, special cost behavior.
- Any special values they place on goods and services; for example, special revenue behavior.

If no groups of customers or markets pose specific demands, there is no need for this dimension to the analysis, since the profitability of each individual customer is simply determined by the cost of its product mix and its revenue.

It is unusual, however, for affairs to be so simple, because:

- Large customers are in a position to impose their own conditions on suppliers, and these will involve particular costs pricing structures.
- Different markets—for example, inland or export—will almost always involve different activities.

The key to dividing the customers into groups is to identify customers who place similar demands on the organization; some of these groups may represent a large proportion of the revenue of the organization. This is not a problem as long as the groups are genuinely homogeneous.

When grouping customers in this way, it is essential that the groups are compatible with the market segments which the organization recognizes in its management of the marketing department, since the marketing expenditure, which can often be a considerable cost, will already have been allocated to existing segments. If the project team uses segments compatible with existing classifications, the cost allocation and hence the calculation of segment profitability becomes straightforward. Compatibility between the proposed and existing classification does not imply that they are the same, only that one classification can be easily mapped onto the other.

Distribution Channels

Often, the distribution channels of an organization are customer or market specific, but it may be the case that particular customers or markets receive goods through more than one distribution channel. Where these channels have different revenue and cost characteristics, it is necessary to recognize these so that later the parts of the business which support these channels can be examined separately.

The classification of these segments is usually quite straightforward since the number of different types of channels is frequently quite small. Examples for a retail business might include:

- Collection by the customer.
- Delivery to the customer's distribution depots.
- Delivery to the customer's retail outlets.

These might multiply however if distribution revenue or costs depend on a geographic zone. In this case, it is necessary to segment the customer base into zones depending on the distance of delivery and the charges made.

Products and Services

Many, often most, support activities can be related to particular product or service ranges, as opposed to customers. The broad product or service ranges need to be identified. In defining the product ranges it is necessary to consider whether:

- A particular group of products or services places a special demand on the support activities.
- There is a need to calculate product or service profitability for a particular range, perhaps to review pricing policy.

In practice, there is usually little difficulty in drawing up the list of main product ranges to be analyzed for manufacturing and most service companies. However, some organizations do not think in terms of either products or services; such a case would be an organization selling one product. The response is simply not to define any product or service segments but to concentrate the analysis in other areas; for example, distribution channels.

Other Types of Segments

Other types of division can be created; for example, different suppliers to the organization. If the support activities to maintain different suppliers varied dramatically, it would be necessary to analyze this in order to control the support activities and costs. Doing so would require the major supplier groups to be identified as business segments so costs could be traced separately.

Later in this chapter, we will also discuss another major type of classification—the business process. Tracing revenues and costs to business processes is done independently of the allocations to the business segments; in other words, the whole of the revenue and costs amount is allocated to business processes in a second and independent exercise.

CRITICAL SUCCESS FACTORS

Competitive Position

The critical success factors are simply a statement of what the organization must achieve if it is to meet its objectives. Most of these factors will refer to customer requirements. In the private sector, this will in turn relate to buyer behavior.

While the phrase *critical success factor* may be unfamiliar to some readers, the concept is almost certainly not. It has occurred in many different forms, as illustrated by the classifications given below:

- *Cost, time, and quality.* In project-related environments, this is a common division. Different customers will have a different balance of expectations. For example, "a man on the moon by the end of the decade" was a case of absolute priority to time and quality, regardless of cost. In other cases, a customer may need something on time and to budget, but is prepared to compromise on quality. In delivering a specific product or service, it is essential to understand the customer's own priorities in these terms; if this is not done, the final result may be judged a failure, simply because there was the wrong emphasis.
- *Price, position, product, and promotion/packaging.* Since most success factors are linked to customer satisfaction, it is not surprising that the "Four Ps" of the marketing mix, concerned with influencing buyer behavior, can be used as a framework for analysis. Indeed, the Four Ps are re-expressions of the cost, time, quality formula in corresponding order, with the last term, quality, covering both "product" and "promotion/packaging" categories in the marketing mix. A further restatement of the concept is given in the third classification below.
- *Cost, delivery, and specification/quality.* This classification, which uses the language of supply chain performance, is similar to the previous two. Converting from the marketing mix terminology, "price" and "cost" are linked, as are "position" and "delivery" and, finally, "product" and "promotion/packaging" are equivalent to "specification/quality." This classification also reflects a division of the expectations of customers at the end of the supply chain. A customer may accept poor delivery arrangements for low cost but expect a high-quality product; for example, driving to a discount warehouse to buy a consumer durable. Or a customer may alternatively accept poor quality in return for rapid delivery; for example, visiting a fast-food bar in preference to waiting in a restaurant.

The classifications used are a matter of convenience only, but adopting a classification that is familiar to the managers within the organization and its customers helps explain the concept of critical success factors. To assist in this discussion, we will now give some practical examples of critical success factors. They have been divided into the categories of cost, time, and quality. The factors are summarized in Figure 2–3.

Cost Factors

There may be a few customers for whom cost is no object but most are concerned with value for money. The numerator, value, is concerned with both timeliness and quality, which are discussed below. The denominator, cost, seems straightforward but has many aspects to it. The relevant cost will depend on the product or service being purchased and the sophistication of the buyer:

FIGURE 2–3
Critical Success Factors

Cost	Time	Quality
Initial purchase cost Life-cycle cost Recurring/Nonrecurring cost	Quotation lead time Design lead time Innovation date Delivery lead time Support response time	Closeness of fit of specification to need Conformance to specification Reliability of product Delivery reliability Customer service Promotion and packaging Product/service support

- *Initial purchase cost.* For consumer goods, this is the salient cost. When this is understood by manufacturers and retailers, the response is often to lower initial purchase prices and raise support costs! The most extreme example is a major film manufacturer which sold cameras at cost so as to increase the subsequent sales of film.
- *Life-cycle costs.* To avoid the ploy described above, the more sophisticated buyer will estimate the total cost involved in owning a product for a period, accounting for support costs, resale value, and so forth.
- *Recurring and nonrecurring costs.* Where the volume of future purchases is uncertain, the fixed and variable elements can be separated. This distinction becomes important when potential buyers have very different volume requirements, so a company's cost structure may appear competitive to one customer but not to another.

We will discuss the subject of overhead cost extensively in subsequent chapters as a means to reducing the eventual cost to customers. However, before reducing costs it is necessary to understand which costs are important to the customer. Otherwise, there is the risk of minimizing the wrong type of cost.

Timeliness Factors

The importance of responsiveness in competition is now being fully recognized. Timeliness can be critical all the way through the life cycle of a product or a service, from quotation, to design, to manufacture and finally to after-sales service:

- *Quotations lead time.* In the financial services sector in particular, the ability to offer a rapid quotation—perhaps a property mortgage to a customer in a race to exchange contracts on the property—has become a key competitive parameter. However, providing a quotation can be far from simple; for example, for computer vendors where the configuration of a working system for a particular requirement is not a trivial task.
- *Design lead time.* For manufacturing companies, this can be the most important timeliness parameter of all. The ability to introduce new products consistently more quickly than the competition expands the period during which the product is profitable.
- *Innovation rate.* This is related to the previous parameter of design lead time, though is broader and considers the rate at which a company can change the specifications of its products, as opposed to the time required for a single design change. The company which can develop and deliver products more quickly will succeed even where its prices are not the lowest; they provide high value-added products that command high margins, which are reinvested in yet more superior products.
- *Delivery lead time.* This is a well-recognized performance parameter. The speed of delivery of a standard product, though not a service, can be improved by holding inventory at considerable cost; however, a better approach is to redesign the supply chain processes.
- *Support response time.* The quality of after-sales support will affect a rebuy particularly for capital goods or consumer durables. The most crucial service is usually repair and maintenance; naturally, the timeliness with which this is provided is of prime importance.

Since timeliness is one of the key factors in becoming and remaining competitive, it is an area on which performance measures should be focused. In a later chapter, we explore the whole topic of performance measures, including those concerned with lead time.

Quality Factors

Quality is the elusive element of any product or service. The value attached to quality cannot be disputed but it is often not linked to the specification of the product itself, residing instead in the perception of the product, the outlets through which it is distributed, or the way it is packaged. The critical success factors in this area are therefore varied. They include:

- *Closeness of fit between the product and the customers' need.* The alignment between product and need is more important than generally superior technical performance. One method that has been used to align the technical design of a product and service with

the customers' needs is Quality Function Deployment, which will be discussed later, since it is as relevant to process design as to product design.
- *Conformance to specification.* This is applicable where a formal specification has been drafted. Where this is the case, conformance is essential. The reason is that many customers, in a desire to control their own overheads, wish to avoid incoming part inspection and look to their suppliers to provide conforming parts. Failure to do so can be serious, since a concomitant change is usually to reduce the number of suppliers, and those who cannot supply conforming parts are the first to go. The preferred method of ensuring close conformance to specification is to rely on tight control of the processes leading to delivery, rather than on repeated inspection.
- *Reliability of the product.* Where a physical product is delivered, reliability is usually a factor which influences customer satisfaction. One method which is used to analyze and improve this performance is Failure Mode Effect Analysis, which rigorously catalogs the possible failures, their likelihood, and their effect.
- *Delivery reliability.* The ability to stick to delivery schedules or delivery promises clearly is a buying point in most industries. To achieve it, the first step is to ensure that the original schedule or promise is realistic, rather than that necessary to gain the order. Once this is assured, the task then becomes one of control of the underlying processes.
- *Customer service.* This is a very broad parameter and covers both the quality of experience the customers receive from the company and its responsiveness to the customers' needs.
- *Promotion and packaging.* For many goods, the specification of the product is irrelevant. The purchase, and hence the success of the company, depends on the perception presented by the promotion and the packaging.
- *Product/service support.* Finally, a customer will often not view the purchase of a product or a service as an isolated transaction. There is an expectation of subsequent support. This is particularly the case in the purchase of large equipment. Succeeding in this area is not only a matter of performance but also of perception. Improving the way the customer views the quality of support is a matter for "customer care" programs.

The customer's expectation of product or service performance is central to the rational control of the organization because these expectations, and the subsequent design of product or service itself, are the main determinants of the administrative activities necessary to support production and delivery. Mismeasurement of customers' expectations in this area can lead to the operation of an overhead structure that is not competitive compared to a rival which has understood the customers' requirements correctly.

Treatment of Different Markets

An important point in considering the critical success factors is that, even for the same product or service, the factors will differ between markets. For example, a car when sold to the consumer market may be evaluated on initial cost, but a leasing company will calculate the life-cycle cost. On taking delivery, the leasing company buyer may place great store on reliability of delivery, whereas the consumer market may be more interested in delivery lead time.

While a different set of factors will not always be needed for each market or customer, the potential for different requirements needs to be recognized and accounted for in the analysis. This point is explored further in the case study at the end of the final chapter.

CUSTOMER REQUIREMENTS

Introduction

Once the critical success factors have been identified, the next stage is to translate them into specific customer requirements. Doing so requires an understanding of the buying behavior of the customers in each of the markets the organization serves.

The only way to understand buying is to talk to customers; this can be done informally or through market research programs. To the traditional mind, the use of market research to control administrative functions would seem bizarre, but of course once such functions are accepted as potentially adding value then the first step must be to find out what, in particular, the customer finds valuable.

This is best illustrated by the parallel with "value engineering." The author was once commissioned to carry out a value-engineering exercise on a large piece of capital machinery. Large amounts of cost had been added to the design to create various advanced features, not least a large free-standing control console, which was viewed as a major step forward. While this was the pride of the design department, no feedback had been obtained from customers on the worth of these additions, despite the fact that there were several local customers willing to give a few hours of their time. The results of the discussions with the customers were startling. Many of the expensive "advanced features" were irrelevant, and the free-standing control console in particular was viewed as a positive nuisance because it blocked the factory aisles! The lesson was simple: A few hours in the company of the customer is time well spent.

There are two stages to analyzing customer requirements:

- The first is to translate, if necessary, the success factors into qualities recognized by the customer and to add sufficient detail to allow the customer to state his or her preferences unambiguously.
- The second is to measure the importance the customer attaches to the different requirements.

After outlining the theory of buyer behavior, we describe these two steps: the identification of the requirements and their quantification. We then outline a specialized measurement technique, conjoint analysis, which may be useful to some readers.

Buyer Behavior

This section considers the theoretical foundation for the analysis of buyer behavior and customer requirements. It is not essential to understand the material to conduct the program; however, it should be enlightening for those readers who wish to understand the basic principles behind setting customer service levels.

There are different approaches to the analysis of buyer behavior. Some are concerned with psychological and social motivations; however, to examine customer preferences on overheads, we are concerned with economic motivation. The framework for this examination is provided by utility theory, which is a major element of economics.

The "utility" of an item refers to its usefulness, or value, expressed in monetary terms. Curiously, despite the heavy use of the term *value*, its measurement, in terms of utility, is rarely considered. The simplest arrangement assumes that the value of some goods is proportional to the quantity possessed; in other words, the relation between utility and quantity is linear. For most goods, this is not the case: the amount paid for, and hence the value of, the thousandth item would be less than for the first. Therefore, for this case, the marginal utility decreases with the quantity consumed.

In economics, this is referred to as The Law of Diminishing Marginal Utility. Unlike the laws of physics, however, the laws of economics can be broken! A minor exception concerns necessities, which have an infinite marginal utility for the necessary quantity; for example, as Mark Twain observed "Each person is born to one possession which outvalues all others—his last breath." The second exception concerns small initial quantities of an item which is not a necessity. It is possible that small quantities are viewed as not worth having, so have a small marginal utility, while moderate quantities have a larger marginal utility.

We now have a basis for evaluating the performance of the organization in the eyes of its customers, which is shown in Figure 2–4. For a given parameter—for example, lead time—there will be:

FIGURE 2-4
Utility Model

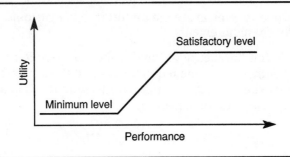

- A minimum level of performance, below which the customer will not buy; for performance below this level there is zero marginal utility.
- A range of performance, in which increasing performance leads to increasing value; there is positive marginal utility.
- A high level of performance, beyond which performance has no value; there is a zero marginal utility.

For each element of performance, the ideal situation is to be able to identify the high and low breakpoints and the value the customer attaches to increasing performance in the range between them.

Identification of Customer Requirements

We have already defined the critical success factors as a statement of what the business must achieve if it is to meet its objectives. This is one step away from a statement of customer requirements, which is more detailed. So, for example, if "prompt delivery" is a critical success factor, this needs amplification to show how rapid delivery should be.

The next step is to ask customers to value the different requirements. The simplest method is to ask them to rank their requirements in order of importance; for example, particular product features, levels of delivery performance, and so on. This can be quite useful in clarifying customer needs. This in turn can show the emphasis of the overhead activities required to meet these needs and the level of performance that is required. However, the method is rather crude.

An obvious refinement is for customers to quantify their expectations of performance. So, for example:

- Cost expectations need to be quantified, either in terms of an absolute level of cost or as a maximum permissible uplift on the minimum available price; for example, a customer could conceive

paying up to 120 percent of the minimum available if other conditions were right;
- Timeliness needs to be broken down into bands. For example, delivery time may be important, but it is necessary to ascertain the proportion of the customers who require same day delivery, next day delivery, or delivery within the week. When analyzing the expectations on product introduction, there needs to be a view on the frequency of new product introduction that is preferred;
- The quality requirements need to be expressed in terms of the permissible degree and frequency of deviation.

As discussed in the previous section, this quantification will have two aspects, namely the minimum level of performance below which the customer will not purchase, and the level of performance beyond which no additional value is perceived.

This then allows the organization to set minimum levels of performance and also to understand the level beyond which it is not worthwhile to improve. For most organizations, achieving this much would be a major advance on their current state of knowledge and is sufficient for an initial program to control overheads.

It is possible, however, to take the understanding of customer requirements further; there is still not enough information for the organization to optimize the customer service levels, in the sense of providing the best value for the money. Doing this requires knowledge of how much more a customer would pay if the product specification or delivery were improved by a particular amount. The service levels within a particular parameter can be adjusted for maximum profitability by identifying the service level which provides the largest difference between revenue and cost.

The technique, called conjoint analysis, is discussed in the next section. It has been used extensively in product design and is equally applicable to process design.

Conjoint Analysis

It is certainly not essential for the success of this program to use conjoint analysis. The overview of the technique is included to show how to calculate information on customer requirements that is often sought but rarely available, namely how much a customer will pay for some element of service.

In an ideal world, customers would be able to place a value on each of their requirements. So if they claimed to prefer shorter delivery lead time, the value of each degree of reduction could be given, up to the level when any further reduction would not be useful. In practice, customers are not able to do this; the question is too abstract. In response to this difficulty, conjoint analysis has been developed; it infers the values which customers place on different requirements from their response to a series of questions.

The first step is to identify the set of customer requirements to be valued. If there has already been an exercise to rank or score customer requirements then this information will be available, otherwise it will have to be collected. This must be the subject of some preliminary market research. The main danger is that a requirement is not included in the analysis, because this will not become apparent subsequently. The inclusion of a superfluous customer requirement is less serious, though it does unnecessarily complicate the analysis.

A series of questions is then formed: Different combinations of the stated requirements (usually termed attributes) are grouped and the customer is asked to choose between the combinations. The groups of attributes are chosen so that the relative merits, in the eyes of the customer, of each of the attributes within the group can be evaluated. For example, the relative merits of particular specifications or delivery options are ranked against each other.

A very simplified example illustrates the use of conjoint analysis. A delivery service may have two key attributes, customer-collects or home-delivery and a lead-time of one, or two or three days. There are six possible combinations of attributes and users can be asked to rank their preference. The outcome may be as shown in Table 2–1.

This table shows that customers regard a three-day lead time as unattractive, regardless of the delivery option. However, the attractiveness of a one-day lead time is not absolute: A one-day delivery lead time with the customer collecting is less attractive than a two-day lead time with a home delivery service.

These values can be inferred from the incremental scores. Providing home delivery scores +1.5, which is less than the +2.5 increment for moving from a three- to two-day lead time but greater than the +1.0 increment for moving from a two- to one-day lead time.

TABLE 2–1
Conjoint Analysis Example

	3 Days	2 Days	1 Day	Average	Increment
Customer collects	0	2	3	1.7	•
Home delivery	1	4	5	3.3	+1.5
Average	0.5	3.0	4.0	2.5	•
Increment	•	+2.5	+1.0	•	•

FIGURE 2-5
Striking a Cost Versus Service Level Trade-off

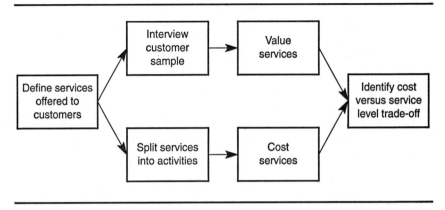

When financial parameters are introduced into the analysis, it becomes possible to quantify the value the customer places on particular attributes and then compare this with the cost of providing these attributes. This is illustrated in Figure 2-5.

PROCESSES

Introduction

We have said that this program uses a process approach. By this, we mean that the method is primarily concerned with processes and activities. The former represent a top-level view of how to satisfy the customers' requirements and the latter an analysis of what actually occurs in the organization in order to meet those requirements.

Now that the needs of the customer have been clarified, we can propose a set of processes which serve them. We first define a process and then give examples of some typical processes. Of course, not all the processes listed will be applicable to any one organization; indeed, many of the sample processes represent different ways of slicing the same cake.

Definition

At a simplified level, a process is a coordinated set of activities which meets a customer requirement. This simple definition captures the essence of a process, namely:

- It is the means by which a customer is satisfied, which has been the subject of our discussions so far.
- A process consists of component activities, which require coordination and control. For a process to function well, not only must the component activities be functioning well, but they must also be linked and coordinated smoothly.

Following the logic of this approach, a process will only have been identified if it fulfils an external requirement. As a first assumption, this has much to commend it, because it encourages an outward-facing view. Nonetheless, the question arises whether there are processes, or individual activities, which do not work towards satisfying a customer requirement. There are, for example:

- External bodies, who are not customers in the common sense of the word, but whose requirements need to be satisfied; for example, there may be some activities which are involved with supply of shareholders' information. There are also other interested parties—for example, the workforce, the local community—who are generally referred to as stakeholders.
- Groups of activities which are necessary for the growth of the organization but which do not have an immediate customer. Examples would include developing new products or services, and customers and markets.
- The operation of internal systems for the eventual benefit of a customer; for example, the financial management function or the information technology systems.

In summary, therefore, our definition of a process given above has to include stakeholders as well as customers in the literal sense, future customers as well as present customers, and the maintenance of a business infrastructure which permits customer requirements to be satisfied. Notwithstanding this caveat, however, the emphasis within the organization should always be on the satisfaction of genuine customers who exist today.

Process Identification

The next step is to identify the key processes within the organization. This has to be done in the context of a particular organization. However, we now discuss some sample processes which will serve to get the ball rolling when trying to identify processes which are specific to an organization.

In identifying processes, and subsequently making models of them, there are some basic choices of approach:

- *To-be versus as-is.* A to-be model is an assessment of the processes as they are intended to be; whereas, an as-is model is a statement of

the processes as they actually are. In business process reengineering, the to-be model represents the ideal, though this is simply one option; the degree of innovation to be introduced into the to-be model is a matter of judgment.
- *Top-down versus bottom-up.* A top-down model is built by taking the overall function of a process and successively breaking it down to lower levels of detail. A bottom-up model is built by defining the lowest level of activity and building these up into an overall process by defining the interrelationships between activities.
- *Logical versus physical.* A logical model is a statement of the processing required to deliver a given function. A physical model is a statement of the process which actually exists, which may contain unnecessary complexity and redundancy.

These dichotomies are similar but not congruent. To-be models are usually built from the top down and represent a logical view; as-is models are typically built from the bottom up and give a physical view. In this step and in Step 3, Radical Change, the team will be adopting the to-be, top-down, logical approach. The degree of innovation in the to-be model depends on the radicalism of the change being contemplated.

The question also arises whether it is realistic to even consider processes for a general organization or if processes need to be specific to an industry. The answer depends on the level of detail required; in choosing the level of analysis there is an excellent motto to bear in mind, "relevance over precision"; in other words, avoid wasting time on irrelevant precision. We envisage between 5 and 20 processes being identified; the lower figure represents a fairly superficial top-down view of the organization and the higher figure a relatively detailed top-down view. Nonetheless, even with the higher figure, we are only considering very broad processes, many of which will apply to different corporations.

It must be stressed that the general processes given below are only a guide; not all will be relevant to any one organization, and there will be some processes that are relevant to a company which are not covered in the sample given below. For convenience, we group them into broad categories:

- *Order fulfillment*, namely the coordination of the activities which take a customer order and fill it.
- *Customer development*, which spans obtaining customers, understanding their requirements, and maintaining contact after the sale has been completed.
- *Business development*, which covers developing markets and products within the organization.
- *Business maintenance*, which includes the processes concerned with keeping the organization intact.

FIGURE 2-6
Number of Processes and Activities

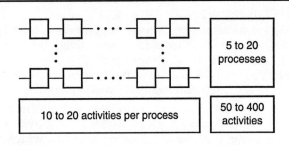

These divisions are appropriate to many, but not all, industry sectors. In the retail sector, for example, it is likely that the process names and divisions would reflect the traditional distinctions between merchandising, distribution, and store management.

The identification of the processes relevant to the particular corporation is only the first stage in the analysis of the processes. During Step 2, Internal Analysis, we examine the activities of the company in detail; we identify between 50 and 400 individual activities, depending on the level of detail adopted, and link these to the 5 to 20 processes. In doing so we break down each top-down process into between 10 and 20 activities, analyzed from the bottom up. This synthesis is illustrated in Figure 2-6.

Order Fulfillment

These processes refer to the fundamental operations of most businesses; namely, taking an order and meeting it. It would be possible to have a single process spanning the whole company, from sales order entry to delivery; this would be appropriate if the logistics task was relatively simple, perhaps the dispatch of an order from stock from a single location. However, for a more complex supply chain, a more detailed approach is necessary. The processes might include:

- *Define customers' product or service requirements.* This is appropriate where the contents of an order need careful definition, especially where there are many different options which are available and there must be consistency with existing equipment.
- *Agree on delivery and schedule operations.* This is one of the more complex processes which involves agreeing the schedules timings with the customer and planning the operations to ensure they are met. Unfortunately management control of this process can often be

split, with the sales function agreeing delivery and the production function scheduling the operations.
- *Manage operations capacity.* This refers to the management, as opposed to the scheduling, of the operations, e.g., a manufacturing plant. This can be considered as a self-contained process, whereby orders up to a certain level are placed on the plant, and it is then the responsibility of the plant management to deliver.
- *Procure material.* This is similar in principle to "manage operations capacity": a requirement for material is identified and it is then a separate responsibility to ensure that the material is available at the required time at the best price.
- *Supervise inventory.* Once the inventory levels at the different points in the supply chain have been set, there remains the task of supervising the storage locations and the movement of material between them. If this is a minor part of the business the process can be included within manage operations capacity.

When dividing up the supply chain into individual processes, it is worth considering who is responsible for key parameters in the business, assuming that managerial responsibility is also divided along process lines. In the previous example, responsibility for the levels of inventory would be held within the "Agree on delivery and schedule operations" process; the holder of the responsibility would have discretion over the trade-offs between inventory holding and levels of customer service, choosing perhaps to increase the availability of products by increasing the levels of inventory held. The organization may choose to limit this discretion by placing bounds on either the maximum level of inventory held or on minimum levels of customer service; probably constraints will be placed on both, though the conflicting constraints must be compatible and realistic.

Remaining with the division of processes given above, it is less obvious who is responsible for purchased material costs, which may well amount to over half the costs of the company! While the manager of "procure material" obviously holds some responsibility, the price obtained for a given material will depend on the delivery requirements; if the supply chain is arranged so that material has to be obtained at short notice, prices will rise.

It should be emphasised that the processes given above are merely examples of a possible division of the organization and that others are possible. For example, for organizations for whom outsourcing is only a minor facet of their business, a single-process "Procure material" would suffice. Where, however, procurement is a substantial part of the overall organization, the management of suppliers needs to be resolved in greater detail; processes such as "Identify suppliers" and "Manage suppliers" would be used.

Customer Development

Although most processes are concerned with satisfying requirements of existing customers, some are specifically concerned with developing the customer base. We include here those processes which work to satisfy a customer other than through the operation of the supply chain:

- *Acquire customers.* Once decisions have been taken on the markets in which the company is to operate and the products which it is to offer, there remains the critical process of acquiring new customers. The input to the process can be considered as a number of defined market segments and a given product or service range; the output is a series of new customers. The activities undertaken will vary and will often include the activities of the field sales force.
- *Identify customers' requirements.* This process exists in organizations where the onus is on the supplier to identify the customers' needs, as opposed to simply matching a portfolio of products to needs which have already been identified. This is not common, since in most industries this diagnostic phase is the responsibility of the potential customer. It is not always the case though; for example, in the professional services sector where a key winning factor is to identify the problem.
- *Support customers.* This is sometimes part of the ongoing relationship that the sales function forms with the customer; in other cases the after-sales support is relatively technical, as with computer hardware and software sales. Sometimes this takes on more of the characteristics of a logistics exercise and can be termed *logistics support*; for example, the support of heavy construction equipment in the field.

There are also important questions regarding the division of responsibility between these processes. One question is the degree of responsibility the "acquire customers" process should have for general marketing. Where the link between acquiring particular customers and eventual sales is weak—for example, for a manufacturer or wholesaler of branded retail goods, whose eventual sales depend on the number of purchases by consumers—the emphasis is upon brand management, and the control of marketing expenditure should reside there. However, where sales are made to the ultimate customers directly, there is an advantage in a division of authority which separates the product portfolio planning and the actual implementation of the marketing and sales programs. In this case, much of the marketing budget should then be controlled within the "acquire customers" process.

A second question is whether sales order entry should fall within "acquire customers" or within the supply chain management processes. The author's view is that sales order entry has more in common with the logistics processes than with the sales function. Furthermore, for the managers of the logistics processes to have a span of control which matches their responsibilities, they should have control of order entry, since:

- They will be responsible for meeting lead-time promises, and therefore the time it takes an order to clear the sales office is an important part of this total time.
- Poor quality of sales order entry is a common problem of errors occurring downstream in the supply chain, and therefore it is advantageous if the activity is controlled by those who will be most affected by the poor quality.

Frequently, there is reluctance, however, in assigning responsibility for order entry to the logistics functions. One reason for this is that the sales function is measured on the value of orders taken and may wish to retain the ability to make any promise on specification, delivery, or price necessary to obtain an order. The subsequent problems are clear enough.

Business Development

Some processes are concerned with the development of the future business, in terms of products and markets. These processes cannot be related to current customers, but nonetheless they are necessary. In many organizations, the responsibilities for these processes are diffused across the organization, and consequently they are not carried out well. The first step to remedying this situation is to recognize the key business development processes, which may include:

- *Plan products*. The product and service origination process spans market research and selection, concept generation, specification, and setting up of distribution networks where necessary. It also includes abandonment, an important decision which unfortunately is frequently carried out by default. It would usually be impractical to remedy this by creating a product planning department or directorate because the task is inherently multidisciplinary especially in linking strategies for marketing, products, and manufacturing. However, the process of managing the product portfolio can be recognized and responsibility assigned for its management, even though the participants in the process will have other responsibilities.
- *Manage brands*. For branded goods, much of the product planning and marketing referred to above, of course, revolves around the brands, and brand management becomes a process in its own right. This would usually encompass the product planning described above, as well as responsibility for accepting the design of products and packaging, pricing policy, and the choice of distribution outlets.
- *Develop product*. The importance of product development in both manufacturing and service companies is seldom disputed. The

potential for high margins for advanced products is well recognized. Furthermore, product development is crucial in the control of future cost. It has been estimated for manufacturing companies that some 80 percent of a product's manufacturing cost is committed once the design is completed. It is important to recognize that while management responsibility for the whole process must be clear, the process itself needs to be multidisciplinary and that product or service design carried out in isolation will have poor results.

These processes pose special problems in the costing of the products or services. If a cost is being incurred for the benefit of a future product or service, there is no logical way to relate it to the present product ranges. Therefore, any allocation of development cost is bound to be arbitrary. If it is necessary to properly allocate development costs to individual products, a form of life-cycle costing is required.

Business Maintenance

A few internal processes must be undertaken for the organization to continue; a difficult balance has to be struck. On the one hand, these groups of activities do not add value directly; but on the other hand, if they were not carried out at all, customers would not be served. The main processes include:

- *Manage human resource.* Little mention has yet been made of the stuff of which processes are made, namely people. A decision needs to be made on whether the organization adopts a development perspective, whereby individuals are carefully recruited and then developed, or if it adopts a more laissez-faire attitude. If the former course is selected, human resource development is an important process. While it might seem the former course provides a natural advantage, it often seems that the disadvantages of inbreeding implied by concentrated internal development more than outweigh the benefits.
- *Manage finances.* The financial management function usually appears self-contained within an organization. Most of this function falls naturally within the financial management process, but not all. For example, the debt collection activity can be viewed as the final stage of the supply-chain management process. The importance of financial management is rarely disputed, especially since many view it as a source of profit equal to operations management. The only danger is that financial management can be too dominant and detached from the day-to-day operations of the organization. If this happens, the organization begins to be run by proxy, substituting financial measures for those which measure the parameters which matter to the customer.
- *Maintain infrastructure.* There will always be a need to maintain a physical and information infrastructure to allow for the coordina-

tion of the business. When comparative studies are made, it is startling how wide the variation can be between different organizations carrying out identical tasks.

It is in this area that the traditional view of administrative control is most appropriate. If business maintenance costs do not add value to the customer directly, even though they support other processes which do, the organization should minimize these costs without compromising the level of customer service.

Summary

We have outlined the principle of processes and provided some examples. The actual processes chosen for a particular organization will depend on its basis of competition and will need to be tailored to the organization. An important consideration to be borne in mind when devising processes is to understand in which process the responsibility for certain parameters resides; for example, the responsibility for inventory levels, prices of purchased material and delivery reliability.

Typically, between 5 and 20 major processes will be used to encompass the activities of the organization.

BENCHMARKING

Benefits

The new interest in benchmarking arises from a need to inform managers whether they are the best in the world in particular processes and if not, the usual case, to determine who is better and by what margin. For those organizations which do not have to compete for their existence, the reward for the exercise is simply the knowledge that the organization is fulfilling its role in the best way possible. However, for most private sector organizations, the benefit is less high minded—it is the survival of the organization itself.

The threat to survival has grown with the advent of global competition. When companies only had to compete with those in their vicinity, they supplied a local market; the managers of the company were generally aware of how good their own operations were compared to a competitor. If a more distant company operated more efficiently, it would not be a matter of immediate concern since the distant competitor could not threaten sales to local customers. This has now changed with the lowering of trade barriers and improvement in communications, with the result that companies now compete with organizations in parts of the world of which they know nothing. This may be apparent to companies who already supply to the international market, but it is equally applicable to those who supply a local market because there is nothing to prevent their customers from sourcing components from international competition.

In these circumstances, there is naturally a need for management to find out how good they really are, not just compared to the competitor in the same region or nation, but the world, and on a continous basis. This is the rationale behind benchmarking.

Before we discuss how to do this, we first outline the different types of benchmarks available.

Benchmark Types

Benchmarks differ in the extent of the comparison undertaken. We now outline the different types of benchmark available, and it will become apparent that much old wine is in new bottles. We can categorize benchmarks, beginning with those with relatively narrow horizons and finishing with those which take a broad view:

- *Ideal benchmarks*. As a desktop exercise, it can be worth considering the absolutely ideal level of performance, assuming all the constraints are removed. This is frequently done in work study, where the ideal throughput of a function or a machine is calculated, assuming no breakdowns or interruptions. This ideal standard is then adjusted to allow for a certain amount of lost time that will always occur in practice, in order to set the real target. Carrying this out for a whole process requires more imagination, but can point the way for future development. For example, some years ago in the U.K. it generally took six weeks to offer a mortgage loan on a property; now it can be done within the day, assuming all the documentation is in order. Setting an ideal benchmark of same-day service would have seemed absurd in the past, but this level of performance has actually been achieved.
- *Internal benchmarks*. These are comparisons between different parts of the same company. Such exercises are well established and have the advantage that the management of the company have the knowledge to make meaningful comparisons, without being misled by anomalies. This last point touches an oft-repeated adage in benchmarking, namely that "You cannot separate the numbers from the people." The disadvantage of internal benchmarks is, of course, that there is little understanding of what is being achieved elsewhere in the world. If the company is genuinely among the best in the world in certain functions, suitable comparisons exist within the organization; for the vast majority of organizations, however, internal benchmarks are insufficient.
- *Best practice surveys*. It is possible for companies to participate in surveys on their adoption of modern practice, often through the use

of a trade association. The drawback is that the results do not focus on actual performance—the output, but only on working practices— the input. To overcome this, comparisons of performance are also sought, sometimes in ratio form.
- *Ratio and performance comparisons.* This is not a new idea. Many companies have long subscribed, through the medium of a third party, to reports on comparative business ratios and other performance indicators. Under this arrangement, companies transform financial information into ratio form and report on other parameters by completing a questionnaire. They then submit the information to a third party, which publishes the information in anonymous form. Each participant can then compare its own performance with that of others but is unaware of the actual identity of each comparative organization.
- *Industry benchmarks.* These involve the comparison of an organization with others in the same industry or service sector. On the positive side, interesting comparisons can be drawn between organizations because on the whole they undertake broadly similar activities. On the negative side, there is only the opportunity to define the level of performance that is "good enough"—as good as any current competitor; benchmarking within a sector does not help define the level of performance which is best practice for a given process, across all industries. Furthermore, there are problems in sharing confidential information with competitors, although this can be ameliorated through the use of third parties. Active third-party involvement is essential to overcome the confidentiality issue, which would otherwise frustrate the exercise. This is because when creating benchmarks it is necessary to separate out the differences in cost which are controllable and those which reflect historical factors; for example, in comparing the costs between organizations where one is using fully depreciated equipment while the other is not. To separate the controllable and noncontrollable differences between organizations involves working at a close level of detail, and this is likely to involve a sharing of information that would prove unacceptable for competitors, unless a third party carried out the analysis.
- *Process benchmarks.* It is in this area that most of the latest interest in benchmarking has arisen. The basic change in thinking is that once a corporation is defined from a process viewpoint, it is then possible to compare the performance in those processes not only with those in the same industry, but also in other industries. The steps in doing so are to identify the key processes of the organization, research the best performers in the world, regardless of industry, contact them, and arrange visits by a benchmarking team. Benchmarking in this way has the dual advantages of avoiding the situation where competitors are expected to divulge confidential information and allowing a comparison to be made with the best performer across all industries, thereby offering the prospect for the company to move ahead of its own competition as opposed to

drawing level with it. The only difficulty is in selecting the right processes and comparator organizations; this is discussed in the next section.

Only the last item—the concept of benchmarking processes against the "world-class" standards—is genuinely novel; however, all are useful. We confine the subsequent discussion to process benchmarking since the other types will already be familiar.

Selection of Processes

It is impractical to benchmark every process of an organization, and therefore one or more must be selected for the procedure. We now discuss the criteria for selection.

Perhaps the most important criterion is that the process outputs must be relevant to the critical success factors of the organization. An analysis has already been made of the factors on which the organization competes; if a particular process affects several of these factors in a major manner, it is a candidate for a benchmarking.

Beyond this, there is an issue of the general level of resource consumed. For example, some processes may be critical, but satisfactory results can be achieved by committing additional resource, while the cost of the process remains within reasonable bounds. In such a case, benchmarking would not be worthwhile, and instead attention would turn to those processes which consumed a large amount of human or capital resource and where increases in productivity would substantially improve performance.

The final point, which may smack of appeasement, is that the exercise should begin as a process where the people concerned view it positively. If benchmarking is a new departure within the organization, perhaps one which has not been outward looking in the past, then the first exercise must be a success. This will not happen where those involved in the process are likely to be resistant to change and who regard a comparison with outside practice as either threatening or irrelevant. The first benchmarking assignment must therefore concentrate on a process where the participants are eager to change and prove themselves. If none of the key processes in the organization are operated by such people, the prospective benchmarking enthusiast should rapidly find another job!

Selection of Comparable Organizations

Once the processes which are candidates for benchmarking have been identified, the next step is to identify comparable organizations. There are two major criteria:

- They are good performers in their own business, which may be very specialized.
- Their success depends on competence in the process of interest.

To illustrate with a practical example from the author's own experience, where would a benchmarking company be found for the efficient design, in terms of space and power, of electric motors? Thinking laterally, compactness and efficiency (which is tantamount to coolness) is of central importance to dental drills, where a dentist judges a design on the convenience and comfort of the drill. Sure enough, a visit to one of the world's leading manufacturers of such equipment proved an education to a motor designer (who would have considered himself an expert within his own country) on the degrees of compactness and efficiency that were possible; the potential for improvement was believed because of the evidence seen with his own eyes.

Within this anecdote, there are lessons:

- Seek out international comparison. Within national boundaries, word of good practice will already have traveled through movement of employees or professional associations.
- Seeing is believing. Whereas reported comment on best practice elsewhere can be counterproductive, if employees are taken to see what is possible from people such as themselves, with the opportunity for discussion, the results are likely to be more encouraging.

The search for comparable organizations can be conducted by reviewing press cuttings, industry statistics, or membership of various trade and industry associations. The problem with this approach is that at the end of the search there has to be a cold call, which may be treated with suspicion and result in rebuff. Not surprisingly, the most fruitful groups are forums of companies which have declared an interest in benchmarking from the outset.

Before approaching a prospective benchmarking partner, it pays to anticipate the question What's in it for me? There has to be benefit on both sides. This could encompass the exchange of best practice across different processes, which in turn is likely to be more applicable where there is a general similarity between the organizations. If all else fails, appeal to the prospect of publicity! Apart from the vanity of those who would be involved in the project, the appearance at various conferences generally provides a level of publicity and credibility that would cost a fortune if it were paid for through advertising.

Comparison Issues

The benchmarking exercise should be concerned with measuring the aspects of each activity which contribute to satisfying the requirements of the customer in terms of time, cost, and quality. This has to be done at the detailed level, since it is at this level that most improvements become apparent.

The fact that comparison is to be made at a detailed level tends to make general guidelines of limited use. However, there are four main issues which are always of interest:

- *Product or service structure.* Many differences in performance can be traced directly back to the structure of the product or service that is to be delivered. This fact is probably less of a surprise than the degree of influence that the original design of the product or service actually holds; we have already remarked that some 80 percent of the operating cost of the organization can be predetermined or committed once the product or service design is complete.
- *Process structure.* The same product or service can be produced and supported by differing overhead processes. Some of the variation in overhead processes will arise from differing characteristics of the products or services being delivered. However, there may be other factors, such as an overhead structure that was designed to support a greater or lesser scale of activity than that which occurs at present.
- *Level of complexity.* The degree of variety a process must deal with has a major influence on cost and performance. Processes may have been designed to deal with a different degree of variety of product or service than occurs at present. This often happens where there has been a proliferation in product or service range without a commensurate increase in volume. This leads to inefficiencies if there is a lengthy preparatory setup period for the support of each product or service.
- *Human and capital resources.* This comparison has to be made in the context of the differing product and process structures remarked on previously. In practice, it is very difficult to disentangle the differences in resources from structural differences and the effects of scale, mix, and so on. One technique which is proposed later is the use of activity-based costing to disaggregate processes into their component parts so as to examine such effects in detail.

These four factors are concerned with the objective and the quantifiable factors which affect a process. This is only part of the story. The other part of the story is concerned with the attitudes of the people within the organization. This would include factors such as motivation, the ability of individuals to work with each other, and the sense of competition that exists between the different parts of the organization and between the organization and outside.

It is important to take note of both the objective and the more subjective factors. The latter can differ considerably for no reason other than history; this was brought home to the author in a comparative analysis of three electricity utilities. The functions of each electricity utility were identical, and their structures were similar, but the attitudes which prevailed were very different. In one, a "let's get down to do it" culture prevailed with the emphasis being placed on results; in the second, a sense of formality and procedures prevailed, with the head of the organization being addressed in formal terms; in the third, there was a sense of informality but one that was not associated with an impetus for change. None of these differences had a logical cause, nor could they be easily "proved," but their existence was not in doubt and was a major contributor to the differences between the companies.

Practical Matters

Even when suitable comparator organizations have been found and they agree to cooperate, there remains the question of how to conduct the benchmarking exercise. The subsequent description assumes that a decision has been made to visit the comparator, as opposed to working through questionnaires. There is no doubt that personal visits are the more useful route.

The first point is that it is worthwhile to visit more than one comparable company so as to avoid being misled by idiosyncrasies within one organization. There is no maximum number, but obviously a law of diminishing returns begins to operate. Two companies can be considered to be the bare minimum, though more than four is unlikely to be economical.

Prior organization is essential; the benchmarking delegation cannot simply arrive and wander around. It is best that a preliminary assessment is made by a senior manager, who will draft out a program in conjunction with the benchmarking company. This needs to cover what should be included as well as an understanding of areas which are off limits. Once this brief has been drafted, it should then be passed to the benchmarking team who can elaborate on the areas they wish to examine and draft a request for information which can be sent ahead. This may seem a tall order, particularly where there is a limited understanding of the processes which actually exist at the target company, but it makes the time spent at the company (which must necessarily be kept short) far more productive.

The team itself should be drawn from middle management, supervisors, and experienced operators. The inclusion of relatively junior staff is essential if the exercise is to produce real change within the company. If too senior a team is used, there may well be a reaction against the exercise back at the company with it being viewed as a stick to be used against the workforce.

During the visit, it is essential that attention does not wander away from the selected areas. Observations need to be documented and a time in the day allocated to this. The duration of the visits will of course vary, though a period of one or two intensive days is usually sufficient.

After the visit, it is essential to summarize the findings and report back. A dual reporting line is useful: one to senior management on the main findings, so they are reassured about the value of the visit, and a second report to those involved in the operation of the processes so as to spread best practice. The latter is best done verbally to the group involved in the operation; this assumes that there are such groups in place who meet to sponsor continual improvement within the organization; if not, one should be set up and made operational prior to the benchmarking visits; otherwise, the usefulness of the exercise will be limited.

Relevance of Activity-based Costing

On encountering the comparable organization, the first observation is bound to be the difficulty in comparing like with like. Departments and responsibilities are likely to differ from the familiar, and these differences have to be identified before valid comparisons can be made. So, for example, a comparison between two purchasing departments is likely to founder on the fact that they undertake different activities; for example, one organization may spend time prequalifying vendors while another does not.

It is therefore necessary to consider the activities, and their costs, taking place within the areas under review. In the next chapters, we outline in detail an activity-based costing approach, which is far more involved than would be necessary for calculating benchmarks. Here we simply note the advantages that activity-based costing provides. It gives:

- A common language for comparison across different organizations. Activities form the basic units of an organization, and as long as there are clear definitions of activities at a sufficiently close level of detail, it is possible to apply these common definitions in different organizations and arrive at valid comparisons of resource cost and process structure.
- A method for analyzing the effects of experience curves. Experience curves apply at the activity, not product or service, level. Quite often, the question of experience curves enters into benchmarking, and it is necessary to resolve these issues at the level of particular activities.
- A way of understanding the different emphasis that an organization places within a given function; for example, whether a company spends a great deal of its time expediting deliveries from suppliers, or alternatively, concentrates on educating suppliers to deliver product or services on time.

The principles and techniques of activity-based costing will form a major part of subsequent chapters, where it will become apparent that the topic is not only of use in explaining differences between organizations, but also in improving the performance of a given organization in detail.

Continuous Benchmarking

So far, the description of benchmarking has been highly pragmatic and has concentrated on the tasks which have to be undertaken by those wishing to start benchmarking for the first time. It needs to be emphasised, however, that benchmarking is a continuous process in its own right and not a single exercise.

The best vehicle for undertaking this is a quality program, where the search for continuous improvement can include the systematic search for examples of the best practice of other organizations.

INFORMATION REQUIREMENTS

Need for Information

The final step of the program involves the setting up of a sustainable system for the control of overheads. This, of course, requires the systematic generation of information to support decisions within each process. Now that business processes have been defined for the organization, it becomes possible to understand the types of decisions which have to be undertaken within each process and consequently the type of information required for the processes to function properly. Employing the classification of processes used previously, we now discuss:

- The types of decision which need to be made within each process and a topdown view of the type of information required to support those decisions.
- The performance measures which need to be generated to enable effective management.

Once the information and performance measure needs have been understood, an assessment can be made of the readily available systems which might support the management of the process.

Identifying the high-level information requirements is the first stage in defining an information systems strategy and an information technology strategy for the organization, which are necessary to avoid duplication and incompatibility. It is, however, only a preliminary stage; the detailed assessment of information requirements takes place in Step 2.

Order Fulfillment

The supply chain is usually the most information- and decision-intensive part of the business, demanding information on capacity planning, resource scheduling, and sometimes inventory levels. The sample processes given in the "Processes" section of this chapter were: define customers' products or service requirements, agree on delivery and schedule operations, manage operations capacity, procure material, and supervise inventory. We now discuss each of these in turn.

Define customers' product or service requirements. The decision is to choose which of the company's products or services will meet the customers' needs. This requires information on both the product and its relevance to the customer. The demands on the company's information systems are not great, but the work can be complex and mistakes very costly. The information systems required by the process are concerned with:

- The specification of the product and, where appropriate, configuration control.
- Composition of a quotation or sales order.

The main performance measures required for the management of the process relate to the cost of quality associated with:

- Specifying products which are either not compatible with the installed base or are not fit for purpose.
- Incorrect composition of the order.

This area can be a problem in manufacturing companies, where a complex product offering may need to be configured for a particular circumstance.

Agree on delivery and schedule operations. The decisions in this area are particularly complex, involving a decision on when the company can commit to delivery and the deployment of capacity so as to best meet the various commitments.

Unsurprisingly, this is a very information-intensive process. For make-to-order operations, in both the manufacturing and service sectors, setting a delivery date requires knowledge of resource and equipment availability; once a feasible date has been given for delivery, the order has to be incorporated into a master schedule for the operating units. For make-to-stock operations and wholesale or retail businesses, agreeing on delivery requires knowledge of stock levels and future commitments. In many companies, the information systems are already well developed. The most developed systems occur in manufacturing, in the form of Manufacturing Resource Planning systems, which provide:

- Master scheduling, which compiles a list of items which the organization intends to produce.
- Capacity planning, which confirms the master schedule is compatible with the available capacity.

- Material resource planning, which computes the material requirements needed to fulfil the master schedule. A closely related system is stock control, which can be used to supplement or substitute for material resource planning.
- Capacity requirements planning, which computes a detailed consumption of resource by work center.
- Operations scheduling, which produces "work-to" lists for each operating unit.

These subsystems, with the exception of material requirements planning, are fully applicable to the white-collar functions of service companies.

The performance parameters for this operation are concerned with:

- The reliability of delivery promises. It is necessary to separate the effects of unrealistic promises and poor coordination from the failure of the operational capacity to deliver.
- The response times offered to customers, given the level of inventory held, if this is relevant.

In the past, great importance was also placed on the level of utilization of the operations capacity; the schedules should not overutilize (through the use of overtime) or underutilize the available operational capacity. This is now given a lower priority, and the emphasis has shifted to being flexible to the customer's needs.

Manage operations capacity. The decisions in this area are concerned with tracking the physical operations and controlling them to ensure that actual performance complies to the schedule. While the process is certainly information intensive, there are fundamental differences in approach to the control of this process. One way favors a top-down directive approach and requires work-in-progress tracking and the continual updating of the work priorities for each work center. However, this can become too cumbersome, and an alternative way is for information to flow "horizontally" between operators and for working priorities to be developed at the operating level.

Interestingly, Japanese manufacturing companies put greater emphasis on the use of simple visual systems for the day-to-day control of operations as opposed to reliance on direction by computer systems. Nonetheless, there has to be some method of transferring the top-level master schedules to the operating level. One method is to use "pull" systems, whereby customer demands are declared at the final operational stage, and these are fed backwards through the supply chain with each stage making demands on its predecessor. These are described when "just in time" is discussed in Step 3, Radical Change. Assuming a top-down approach is adopted, the information systems necessary to control the operations will include:

- Tracking systems to identify the state and location of work-in-progress.
- Measurement systems to collect information on the resources consumed in the work.
- Variance analysis systems to compare the actual and scheduled work and to highlight backlogs.

In the past, performance measurement has concentrated on:

- Overall conformity to the agreed-on delivery schedule—the proportion of orders which are completed on time.
- The backlog of overdue orders.
- The actual consumption of resource, compared to the standard.
- The level of quality problems which occur.

The focus of the performance measurement is shifting now from an overriding concern with cost to timeliness and quality.

Procure material. The decisions to be taken in this process revolve around the management of the purchasing cycle (which is fully detailed in Step 4, Focused Change). The cycle comprises research, specification, supplier selection, ordering, monitoring, acceptance, and obtaining payment.

The research phase needs to be supported by systems to provide:

- Market intelligence, including the monitoring of market conditions, especially movements in cost indices for monitoring buyer performance and assisting in price negotiations.
- The status of the supplier qualification program, which should be dynamic and include the monitoring of supplier performance and reliability.

For the remaining phases, in manufacturing industry the process makes use of the following systems:

- Material requirements planning, which specifies the items to be purchased and the due date. The preferred supplier is also held within the system, typically in the item master file.
- Purchase order.
- Goods received.
- Purchase ledger.

For service companies, the material requirements and goods received systems will be much simpler, but nonetheless there is still the need to identify the services required and their timing and to take note of their delivery.

The management of the function requires similar information to the previous process, namely conformity to the delivery schedule, the backlog of overdue orders, and the difference between actual expenditure and targeted expenditure.

Supervise inventory. The decisions in this process involve the movement from one location to another, to ensure inventory is being held where it is required and expected. The information systems needed to support the process are those covered by Distribution Resource Planning systems, which cover:

- Stock recording systems, to record the current status of the inventory.
- Distribution planning systems, to plan the deployment and distribution resource.
- Systems using forecasting or ordering information to indicate the inventory requirements in each location.

The success of the inventory management is measured in terms of:

- The nonavailability of items.
- The accuracy of stock records.
- The degree of unnecessary distribution cost.

A further measure is, of course, the level of waste in the inventory, though a distinction has to be made between inventory becoming obsolescent and the deterioration of inventory.

Customer Development

The customer development processes, with the exception of after-sales support, tend to be less demanding on the organization's core information systems. Where systems support is required, it can be developed separately.

The investment in these systems is worthwhile for three reasons:

- They increase the productivity of the sales force, which will either lead to an increase in sales or to a reduction in this expensive resource.
- They lessen the dependence on individual sales people.
- They benefit the business by providing advance warnings of trading conditions. This can be invaluable, since otherwise the view of the market is limited to the forward order book. In industries where there is a long time between an expression of interest and the fruition of an order, the feedback from the sales force can provide a useful indication of future volumes, which could influence investment and recruitment plans.

We now describe the information requirements of the three processes defined earlier: acquire customers, identify customer requirements, and support customers.

Acquire customers. The decisions in this process are mainly concerned with the directing of resource, but the direction is very dependent on market intelligence, including:

- The market's composition, in terms of customers and their characteristics, and location and the purchasing authorities.
- Signals which indicate the intention to buy.

Once the market intelligence is understood, the remaining need is for information to match the resource to the opportunities through a measurement of availability and suitability of each sales representative to the task at hand. This is usually relatively simple.

The measurement of the performance of a sales force requires systems to report on:

- A series of ratios, showing the rate of conversion achieved in the sales process; for example, customer population to number of inquiries, the number of inquiries to the number of quotations, the number of quotations to the number of sales, and so on.
- The net effect of the conversion process: the numbers and value of sales closed, split by product or geographic area and sales representative.

The most difficult task is to separate the proactive sales, created by the efforts of the salespeople, and the reactive portion, where the customer takes the initiative.

Identify customer requirements. The decisions in this process can be highly judgmental, especially given the limited access to information on the potential customer's full situation. In this case, there can be no general statement of the information necessary to effectively manage the process; instead there is a dialogue with the customers to develop a full understanding of their needs. This dialogue is also an opportunity to develop the relationship between company and its customers.

It is also a difficult to measure performance. Assuming potential customers are fair judges of the competence with which their requirements have been identified, two possible measures of success are:

- The strike rate of proposals produced following the investigation into requirements.
- The time and expense involved in the process.

For businesses where there is an expectation that a potential supplier will research the customer's needs, this process will usually be the largest source of activities which do not earn revenue. Effective control is paramount, both to ensure a stream of future business and to avoid wasting resources.

Support customers. The decisions in this area can vary from meeting the customers' needs for physical support to a proactive sales role. Assuming the former case, the decisions require knowledge of the products or services that have been delivered. This history can be very complex, particularly where issues of configuration control are involved as well as a long sequence of updates and changes. Quite often the bulk of the cost of ownership of an item can occur during the support phase; this has prompted interest in continuous acquisition and life-cycle support systems (CALS) to pull together a consistent set of data from the inception of the project.

Performance measurement of the function requires information on the satisfaction of customers. Where delivery of physical components is involved the supply chain performance measures become relevant; for example, availability of items and timeliness of delivery.

Business Development

The business development processes usually do not rely on the collection of large volumes of information, though information may be collected from a wide variety of sources. Instead, the decisions depend on the manipulation of data and the drawing of inferences.

The processes defined earlier were plan products, manage brands, and develop products.

Plan products. These decisions relate to the management of the product life cycle, from inception and development to abandonment. This management of the product portfolio requires information, for each product, on the size and growth in market share and the product profitability or cash flow in order to funnel development expenditure into promising products. The assumptions on sales growth and development expenditure then need to be examined for their business implications.

This process is fundamental to the future business and, consequently, many of the relevant performance measures are at the corporate level; for example, growth and market share. These are not useful for monitoring process performance because they can be affected by many other factors. However, in some cases it is possible to measure the lead or lag the company has compared to its direct competitors, in months or years, and this allows a clearer view of the competence of the product planning process.

Manage brands. The decisions in this process seek to maximize the value of the brand, which in turn depends on maximizing profitability. The main variable elements are, of course, revenue and the distribution and promotion costs; the product cost is usually fixed. Maximizing the profitability requires information to deduce the incremental revenue and costs arising from any prospective action. This process requires diverse information on:

- The environment into which products are being sold, in terms of changes in demography, preferences, and regulations.
- The markets themselves, in terms of size, growth, and competitor products.
- The supply chain, including the availability of goods and the performance of the distribution channels.
- Access to new concepts from which to make proposals for new product development.
- Feedback on the actual product performance compared to the planned performance, broken down into relevant categories; for example, market, distribution channel, and geographic area.

The basic measures of performance are the value and profitability of the brand, as alluded to previously. As with corporate profitability, however, an eye has to be kept on future as well as current profitability.

Develop products. "Decision making" understates what is required in product development, which is an inherently creative process. However, this does not apply to the actual management of the process. Nonetheless, even the process management is difficult and to make it simpler each development project is usually decomposed into a hierarchy of small projects, each having its own input information and its own plan and a set of conditions for defining when the process is complete.

Particularly for engineering companies, this process can be highly information-intensive and demand the use of computer-aided design systems to manage the information and reduce the design lead times. Whatever the systems used, the basic information requirements are:

- The product specification, which the design must meet.
- The process targets and constraints; for example, time frames and resources.
- An understanding of available technologies and components, which may of course involve years of training.
- A comprehensive definition of the current design, in terms of material, geometry, and so on, and access to definitions of past designs. This last point is important for the whole enterprise; by building up a stock of "retained design," not only is design productivity increased, but also the learning and complexity costs are reduced outside the design department.
- An assessment of the degree of completion of the design. This is not always straightforward; input measures—money spent and time taken—are very poor surrogates. The assessment is much easier if the design has been broken down into small tasks because it is at least possible to identify if a subsidiary task has been finished.

Measurement of performance is in terms of cost, time, and quality, with the first of these three factors usually being the least important. The costs associated with late or bad design usually far outweigh the additional costs of getting it right.

Business Maintenance

We have noted that the process view does relatively little to reform the business maintenance functions, since there are no clear definitions and ends or even identifiable customers. However, they do require information with which to operate. The information requirements of the process responsible for human resources, finance, and infrastructure will be close to those of current personnel, accounting, and administration departments. For completeness, we describe these because they will have a bearing on the information strategy of the organization.

The three business maintenance processes highlighted earlier are manage human resources, manage finances, and maintain infrastructure.

Manage human resources. The decisions taken within this process vary according to the division between staff and line functions. The minimum information requirement needs systems to report on:

- The current workforce, their grade, pay, age, and so on.
- Human resource requirements to drive the recruitment process.
- Appraisal and training needs.
- Prevailing rates of pay for the various grades of staff.
- Legislation governing employment law.

There is a second type of information, which is less commonly collected; this is on the attitudes within the organization. This information can either be collected by occasional surveys or by use of the appraisal system and by exit interviews with departing personnel.

Manage finances. In nearly all organizations, the financial management systems are well developed because these systems are the mainstay of decision making throughout the organization, not just within the finance function. The systems provide for:

- Planning, ideally with the top-level strategic plan cascading down into a series of lower level short- and long-term plans. In this way, the organization can work in unison and confirm that all the proposed actions are affordable.
- Monitoring of actual performance against planned performance and ensuring there is clear accountability.
- Enabling competent financial management of the organization.

The core of these systems are the general or nominal ledgers, connected to which are the sales and purchase ledgers. Ideally, although it is not essential, other systems—for example, asset management and budgeting and forecasting systems—should be consistent and integrated with the ledger systems.

The performance of the three functions is measured by the degree of coordination achieved, the integrity of the information, and the financing charges.

Maintain infrastructure. The decisions involved with providing the general administration and information systems are varied, but their underlying principle is an understanding of the requirements of the business, the current state of the infrastructure, and a viable path to meet those needs from the present position. The basic information requirements are therefore:

- A statement of the needs of the organization, derived from an exercise such as this.
- A compilation of the current systems and assets.
- The opportunities presented by current technology and the constraints faced in the development.

The performance of this function is difficult to measure, since shortcomings will be felt by a general lowering of efficiency throughout the organization. Even if there are no serious complaints, this does not mean that opportunities have not been missed or that the same result could be achieved at lower cost. Nonetheless, the only feasible measures relate to the degree of satisfaction among the users of the various services provided.

Survey of Available Systems and Technologies

We have discussed at length the type of decisions to be made in each process and the types of information required to support these decisions. This enables a survey to be made of the market to understand the relevant:

- Types of system that are available to assist in the management of the process. While it might be thought that this risks prejudging the eventual systems solution, most types of system are available on a variety of platforms (that is, hardware plus operating system), so it is unlikely that any constraints on a future system will be introduced.
- Available technologies. These are not confined to data processing or storage, but include input/output technologies and communication.

It can be useful to be aware of this before Step 2 is undertaken, since they can then be discussed during the interview program. Becoming aware of the wider possibilities early on in the program increases the likelihood of innovative solutions before thinking has been conditioned by current practice.

SENSITIVITY ANALYSIS

Introduction

Finally, thought needs to be given to the sensitivity of the results of the external review to change. There is little point in conducting a thorough review based on current information if the changes in the offing are likely to alter the conclusions beyond recognition.

We do not propose a sophisticated methodology for this assessment. It is important, though, to review the conclusions at the end of this step and understand their sensitivity to key assumptions.

Method

The usual method of undertaking a sensitivity analysis is to identify all the input parameters to an analysis, vary them, and observe the effect on the outputs. The assumptions behind those input parameters that have a disproportionate effect on the output are then examined more closely. This approach is ideal where there are a small number of inputs, usually quantitative, and the relationship between input and output is clearly understood and often encoded in a spreadsheet. It is less easy to apply when there are a large number of factors which have influenced a decision, perhaps in a judgmental way.

In these cases, it is preferable to start from the conclusion of the planning exercise and identify the main premises on which it is based and to examine these in a level of detail proportional to their influence.

Critical Areas

In practice, the main changes are likely to be in the area of corporate strategy and technology. A decision to vertically integrate, the entry or exit of a competitor from the market, or a decision to adopt widespread outsourcing of internal activities could well affect the conclusions on customer requirements, key processes, or information requirements. In a similar way, major advances in technology can create new opportunities and threats.

BENCHMARKING CASE STUDY

Background

The company is engaged in the generation of electricity, mostly from coal power stations of similar design. The generation operations as a whole employ over 10,000 people, of whom the vast majority work in power stations.

The stations themselves are widely distributed throughout the country and the local management has to be largely autonomous. As a result of this autonomy and the relatively small size of the central staff, each power station has tended to follow its own course.

Objectives

A large cost reduction target has been imposed on the generating function, to be implemented over several years. The chief concern of management is that, in enforcing cost reductions, the temptation will be for local management to choose the easy short-term options. This is a major hazard because a key function of the management is the stewardship of the capital assets: If the assets begin to be neglected, to achieve short-term cost savings, this would not be detected until the damage has been caused and the cost to retrieve the situation would be enormous.

The objective is, therefore, to seek ways of ensuring that dispersed and autonomous local management adopt the proposed cost savings and do so in a way that does not jeopardize the capital base of the company.

Approach

The first step is to extract from the company's general ledger systems the costs incurred and the number of people employed in each cost center (unusually employee information is held on the ledger systems). The cost center structure is not uniform across all the power stations, as a result of the local autonomy, but the cost centers have been resolved down to a fine level of detail and have clearly descriptive titles.

It is essential to have a uniform system of cost analysis, and therefore we define the broad activities required to run a power station. This is done in conjunction with the staff of one of the power stations. The ledger systems divide the costs into operations, maintenance, and administration; and the activities maintain this distinction. The activities defined for each category are shown in Figure 2-7. Once the broad activities are clear, the next stage is, for each power station, to map the detailed cost centers onto the activities; this is done with the assistance of the staff of each power station, mostly by means of conversations over the telephone.

We now turn our attention to the cost information itself. It is held down to a very fine level of detail, and it would be overwhelming to extract it without significant aggregation. Therefore, the information is aggregated into broad categories which we call "cost elements" prior to extraction from the system. These are staff cost, materials, expenses, and contracts. The detailed cost lines are then aggregated into these broad

FIGURE 2-7 Sample Activity Library

Operations	Maintenance	Administration
• OA Operate Power Station 　* OA1 Production Planning, General Management 　* OA2 Shift Management and Training 　* OA3 Technical and Chemical Services 　* OA4 Fuel Operations 　* OA5 Waste Operations 　* OA6 Coolant Operations 　* OA7 Cleaning 　* OA8 Miscellaneous • OB Monitor Performance 　* OB1 Monitor Performance 　* OB2 Enhance Performance 　* OB3 Staff Safety • OC Sell Electricity 　* OC1 Sell Electricity	• MA General 　* MA1 Headquarters Maintenance 　* MA2 Power Station General Maintenance 　* MA3 Power Station Inspection and Testing 　* MA4 Projects 　* MA5 Training • MB Control and Instrumentation 　* MB1 Control and Instrumentation Maintenance 　* MB2 Protection and Measurement Maintenance • MC Mechanical 　* MC1 Mechanical 　* MC2 Corrosion Protection 　* MC3 Welding 　* MC4 Workshop and Outside Plant • MD Electrical 　* MD1 Electrical 　* MD2 Workshop and Outside Plant • ME Chemical/Civil 　* ME1 Chemical 　* ME2 Civil • MF Extension of Plant 　* MF1 Plant Life 　* MF2 Power Station Projects • MG Dismantle Plant 　* MG1 Dismantle Plant • MH Materials Management 　* MH1 Contracts 　* MH2 Purchasing 　* MH3 Inventory Management	• AA Human Resources 　* AA1 Management Planning and Development 　* AA2 Training 　* AA3 Employee Relations 　* AA4 Employee Benefits 　* AA5 Safety Risk Management • AB Finance 　* AB1 Management 　* AB2 Finance 　* AB3 Systems 　* AB4 General • AC Administration 　* AC1 General and Management 　* AC2 Office Services 　* AC3 Communications 　* AC4 Document Management 　* AC5 Security 　* AC6 Transport 　* AC7 Horticulture 　* AC8 Plant and Technical Support 　* AC9 Commercial Management
12 activities	21 activities	18 activities

categories. In doing so, the balance sheet items; the revenue items; and the finance charges, which are also held within the ledger systems, are dropped from the analysis.

Programming

The aggregation of the raw ledger data from individual cost lines into cost elements and from detailed cost centers into activities requires some programming.

Aggregating cost lines into cost elements is carried out in the ledger systems. The code each of the individual cost lines is allocated to a particular cost element and a program is run to sum the ledger costs of each line. Fortunately in this case, the detailed lines were already arranged in a sequence that bears a strong resemblance to the cost elements which were to be used in the analysis. The program, therefore, is not particularly complex and comprises a series of "if" statements to identify if the ledger code of a particular cost line is in a relevant range.

The second task is carried out after transfer of the aggregated data to a PC database application. A mapping is established for each power station, which relates each cost center (whose costs have now been aggregated into broad cost elements) to a particular activity.

The full-time equivalent figures are treated in a very similar way. The headcount, split by grade, is recorded by cost center in the ledger systems and is also passed over to the PC database application. The application aggregates the employment figures into staffing levels by activity.

At the end of these exercises, the company now has, for the first time, an ability to compare the costs and staffing levels in a uniform way across all the power stations. The form of the analysis is shown in Figure 2–8.

FIGURE 2–8
Activity Analysis

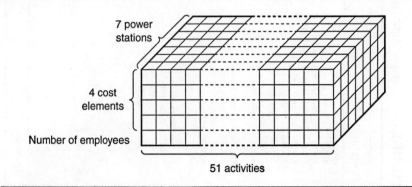

Internal Benchmarks

With a common classification of costs and human resources, it is now possible to form internal benchmarks; the comparison is restricted to power stations of similar design. The comparison can be carried out at the activity level, using either costs or number of employees. For brevity, we consider the employees' comparisons only. Figure 2–9 shows the comparison in staffing levels between almost identical power stations. The first conclusion is that the differences in staffing are surprisingly large and merit further investigation. Figure 2–9 also groups the activities into three categories:

- Operations concerned with the running of the power station.
- Maintenance concerned with protecting the asset base.
- Administration, containing support and policy activities.

Furthermore, the major differences in manpower occur in the area of administration activities. This highlights the consequences of total devolution of management to individual power station managers. The managers are taking their own views on retention of surplus staff, the appropriate level of training required and the need for support activities.

The next step is to obtain more detail by seeking a world-class benchmark to provide an indication of the appropriate level of staffing for each activity.

FIGURE 2–9
Comparison of Power Station Staffing

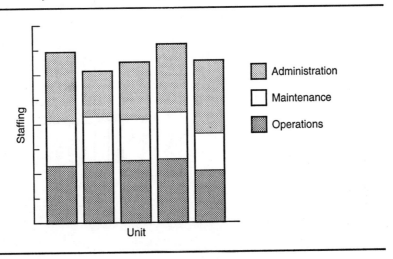

FIGURE 2–10 *Power Station Model*

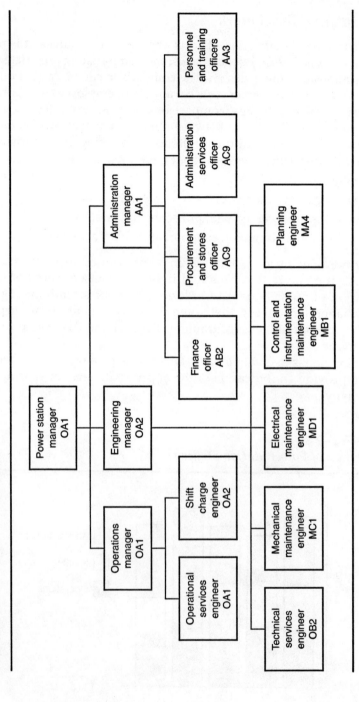

Benchmarking Case Study

World-class Benchmarks

An engineering manager of many years' experience of operating coal power stations is asked to define an ideal organizational structure, with the only constraint being the physical design of the power station. This definition includes every single employee required in the station; the top level is shown in Figure 2–10. The structure is very different from that currently in place within the company, though the structures in individual power stations also differ between themselves.

This would ordinarily create a problem for comparison; however, since the activity library has now been defined, it is a simple matter to map the world-class organization on the activity structure giving a set of world-class activity benchmarks; the mappings are also shown in Figure 2–10.

A comparison is then made with the staffing levels for the activities in a typical power station, as shown in Figure 2–11. The world-class benchmark suggests significant reductions in staffing are possible overall but, more usefully, the company can see which of its activities are overstaffed and also which are understaffed. The latter include some maintenance activities, where there is a danger that the capital base of the company could be endangered if the level of maintenance is not improved.

FIGURE 2–11
Comparison of Model with Actual

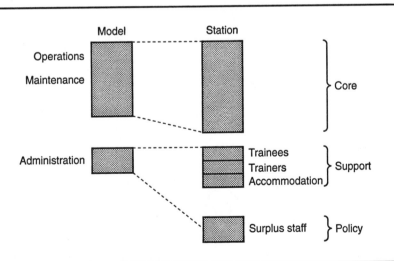

Conclusion

The management is left with two key conclusions:

- There is a need to set firm policy guidelines for managers, which determine the boundaries on the discretion they are able to exercise.
- The staffing of some activities is out of balance with the world-class ideal and, after allowing for specific local conditions, the levels need adjustment.

Finally, these conclusions have had to be formed as a result of a single exercise. There is a need in future to adopt an activity-based budgeting approach, where the cost centers refer to a specific activity. In this way, not only will the comparisons between power stations become far easier, but also a comparison can be made continually between each power station and the world-class benchmark.

Chapter Three

Activity Analysis

The thing that hath been, it is that that shall be; and that which is done is that which shall be done: and there is no new thing under the sun.

ECCLESIASTES *1:9*

INTRODUCTION

Objectives

The basic purpose of this step is very simple: We want to find out what is being done within the organization, why, how well, and for what cost. While organizational structures can vary widely, in a potentially distracting way, the basic activities of companies in the same industry are largely the same and, subject to technological advance, will remain so.

We must first define the boundaries of our study and then define the costs which are being incurred within this boundary. These costs are referred to as the cost base. We then research, by means of interview, the activities which cause these costs to be incurred. Once this is done, we can then relate the two and calculate the activity costs of the organization, allowing managers a view for the first time of what is being done and how much it is costing.

However, the calculation of activity costs is only the start. It is also possible to trace these costs to customers, products, or the other segments of the organization defined earlier. The project team can calculate product and customer profitability to a higher degree of accuracy than has been done before. In fact, this is usually one of the key deliverables of the project.

A further enhancement is to consider, for each activity, its:

- Attributes, which are simply features of an activity which can be recorded for subsequent analysis.
- Cost drivers, namely the factors within the company which influence the level of cost.

A further objective is to link the top-down process view to the detailed bottom-up activity analysis. Once this is done, the project team will be in a unique position, to:

- Combine the breadth of understanding only available to senior management with the knowledge of detail available to departmental managers.
- Relate the activities carried out within the organization to the satisfaction of the needs of customers.

We then analyze the company's information requirements, its current systems, its data, and its data-processing requirements. Although we considered the decision-making and process-information requirements in Step 1, External Review, this was only at a very superficial level. The detailed analysis of the information systems will be carried out in this step.

It will become apparent that the data storage and data processing requirements of the project team are far from trivial; therefore, we discuss the use of IT support tools to facilitate the process.

Deliverables

During this step, illustrated in Figure 3–1, the project team will define the following information:

- The departments which fall within the scope of the exercise.
- The cost base of the overhead structure.
- An activity map of the overhead structure.
- The activity costs.
- The attributes and drivers of the activities.
- The links between activities and their associated processes defined in Step 1.
- The costs of each cost object: customer, distribution channel, or product family.
- The segment profitabilities.
- The requirements for information systems and technologies.
- A database of costs and other information.

Issues

The framework for reporting the deliverables listed above is the activity map of the corporation. By building this map and using it to analyze all the costs and performance and information issues of the organization, the project team will form a consistent view of the whole company. This view, though broad, can focus down on the basic unit of the operation of the company: the activity.

There is also a great emphasis on building a cost model of the company. Unless the costs of each activity are properly understood, and these costs used to calculate the profitability of the products, customers, or distribution channels, the full range of decisions on changing the

FIGURE 3–1
Activity Analysis

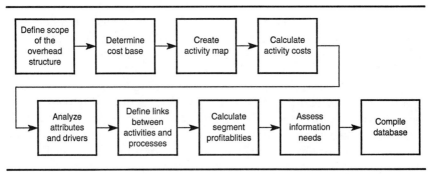

overhead structure cannot be made. However, after the cost model has been built, the influences on the cost and performance can be understood, and overheads can be controlled without resorting to crude across-the-board cuts or simply demanding higher performance for the same resource consumption.

The outcome of the reporting of the activity-based costs for the first time usually prompts many changes in priority within the organization. Prior to their calculation, managers have a view limited to their own area.

Before beginning the description of the actions to be taken in Step 2, Activity Analysis, it is useful, but not essential, to consider the nature of "cost"; below, we discuss the ways in which it has been measured in the past, namely full-absorption costing and marginal costing, and how it is to be measured in the future using activity-based costing.

The Nature of Cost

Much of the subsequent analysis will be concerned with the subject of costs, which is a concept more subtle than is often imagined. The apparent precision with which costs are calculated suggests to many that they are accurate and "true." In fact this is not the case, for two reasons:

- The method of calculation does not usually reflect how costs are caused by the activities of the company. This can be tackled by adopting better methods for the calculation of costs, and we later advocate the use of activity-based costing for this purpose.
- More fundamentally, there is no such thing as a single "true cost." This goes to the very heart of what constitutes a cost.

A cost is a number which is used to support a decision. How that number is calculated depends on the decision which is to be taken; in other words when asked What is the cost of this? the first response must be What do you want to know for?

Usually, the cost will be used to support a decision to be taken on whether to adopt one or two different courses of action. The calculated cost represents the difference in expenditure between these two different courses. This cost is often called a "differential cost." This is closely related to the concept of "marginal cost," which is the difference between the costs involved in maintaining the status quo and adopting a new course of action.

In the language of economics, we are searching for the "long-run marginal cost" between the different courses of action. However for the economist, the cost is the "opportunity cost," or the value forgone of the benefits of the best alternative use of resources. This view of costs cannot be faulted in principle, though accountants tend to feel uneasy about such definitions because of the lack of documentary evidence for adopting a particular figure as the "cost." Furthermore, economists are quick to point out that when calculating costs to support future decisions, historical expenditure should be ignored: Only future costs and benefits are relevant. To illustrate, a reliable (but unconfirmed) anecdote reports that at one time the first essay for first-year students at the London School of Economics was "'Deidre, you must marry me. I have spent three hundred pounds courting you.' Discuss." The theme of the essay was that historical costs are "sunk," cannot be recovered, and therefore should not affect future investment of expenditure.

The arcane differences between accountants and economists need not trouble us. For practical purposes, when calculating costs it is necessary to:

- Regard the cost of a resource as the price paid for it, except where issues of obsolescence are involved.
- Examine historical expenditure to understand which relate to the normal activity and the rest which should now be written off as no longer relevant. The former needs to be considered even if it refers to assets or material which have no alternative use, since it represents costs which must be recovered if production is to continue in the future; for example, to allow for the purchase of new machinery or material once the current stock is exhausted.
- Carefully define the decision which is to be made on the basis of the cost calculation.

On the last point, in many cases the decision to be made is implicit rather than explicit. For example, when calculating a "product cost" the implicit decision is usually to determine the minimum selling price for the item; if, however, the purpose were to consider product deletion, care would have to be taken to differentiate between those costs which would disappear if a certain product were deleted and those that would remain.

In the subsequent discussion of product cost, we will assume, however, that the purpose of the objective is to trace all of the costs of the company to the products, customers or distribution channels in a way which reflects why costs were actually incurred.

We now discuss the two bases on which costs are usually calculated, namely the full-absorption basis and the marginal basis. Neither is satisfactory, for different reasons. We then introduce a third method which is finding increasing acceptance, namely activity-based costing.

Full-absorption Costing and Its Problems

Full-absorption costing separates costs into direct costs and indirect costs.

Direct costs. These are allocated to a product individually. Significant direct costs include materials and direct employees. Allocating direct costs to products is of course the general aim in any costing system. When direct costs formed the major proportion of total costs, there was little to discuss about costing systems—the task was simple.

Indirect costs. Costs are indirect when it is uneconomic or impracticable to relate a cost to a particular product or service. Under full-absorption costing, the response is to use a two-step process whereby:

- Particular types of cost—for example, heating or rent—are allocated or apportioned to various cost centers, typically either production departments or service departments. In the case of service departments, costs are subsequently further allocated or apportioned to the production departments. If costs need to be apportioned, this is done on a representative base; for example, rent and heating costs are typically apportioned on the basis of floor area.
- The allocated and apportioned costs are then "absorbed" from a production-related cost center into the product cost, on the basis of a parameter such as direct staff hours, machine hours, or direct labor costs.

The problem arises from the relative sizes of the absorbed cost in a modern business. To illustrate, when direct labor cost is used for absorption purposes, the indirect costs are typically 350 percent the magnitude of the base used for the absorption!

The absorption of indirect costs into product costs can be highly misleading. This is not just because the indirect cost is far in excess of the cost on which the absorption was based, but also because the indirect costs do not vary in the same fashion as the base on which they are being apportioned. The bases used nearly all vary with the volume of goods being produced; for example, the number of direct labor or machine hours. However, many indirect costs do not vary in linear proportion to volume, but instead vary in proportion to the rate of clerical transactions; for example, these costs would vary only slightly if it was decided to double the production volume of a single product, but may well double if it was decided to add a second product range.

Producing misleading information in this way can have a dramatic effect on long-term overhead costs. Taking an example from manufacturing industry, the costing system will suggest to the product designers that in order to minimize product cost, they must reduce the number of direct labor and machine hours and so reduce both the direct and the absorbed costs. In fact decreasing the former could well increase the latter; such an event could arise if the designer chose to:

- Specify an externally manufactured component, which had no in-house manufacturing associated with it, but which involved considerable procurement effort;
- Reduce the direct labor, but in a way that resulted in a large increase in the number of parts, which is a major influence on the level of indirect cost.

Even if the designers ignore the costing system and follow their instinct, the resulting product will be overcosted and may fail if the minimum selling price is set on the basis of the outputs of the cost system, due to inadequate sales and volume being achieved.

The previous example explored the damage a full-absorption costing system can do when it is used for the purpose for which it was intended, namely product costing. More dangers appear if the costing system is used as a source of general performance measures. This usually happens in the case when the organization is driven by the need to perform well in periodic financial reporting, as is the case for most publicly quoted companies.

We continue to use examples drawn from manufacturing industry because it tends to be a very demanding environment for costing systems. The potential problems may include:

- The temptation to produce for stock, even where there is no clear demand, so as to enhance overhead recovery in the production facility. As a result of the accounting standards for the valuation of stock, overheads involved in production are considered "absorbed" into units produced as opposed to being fully written off in the relevant period; this even applies to time-based overheads which would have occurred at the same rate, regardless of production. Because underutilization of the production facility will lead to lower profitability, there is a temptation to keep the facility fully occupied even if there is no immediate market for the goods. Many an inventory reduction program has foundered on the needs to maintain factory utilization in a quiet period.
- The need to maximize the standard hours of production in a period can lead to a preference for large batch sizes so as to reduce setup times as a proportion of total hours. Apart from leading to excess inventory, this can reduce their responsiveness to customers in a make-to-order environment.

Introduction

- The use of the cost information for decisions on operating procedure. A classic misuse of the costs is by operations staff seeking to minimize the cost of each item and selecting the process route with the lowest cost. This will normally result in the use of old fully depreciated equipment and lead to the paradoxical result that the best equipment is the least utilized.

To summarize, full-absorption systems provide a rich seam of misinformation, which is misleading even when used for its main purpose of product costing and capable of further damage if it is applied to create performance measures.

The fundamental shortcoming of these systems is that they do not recognise causality: The principles of their calculation do not recognize why costs are incurred.

Marginal Costing and Its Problems

Given such vagaries, many companies choose to adopt a "marginal costing" system. Under this system, costs are classified as either fixed or variable. Fixed costs are those which are deemed not to vary with the volume of production, while variable costs do. To a first approximation, direct costs can be considered variable, and indirect costs can be considered fixed. The company then seeks to maximize the contribution towards fixed costs, where contribution is defined as the difference between revenue and variable cost. While this certainly circumvents the problem of dealing with indirect costs, it hardly solves it. It has the major disadvantage that much of the administrative cost, including labor cost, is now classified as fixed, and therefore excluded from the analysis. This rather misses the point that many of the labor elements of indirect cost are far from fixed: not only are they controllable, they are variable, but in proportion to parameters other than volume.

Moving back to the language of the economist, if the objective is to calculate the long-run marginal or differential cost between two different courses of action, this will not be achieved if costs which are variable in the long run are mistakenly classified as fixed. Doing so will flatter the course of action which gives a lower short-run variable cost (which is simple to identify) even though it has high long-run variable costs, because the latter will have been classified as fixed and therefore irrelevant to the decision. The classic case where this occurs is in the addition of new products or services to an organization's portfolio. The short-term cost may appear small compared to the increased revenue, but the long-term variable costs of supporting systems to deal with the increased complexity go unrecognized.

As with full-absorption costing, many of the problems of marginal costing occur when the information is misused. For marginal costing, the most common error occurs when marginal costing is transformed into marginal pricing. Marginal pricing is the temptation of organizations operating at undercapacity. Where there is the prospect of time-related overhead costs being incurred but not recovered, there is the option to fill empty capacity with orders which show a positive contribution but whose prices do not allow for covering fixed costs.

The danger is that, if this is repeated, the organization will never recover its fixed costs. The main obstacle of marginal pricing is that news travels fast, and if an organization has supplied a product or a service at a price just above marginal cost to one customer, a customer paying full price will demand similar treatment. The response is usually to invent a string of conditions for the lower price to apply, to deny the lower price to full-paying customers. Airline and railway companies are skilled practitioners of this art.

For others, the irony is that marginal pricing is only wise where an organization is working at overcapacity, and the fixed costs are already covered. A common reason for doing this is where the leading supplier in the market wants to move into a monopolistic position; by attacking competitors with prices to which they cannot respond, there is the prospect of driving them out of the market or perhaps lowering the value of the business for an eventual takeover. This highly rewarding anticompetitive practice is given the unflattering soubriquet of "dumping."

Activity-based Costing

We have discussed the difficulties in measuring costs and how the methods used in the past have had their limitations, both in their principles of calculation and in the ways the information has been used. The dissatisfaction with traditional approaches to calculating costs spurred a drive to develop new costing methods. Much of this work has been sponsored by those outside the finance function—the people responsible for the operations of companies have been demanding better cost information. The movement has been successful, and the results of the exercise have gained popularity under the title activity-based costing. There are many reference sources on activity-based costing. Numerous articles have been published by Cooper and Kaplan, two Harvard professors; some of their articles have been summarized in *The Design of Cost Management Systems: Text, Cases & Readings* (Cooper & Kaplan, 1991). A second source of innovation has been the task force set up under the auspices of the Consortium for Advanced Manufacturing—International (CAM-I), whose original findings were published in *Cost Management for Today's Manufacturing* (ed. Berliner & Brimson, 1988). Other references include "Cost Accounting Overhaul" (Fradette et al., 1988), *Activity Accounting* (Brimson, 1991), and *Activity Based Management* (ed. Morrow, 1992).

The activity-based costing methods outlined below are based on the CAM-I approach. The other influence is the use of a series of structured interviews to gather data with the maximum of efficiency, which is a method that has been proven on many assignments. The structural interview method was summarized in "Cost Leadership and Activity Analysis" (Booth, 1992).

Activity-based costing starts with the premise that activity causes cost and activities occur for a reason, namely to provide or to support the provision of a product or service. Therefore, in calculating a product cost, for example, it is necessary to link the performance of an activity with the creation of the product. In forming this link, "tracing factors" are used. Most tracing factors are not connected with the volume of goods produced but to the number of particular transactions; for example, sales orders and purchase orders.

Activity-based costing resolves costs into three categories:

- *Volume-dependent costs*, which equate to the traditional direct staff category.
- *Fixed costs*, which are genuinely of a fixed nature over a short period of time, such as rents and rates.
- *Transaction-dependent costs*, which cover the bulk of indirect staff activities.

It is the last category which is the focus of attention in activity-based costing. Whereas in the past this category was relatively insignificant, its size now merits a proper analytical approach. We now outline such an approach, which is a major part of Step 2.

THE SCOPE OF THE ORGANIZATION

Identifying the Boundaries

During Step 1, External Review, some definition of the organization's boundaries must have been formed, as a necessary step to understanding both the organization's customers and their requirements. Nonetheless, there could still be some ambiguity on the precise scope of the work because the analysis so far has been process based, and processes can cross organizational boundaries. In fact, these interfaces are of crucial importance because they usually represent the main source of poor control. If there is any choice in the matter, the scope of the work should, wherever possible, encompass complete processes. If only fragments of most of the key business processes lie within the boundary, the result will be that the project will optimize parts of the process, perhaps to the detriment of the process as a whole.

Furthermore, there is little point in conducting a project on controlling the organization using a structure over which the sponsors of the team have little control. The control need not be absolute, but it must be substantial. It is possible to bring suppliers within the boundary if there is a close relationship with the supplier; for example, a partnership sourcing type of arrangement.

Of course, these two requirements may be incompatible; those sponsoring the work may only have substantial control over fragments of the processes. In this case, the question must be asked whether the project is better conducted at a higher level within the organization or even whether the organization boundaries are appropriate in the first place.

For many readers, the previous discussion will not apply because it will be quite clear where the boundaries of the corporation lie. We now consider identifying the departmental units that lie within the boundaries of the study.

Defining the Enclosed Structure

The proposed method for calculating activity costs makes heavy use of interviews and discussions with the line managers of the organization. It is therefore essential to define who should be interviewed and on what topic. In so doing we are, in fact, creating an internal structure within the boundaries; this structure consists of a series of centers, termed *activity centers*, which are closely related to the cost centers.

The activity centers should be consistent with the departmental and budgetary framework of the organization, if at all possible. There is no doubt that this makes the ensuing interviews far simpler because the interviewees are being asked to:

- Comment on the activities they are responsible for supervising.
- Allocate a set of costs with which they are familiar.

There will be greater accuracy, accountability, and ownership of the eventual results if there is a clear relation between the activity centers used in the analysis and the familiar structures of the organization.

Sometimes the costs allocated to an activity center do not match those reported for the constituent cost centers. This can happen if all of the costs which fall within a manager's area are not reported, perhaps because the costs are outside his or her control; for example, depreciation. This can be tackled by including the additional costs in separate categories and explaining that these costs are relevant to the operations of the manager's department but are not normally apparent in the usual statements.

Usually, cost centers have to be combined because there are too many centers for the purposes of the analysis. We explain in the following section that this is tackled by aggregating the cost centers and involving all the relevant managers in group interviews. This does not generally present a problem. More difficulty arises where cost centers need to be split, perhaps because the cost center is too large and contains too many dissimilar activities. If cost centers are split, the computational effort and the potential for confusion is considerable. The preferred route is therefore to aggregate existing cost centers where necessary and to avoid splitting of centers.

Distribution of Activity Centers

We have discussed creating a series of activity centers and, if necessary, aggregating cost centers in cases where the existing ones represented too fine a level of detail. This begs the question of what is the appropriate level of detail at which to conduct the data collection.

For the smaller organization—say under 1,000 employees—the number of activity centers will approximate to the number of managers, though sometimes managers may be considered to be in charge of more than one activity center if they control two distinct sets of activities. For example, finance and administration could be considered as separate activity centers even if they reported to the same manager.

The number of activity centers should not, however, increase in direct proportion to the number of employees within the organization: there is a natural limit beyond which the exercise becomes unwieldy. Most exercises are conducted with between 10 and 40 activity centers, and this gives a satisfactory compromise between sufficient detail and prohibitive complexity.

Apart from deciding upon the number of activity centers, decisions have to be made on their distribution. Activity centers should be created where:

- Either a significant amount of overhead cost is incurred,
- Or several key activities are undertaken; in other words, there is significant complexity.

Applying these guidelines will result in the costs of the different activity centers being broadly similar, except where:

- A large amount of cost is incurred in a single homogeneous area. In this case, the activity center would be large because it would not make sense to divide the area. This situation most usually occurs where there is a whitecollar production-type function involved in the processing of large amounts of information in a repetitive way.
- Many distinct activities are taking place in a particular area of the firm. This would justify the creation of an "undersized" activity center.

Where there are multiple sites carrying out similar activities, these sites should have the same activity center structure to permit a comparison across sites. Where there are a large number of sites, it may be necessary

FIGURE 3-2
Activity Centers and Activities

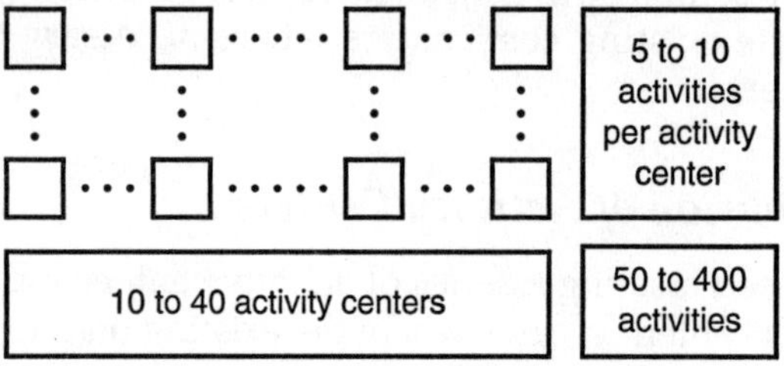

☐ ⋯ ☐ ⋯⋯ ☐ ⋯ ☐ ⋮ ⋮ ⋮ ⋮ ☐ ⋯ ☐ ⋯⋯ ☐ ⋯ ☐	5 to 10 activities per activity center
10 to 40 activity centers	50 to 400 activities

to select a few as models for the rest. This should be viewed as a last resort because it is difficult to make suggestions for improvement at a location which has not even been visited.

To summarize, in creating the activity structure we are seeking to identify between 10 and 40 activity centers, which account for significant areas of cost or complexity and which will usually contain between 5 and 10 activities. The number of activities can therefore vary between 50 for a simple analysis and 400 for a detailed study. This is illustrated in Figure 3-2.

THE COST BASE

The Scope of the Cost Base

The next step, and one that is frustratingly difficult, is to establish the "cost base" of the organization, namely how much cost is being incurred during a period within the declared boundary. As well as establishing how much is being spent, it is also useful to understand what type of resource is being purchased; for example, materials.

Although we are primarily interested in support costs, at this stage there are many advantages in understanding the total cost base of the organization since:

- It allows a view to be taken of the relative significance of the administrative cost, compared to other types of cost.
- There is often not a clear distinction between what can be regarded as support and that which is direct labor. For example, there is little difference for the purposes of cost control between the cost of an operator of a machine-paced work center and the cost of a clerk who schedules work for the center.

- It is far easier to exclude costs from specific analyses than to add back costs not included in the original analysis, which always carries the risk of double counting.

It is straightforward to create categories for direct costs as well as the traditional overhead costs to permit the two categories to be kept apart. Even when a decision is made to examine the total cost in establishing the cost base, there still seems to be room for endless debate on whether it makes sense to include some items, particularly in the area of finance charges. The author's preference is to include these, and to allocate the finance charges on the basis of the capital requirements.

The ideal situation is to be able to reconcile the cost base used in the analysis with that formally reported in the periodic financial statements; this applies equally to private and public sector organizations. If this is achieved, not only is the credibility of the subsequent analysis improved — there is recognition of the "official" figures—but also in calculating activity costs there is reassurance that nothing has been missed. We now discuss which of the various periodic financial statements provides the best source of information.

Period of Analysis

A decision has to be made on the period over which the cost information and the nonfinancial information, which is used to support the tracing of costs, is collected. The most difficult part of the data collection is usually the gathering of the nonfinancial information needed to trace the activity costs. This has a bearing on the choice of period. There is little point in selecting a period in which to analyze costs if there is no nonfinancial information which has been kept for that period or if it cannot be estimated.

Other considerations apply where the company is undergoing change. Where there is a seasonal cycle to the business, the period chosen has to include a whole number of seasons; for example, if there were three seasons per year, the period could either cover four months, eight, or a whole year. If this is not done, any extrapolation will be misleading both in terms of product mix and total volume.

Where there has been a number of exceptional events in the past—for example, unusual orders, product deletions—a period has to be selected which is representative of the future. If there is a general volatility in either volume or mix, taking a relatively long period of time allows these variations to be smoothed out. However, if there are underlying trends, too long a period could obscure these by including too great an amount of outdated information.

Finally, given the advantage of reconciling the cost base with the reported financial statements, if there is a recognized period for the preparation of financial reports, it is useful to arrange for the period for the collection of cost information to coincide. In this way, any queries on the overall sum of costs used can be answered by reference to an accepted document.

Sources of Information

The advantage of reconciling the cost base to the periodic financial statements is that it is likely that the results of the activity analysis exercise will be controversial; if they are not, it is questionable whether the exercise was worthwhile. It is natural that those who feel that their interests will be damaged by the new information will seek to discredit it. One approach is to question the competence of the method which produced the results. However, if the process described in this chapter is followed, there should be little problem in explaining and defending it.

A second approach is to challenge the validity of the input data, and care has to be taken in ensuring that all the data used have an authoritative and traceable origin. Obtaining authoritative nonfinancial information, which is used to trace costs, can be difficult; it is typically collected and stored less thoroughly than financial information. In practice, the nonfinancial information is derived from a variety of systems, and it is the responsibility of the project team to keep track of the managers who supplied it and to ensure that it is consistent. If the cost base is to be based on a future estimate of costs—for example, the forthcoming budget—this requires obtaining the forecasts of the *future* nonfinancial information on which the budget was based; for example, production volume and number of orders.

Turning our attention to the financial information, this is not usually gathered individually. Instead, the task is to identify the most appropriate source documents. There are two common sources:

- *The general ledger*. This is the main document of record of money spent within an organization, and hence it cannot be challenged numerically. Furthermore, it is usually kept to a fine level of detail, and consequently it is often straightforward to aggregate these detailed categories into larger categories needed for the analysis. Its disadvantage is that it is a historical document, and if the organization is in a state of flux, the cost behavior of the past may not resemble that of the future.
- *The budget*. This offers the advantage of being based on estimates of future costs, rather than being a historical record; however, it is often not compiled to such a close level of detail. A further disadvantage is that it is sometimes not accepted within the organization as an accurate picture of future costs. While this would be a sad comment on the competence of the budgeting processes, it is worth considering before adopting the budget as the source of information.

In the subsequent discussion, we will assume that the general ledger is used as the source of financial information.

It is usually the case that information is modified after extraction from the source document. Reasons for this may include the need to negate the effect of cross-charging that can occur within a general ledger and obscure the level of costs which actually occur within a given costs center, or a belief that the ledger costs are not appropriate. We now consider these adjustments to the source data.

Adjustments to the Source Data

Ideally, once the source of the cost information has been settled, it could be used within the analysis without further ado. This is rarely the case, and it is usual to have to manipulate the cost information. This manipulation may not always affect the overall total cost; if it does, reconciliation procedures need to be set up to ensure any additional cost being added or subtracted to the cost base is understood and can be verified.

Taking the case where the total of the cost base does not change, there are two common types of adjustment:

- Removing cross-charges. Frequently, cross-charges (also known as departmental allocations) have been made in the source data that will obscure the actual costs of particular activity centers. For example, the charges for information technology may have been apportioned across many departments, obscuring the total cost of the function. In these cases the cross-charges need to be reversed.
- Apportionment of resource costs. Sometimes particular resource costs will not have been allocated to activity centers; for example, telephone charges and leasing charges. Instead, they remain in the source data as resource costs. Since we wish to trace the activity center costs to activities, these resource costs need to be apportioned to the activity centers. The only exception would be where a particular cost was not to be allocated to the general activities, but preserved in total, for direct allocation to cost objects. This can be done by keeping the cost in a dummy activity for subsequent allocation.

These adjustments are illustrated in Figure 3–3.

Other types of adjustments to the cost base affect the overall total. The two most common reasons are:

- Substitution of a particular cost for a more relevant parameter. For example, it may be felt that the inclusion of depreciation would give a misleading view on the future costs of certain overhead activities because the relevant equipment was fully depreciated and would soon need replacement. In this case, the depreciation figure would be replaced with a charge reflecting the replacement cost of the equipment.

FIGURE 3-3
Adjustment of Allocations

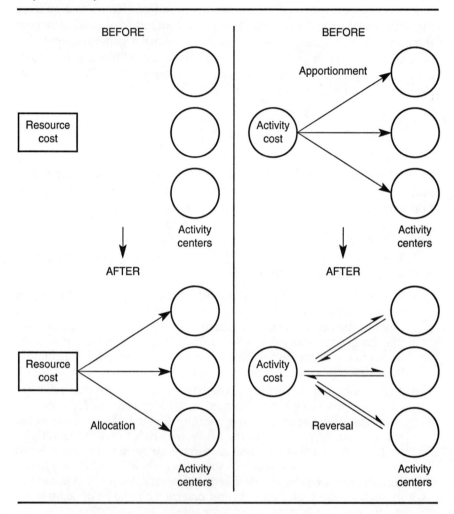

- Avoiding arbitrary cost allocations. In many cases the boundary of the study will have been drawn along familiar financial reporting boundaries, which cut through departments or indeed individuals. When this happens, the department or individual concerned has its cost apportioned accordingly, usually in quite an arbitrary manner. Either these apportionments can be taken at face value, or the gross costs can be included in the study and the activity analysis used to examine whether the existing apportionments are, in fact, accurate.

The necessary adjustments of the source data are usually carried out in a spreadsheet as a preliminary step to the main analysis. As noted above, if changes are made, reconciliation procedures need to be undertaken to check that the total costs have not been accidentally inflated or reduced.

Aggregating Cost Centers into Activity Centers

So far we have explained how to define the scope of the cost base, collect information on it, and make any necessary adjustments. The next step is to transform the cost base from a statement of cost by cost center into a more summarized form—a statement by activity centers.

We have already discussed the principles behind identifying activity centers. There now remains the detailed computational task of transforming the source data from cost center form into activity center form. If the activity centers are simply aggregated cost centers, this is not difficult. Where cost centers have to be split, the task is more complex. This is illustrated in Figure 3–4.

Aggregating Cost Lines into Cost Elements

After the scope of the cost base has been defined, the next step is to determine the types of cost which will be used in the analysis. In the language of activity costing, these different types of cost are referred to as cost elements.

FIGURE 3–4
Forming Activity Centers

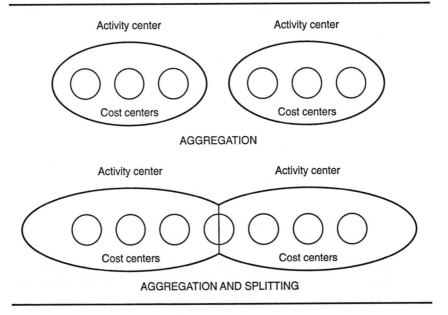

Before we discuss the various available categories, it is worth considering why different categories are needed at all. The reason is that different types of cost within a cost center may need to be traced to different activities in different proportions. For example, it is conceivable that within one activity center, most of the staff cost will be allocated to one activity, most of the travel expenses to another activity, and most of the depreciation charge to a third. In such cases, having more than one cost element is essential if costs are to be traced accurately. However, the message here is to keep it simple, since the complexity of the analysis rises in proportion to the number of types used. Indeed, in cases where the vast majority of cost is related to employment and the remaining costs are generally concerned with employee support—for example, the costs of premises, stationery—it is possible to work with a single cost element.

We now give examples of cost elements which can be used in the analysis of the cost base. Following from the earlier comments, we include categories that can be used to analyze the whole of the cost base, not just the support portion, though once the nonsupport portion has been categorized separately, it may be subsequently excluded from the analysis, if desired.

Not all the cost elements in the following list need be used, and conversely there may well be some which are not included below which would need to be used in a particular organization. Whatever the choice of cost elements, the computational process is to take the source data, which consists of details of cost lines grouped by activity center, and allocate each cost line to the most relevant cost element. The cost lines are then added together to arrive at a summary of the costs within each activity center, stated in cost element form. Possible cost elements include:

- *Direct labor.* The term is usually applied to the employment costs, including noncash benefits—for example, pensions and insurance—of employees who are directly associated with the operations; their time input is recorded by the booking of time and estimated by the use of standard times. In the past, such employees have tended to be manual operators, and the term "direct" is often equated to "manual labor." This can be misleading since it is quite possible for the time of designers to be directly booked to a particular product or service, especially when a job or project costing system is in operation. On the other hand, some manual labor may not be associated with particular products or services, such as machine maintenance. For our purposes, direct labor cost is a cost which can be related to a particular product or service by means of a standard time. If this relation exists, it is possible to link the costs directly to the products, and hence calculate profitability, without the intermediate step of activity analysis (the standard times are themselves a form of activity analysis). Nonetheless, this is not always done, either because the standard times are not trusted or because they do not account for issues such as setup time.

- *Indirect labor.* This refers to the cost of employees who are engaged in activities traditionally described as overheads. Identification of indirect labor is simple once the definition of direct labor is settled; it is simply the remainder of the labor charge which is not deemed to be direct! The question sometimes arises whether indirect labor involved in production should be classified separately to that involved in sales, administration, and distribution. There is no doubt that it is often useful to distinguish between the two. This can be done either by the costs being classified as different cost elements or by means of the attributes described later.
- *Materials and consumables.* Material costs are those which can be directly related to a unit of output. Consumable costs refer to items "consumed" during operations but whose relation to units of output is indirect. Consumable costs are usually small, so they are categorized with materials; however, a separate classification is possible.
- *Facility and supplies expenses.* These comprise charges for administrative support services or facilities. Some expenses represent bought-in services which may otherwise be carried out by indirect labor; others are charges for facilities. There may be merit in separating production expenses from those incurred by sales, administration and distribution.
- *Travel and accommodation.* Where certain activities incur specialist travel costs for a company, perhaps related to selling or, alternatively, to the buying of particular materials, it is worthwhile to treat these expenses as a separate cost element so as to allocate them to these activities.
- *Depreciation.* When machinery or buildings are purchased, their costs are accounted for through a depreciation charge which appears in the financial accounts. This is usually treated as a separate cost element. An alternative course is to employ a capital charge proportional to the cost of replacing the asset to avoid being misled by the use of fully depreciated equipment or by a depreciation policy designed for tax purposes.
- *Other charges.* There is usually a category required for miscellaneous charges which fall within the cost base. One example is the cost of servicing any debt, or other finance charges, that fall within the cost base; another example would be the cost of offering discounts. In many cases, the costs in these categories would be allocated to special dummy activities, rather than the general activities, and then allocated to products or customers directly.

On the last point, the finance charges are linked to the capital requirements of the business and are best traced directly to products or customers via a dummy finance charge activity. The tracing of these costs should reflect the different capital requirements of the products and customers. We now consider how to analyze these capital requirements.

Capital Requirements

In the control of administrative costs, most attention will be paid to the operating costs of the organization—revenue costs deducted from income in order to calculate earnings before interest and tax (EBIT). However, the interest payments, or finance charges, are also administrative costs, which are dependent on the capital requirements of the organization; these cannot be ignored, especially since they are controllable.

To assist in this control, the intention is to trace the finance charges of the company to its products and customers in a way that reflects the need for capital. The various categories of asset used in the analysis and the methods used to trace the costs are:

- *Fixed assets.* This refers to machinery or buildings which have been purchased to support the operation. One measure for the recognition of the contribution of fixed assets towards the finance charge is the gross book value, namely the amount of money originally paid for an asset, which is the amount of money committed and which cannot be used for alternative purposes. Sometimes it is not possible to use the gross book value for tracing purposes. An alternative, though not ideal, is to use the depreciation charge which is proportional to net book value; this is obtained by setting all the cost elements in the model, apart from depreciation, to zero and observing the depreciation cost allocated to each product and customer;
- *Working capital charges.* The three components of working capital (inventory, debtors and creditors) are traced to either products or customers, as follows:

    The amount of inventory by product range is estimated.

    Creditors are traced in a similar way to inventory, namely an estimate is made of the creditors associated with each product range and credit given accordingly.

    The debtors are of course related to customer groups, and it is relatively simple to estimate the average time it takes a particular customer group to pay and hence the capital tied up in each group for a given turnover.

The capital requirements of each individual product and customer are then estimated and used to trace the finance charge. In a similar way, other activity costs will be traced later in the program.

An alternative to tracing the actual finance charge is to apply a nominal capital charge, calculated as a percentage of the capital requirements. This has the disadvantage of losing the reconciliation with the cost base, though it makes the application of the capital charge independent of the debt/equity position adopted by the company; it would be particularly appropriate where the finance charge was in fact a credit item or was subsidized by the holding company. The most appropriate method is that which produces product and customer costs which reflect the different uses of capital.

FIGURE 3–5
Formation of Cost Base

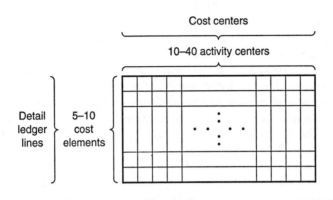

Conclusion

In this section, we have outlined the preliminary steps needed to produce a well-conditioned set of cost information. It began with specifying the boundaries of the cost base, selecting the appropriate period for the analysis, and identifying a reliable source of cost information.

Once this was done, the next step was to specify the structure into which the cost information would be summarized and then to rearrange it in that form. The process is illustrated in Figure 3–5.

THE ACTIVITY MAP

Introduction

"Building an activity map" is a phrase often heard during an activity analysis exercise. It is a graphic phrase and quite a good one. Most "maps" of organizations are organization charts showing how line management responsibilities are defined. While purporting to show everything, they in fact show very little. They do not show what is done, nor how the different activities link together to form the processes which satisfy a customer's requirement. Moreover, it is not apparent that different activities may be duplicated in several departments or that the fulfilment of a simple process will require numerous interfaces between departments.

An activity map is the first step in overcoming these shortcomings. It shows the activities that take place within the company and shows their location. It is the basis for much of the subsequent analysis. We now outline how an activity map is constructed.

The First Interview

Building the activity map will require the participation of a large number of people, between 10 and 40. To limit the drain on their time and to make the task of the project team manageable, it is essential to adopt a formalized approach to the gathering of information.

The best approach is to prepare an information pack and questionnaire which can be sent to all the interviewees for completion prior to the interview, so that the interview itself is confined to answering specific questions and exploring the meaning of the answers given. The pack can be sent in the internal mail, though it will often appear formidable, so a short pre-meeting to talk the manager through the material can be useful.

To set the scene, the information pack must begin by briefly describing the exercise and why it is being undertaken. This formality may seem excessive for smaller organizations, but nonetheless it is surprising how even among a small group of people misunderstandings can arise. The most frequent misunderstanding is that the exercise is the precursor to human resource reductions when in fact there is nothing of the sort in mind.

There should follow a description of the task immediately at hand and how it fits into the overall scheme. This is the first interview which will determine the activities which take place in a particular department, and a subsequent interview will be used to trace costs to these activities and to label the activities with various attributes.

To assist the manager in identifying the activities of his or her department, it is helpful if the manager is supplied with an initial list of activities and is then asked to add and delete activities from this list. We now discuss the use of these activity libraries.

Activity Libraries

An activity library is a standard model of an organization, sometimes referred to as an enterprise model. Models can be built for different industries; for example, banks, public utilities of different sorts, and various manufacturing industries. The implication is that the activities for organizations in a particular field are not organization-dependent, but are largely standard. This is the case if the model is defined precisely, for example; it is not sufficient to have a single manufacturing industry model, there needs to be individual models for various industries such as aerospace, automotive, batch manufacture, process manufacture, and textiles.

If a standard model can be used, it offers many advantages which include:

- *Transfer of experience.* If an organization in a particular sector has been examined previously, there is a great economy of effort involved in retaining this analysis. The list of activities will have

been tried and tested. Where there are differences between the organizations, this itself is a topic for examination.
- *Explanation.* When managers receive the information pack for the first interview, it may appear daunting. A list of activities which can be expected to occur in their departments gives the request for information a tangible foundation. It demonstrates that some thought has been given to the manager's own area.
- *Standardization.* This is the largest benefit of all. There is a danger that during the discussions with different managers the same activity can be called by two different names, and the same names can be given to two different activities. This will invalidate the work and must be avoided. By starting the discussions with a list of activities and their descriptions, the risk of this taking place is minimized.

There are also two disadvantages:
- There is a danger that genuinely unique features of the organization will be ignored as an attempt is made to fit all activities into the standard format.
- It reduces the need for managers to think about the activities which take place in their department.

In the author's view, the use of libraries does provide a net benefit, as long as the drawbacks are considered during the interview.

Interview Conduct

The information pack needs to be sent out a few days before the interview takes place. The interview itself is best kept to an hour's duration, with the possibility of a follow-up if necessary. Longer interviews can lose direction and place an unacceptable load on both the project team and on the interviewee.

After answering preliminary questions, it is necessary to confirm with the managers the activity centers for which they are responsible. Once this is understood, the conversation can then move on to the specific activities within each activity center which the managers have identified as under their control. Usually, there will be between 5 and 10 such activities. A greater number than this should be avoided because subsequently costs will have to be apportioned between activities, and this can be difficult if there are a large number of them.

There should be some degree of commonality between the managers' views of the activities under their control and the initial lists supplied from the activity library. If this is the case, the discussion can then concentrate on the additions and deletions. These need to be discussed carefully, since, after all, they are the first input the managers have made to the project. They are also a sign of operations being carried out in a different way to that which was expected, and this may either show an advancement on previous practice or an area for improvement.

In considering additions to the list, it is important that the new activities have a clear purpose; to illustrate, it would be unwise to add activities such as answering the phone, management, or attending meetings. Instead, the team would want to identify why these events took place. Furthermore, there is little point in adding activities that take up less than 5 percent of an individual's time, unless they form an important part of some other analysis; for example, the attribute analysis.

The interviews have to strike a balance between the gathering of information and obtaining a wider view. Too mechanical an approach will deny the background information that will prove invaluable for identifying opportunities for improvement, but a too discursive approach should not be adopted.

Collation

At the end of the first interview round, the project team will have identified a list of activities taking place in each activity center. In some cases, an activity will be unique, though in other cases it will be seen that an activity is being undertaken across the organization. The information needs to be collated and checked for consistency. If similar functions take place on different sites but they report very different activities, this needs to be investigated.

The finalized activity map needs to be entered into a software support tool, which is used for the storage of information. We describe the uses of such a tool at the end of this chapter.

THE ACTIVITY COSTS

Introduction

The identification of all the activities within a company is the first step in controlling them. However, it is not sufficient simply to identify what activities take place; there must be some indication of their significance. Significance can be measured in different ways. One way is by counting the number of people engaged in the activity. This head-count measure is popular because of its tangibility, though it does suffer from two disadvantages:

- It makes no allowance for different levels of employees engaged in an activity. Expensive employees appear as the same resource as lower-paid employees;
- It does not allow for different practices in buying in external services; for example, it is possible to appear more efficient on a head-count measure simply by subcontracting out services.

For this reason, cost is the preferred parameter for gauging the size of activities. However, head-count analysis is of use in other areas; for example, analyzing the fragmentation of activities.

The Second Interview

The second interview is a far more formidable affair than the first, both for the project team and for managers being interviewed. It is also far more likely to create defensive reactions from the managers being interviewed. In the first interview, we were asking What do you do? which is relatively nonthreatening. Now we are asking How exactly do you spend your budget?

Before the second round of interviews can begin the project team needs to have calculated the costs within each activity center, split into cost elements. The principles behind this have already been described. The actual calculation would usually be undertaken in parallel with building the activity map.

For each interviewee, a documentation pack needs to be prepared, giving a brief summary of the purpose of the interview, namely to link costs to activities, followed by:

- A reminder of the activities the manager has identified as occurring in the activity center.
- A statement of the costs for which the manager is responsible, broken down for each cost element. If it is the intention that the manager verify these costs, it will also be necessary to show how the cost elements have been built up from the individual ledger lines.

The task is to take each cost element and to apportion it across each activity. This is a formidable task, and in most cases the best approach is to start with the labor cost element and take each employee in turn and allocate their time to each activity, perhaps using time-sheet information. In this case, it would be useful to provide the manager with:

- A list of employees in each activity center.
- A matrix which can be filled in to allocate each employee's time between the identified activities.

If the rate of pay of employees differs widely in an activity center this has to be accounted for by obtaining salary information, adjusted to reflect total compensation.

Once the labor cost element has been dealt with, the non-labor cost elements must be allocated. In some cases, these cost elements are traced to activities in the same proportion as employee cost. This is certainly not always the case; for example, some activities may:

- Use a wide area and incur a disproportionate amount of building-related expenses.

- Incur large travel expenses.
- Use capital machinery and so incur depreciation.

The parameters used to trace costs (e.g., employee hours, area, and net book value) are called tracing factors.

The interview documentation has to convey these principles so that the manager can begin to think how to allocate costs from activity center to activity. While it is possible to mail the documentation pack to the manager, its complexity is likely to be confusing. Therefore, it is best to talk the manager through the allocation process when handing over the pack and to return in a few days.

Interview Conduct

Hopefully, there will need to be little discussion over the costs and activities for which managers are responsible, but if there are questions, these need to be dealt with immediately. Once the cost and activities have been agreed on, the meeting can move on to examining the tracing of costs to activities. It is necessary to review the assumptions to check if the most reliable method of relating costs to activities has been found. If the meeting is going well, this discussion on the nature of each activity and their cost behavior is a useful start to discussing attributes and cost drivers, which are the subject of the next section.

ATTRIBUTES AND DRIVERS

Use of Attributes

We have already stressed that controlling overhead activities does not just equate to the monitoring and control of cost. The implication is that any theoretical framework to be used for overhead control must embrace parameters other than cost, and it is to these that we now return our attention.

We first introduce the concept of an attribute, which is the accepted term but which makes the concept sound more complicated than it is. An attribute is simply a characteristic of an activity. This wide definition results in a very diverse choice of attributes, and we discuss some of these below. The common theme, however, is that attributes are ways of collecting information in a structured manner on the activities of an organization. Given the analytical effort involved in the interview process, it would be a waste to stop at calculating the activity costs. There are many other characteristics of activities, knowledge of which would illuminate decisions on alternative ways of organizing the company or on improving the quality of service provided to customers.

Attribute Types

We have already introduced the concept of an attribute. We now give examples of types of attributes. In doing so, their usefulness will become apparent.

Class of activity. Classifications of activity by type vary. Some classifications are binary, the most common being "value-added" and "non-value added," or "primary" and "secondary." The author's own experience of such classification is that they lead to fruitless arguments with individuals who are responsible for activities in the less glamorous category. With this in mind, three-way classifications are sometimes adopted; a common version is to split activities between "core," "support," and "other," where core activities are involved in directly serving customers, and support activities are those which allow core activities to take place. This can work well, but in the author's view a four-way classification is ideal; the core and support activities are retained, but the "other" category is split between:

- "Policy" expenditure, which refers to costs where the level of cost is set by management; for example, research and development.
- "Waste," which refers to activities undertaken to correct mistakes; for example, answering customer complaints.

Once the classification has been decided upon, it is simple to go through the activities and allocate each one to a category.

Location. Where a company operates on multiple locations, it is important to understand what is being done where. Often, many of the opportunities for saving arise from identifying duplication of activities between sites and removing it. Recording, by means of attributes, the locations in which activities take place is the first step in achieving this.

Critical success factors. Some activities are more likely to have an impact on the critical success of the organization than others. Each of the critical success factors can be set up as an attribute and the impact on each activity recorded.

Timing. One use of the activity map will be to relate the demands of an organization's customers to the internal processes, or sequences of activities, which satisfy them. Invariably, the time to deliver a product or service is a key element of this analysis, and the data can be collected during the interview when activity costs are being discussed. One parameter of interest is the time to complete an activity, if appropriate. This can be expanded to include the set-up time—the time needed to start carrying out the activity on a new range of items. Another parameter is the typical amount of time an item must wait before it is worked on. A large amount of information can be collected on timing; the decision on how much to collect depends on how much emphasis needs to be placed on lead-time reduction.

Quality. Obtaining a view on the cost of poor quality is often a key element in reducing overhead costs. The cost of quality is conventionally split between appraisal, prevention, internal failure, and external failure. It is possible to record using attributes, whether or not the activity is affected by any of these categories, and even to estimate the proportion of activity cost falling in each of the four categories. This will allow the total cost of quality to be estimated and identify where it is being incurred. This is certainly a worthwhile start, though the real objective is to find out where the costs are being caused, as opposed to where they are being felt. We will outline how to do this in Step 3, Radical Change.

Cost variability. The cost collection exercise represents a snapshot of costs at a particular time. It is useful to understand how the costs may vary in the future. It is possible to use attributes to record whether costs are fixed in the short term, represent past decisions (e.g., depreciation charges), vary with the volume of production, or vary with the complexity of production. This is particularly useful when considering the effect of volume changes, perhaps arising from product deletions.

Make versus buy. In organizing overhead activities, a recurrent question is whether a particular activity is best carried out internally or whether it is better subcontracted. During the analysis, it is useful to record whether it is practical for the activity to be subcontracted. This will be discussed in more detail in Step 4, Focused Change.

Life-cycle costing. Each activity can be tagged as relevant to a certain phase in the product life cycle, or to none. The buildup of life-cycle cost can then be examined and contrasted to when cost is committed.

Conclusion. In practice, it is unlikely that attributes will be used to analyze all the above parameters, and of course there will some issues particular to an organization that will give rise to specialised attributes. The range of possible attributes is endless. The use of attributes for identifying opportunities for improvement is considered in Step 3.

Types of Driver

One of the most heavily used terms in the lexicon of activity-based costing is *cost driver*. Unfortunately, it has taken on several meanings, the most common of which are as follows:

Attributes and Drivers 111

- A general factor which causes cost to occur for a particular activity. One technique in the control of support activities is to identify drivers which have an influence on a large number of activities. Within this program, this is the meaning given to cost driver.
- A specific factor which causes cost to occur for a particular activity. These factors are not likely to be common across a large number of activities, but are very specific to a particular activity; for example, the number of lines on a sales order. These factors are very useful when matching resources to workload, and will be referred to as activity drivers, although this terminology is not universal.
- A factor which is of use in allocating costs from an activity center to an activity, or from an activity to a cost object such as a product or customer. We have already used the term *tracing factor* for this concept. Of course, in many cases the tracing factors will also be activity drivers.

Each of these terms, *cost driver, activity driver,* and *tracing factor,* will recur as we discuss how to exercise rational control over support activities.

Examples of Cost Drivers

We have defined a cost driver as a general influence on cost. The purpose of collecting information on cost drivers is to see if there are common factors across the organization which influence the level of cost. If there are such factors and they are under the control of the organization, they represent an option for cost reduction.

Typical cost drivers and responses available to management may include:

- *Number of special orders.* In both manufacturing and service industries, it is often the atypical which occupies a disproportionate amount of time. If this is the case, realistic surcharges for special requirements could be imposed.
- *Number of customers.* If there is a substantial overhead in maintaining a particular account—for example, if customer liaison is a major cost—it brings into question the value of continuing with smaller customers. Either such customers could be discontinued, or a discount structure can be adopted which rewards customers who place large amounts of business.
- *Number of orders.* There is often a fixed cost associated with processing an order because of the documentation that has to be generated. If this is a major factor for an organization, a minimum order level is called for.
- *Number of parts.* For those engaged in manufacturing, the costs associated with maintaining records and inventory on a large number of parts are probably all too familiar. However, a similar concept applies to service industries, where a diverse product range can increase support costs because of the consequent complexity of internal systems,

training requirements, and so on. The solution is range rationalization; however, to carry this out requires good product profitability information, which is one of the key outputs of activity analysis.

Other possible cost drivers are less specific. There may be a general feeling of dissatisfaction with the information systems of the company. Alternatively, managers may report their time is wasted by the number of meetings they are required to attend or the time spent briefing senior managers. It is worthwhile recording these more vague causes of cost by noting them as a cost driver. These cost drivers are then used in Step 3 to identify opportunities for improvement across the organization.

Activity Drivers

The primary use of activity drivers is to match resources to workload. When an activity driver has been identified, it is often worth considering whether it represents an input to the activity or an output. To illustrate, a customer service center could either consider the activity driver to be the number of inquiries received or the number of instructions issued. The latter has the advantage that the driver accounts more closely for the actual amount of work involved in each inquiry but has the disadvantage that if it is used to model workload, staff can create workload and hence additional resource for themselves by "keeping busy" through being overzealous in their response to inquiries.

In practice, there is rarely the luxury of choice between the use of a driver related to input or output; usually, the availability of information dictates which is to be used. In Step 4, Focused Change, we will discuss ways in which the workload driver, once identified, can be used to allocate resources to activities in a rational way.

Information Collection and Storage

The collection of data on drivers and attributes is best done in discussion with the managers concerned; classifications by the project team acting in isolation are unlikely to be accepted. The storage of the information is best done on a database, since it then becomes possible to search for patterns in the drivers across the organization. The use of these tools is described later in this chapter.

LINKING ACTIVITIES TO PROCESSES

Background

In Step 1, External Review, the main business processes were defined; the starting point for this definition was the identification of the customers and their requirements. In this step, we have taken a very different view and examined the internal activities of the corporation. It is now necessary to link these two perspectives.

Establishing this linkage is vital. One of the obstacles experienced by practitioners of business process reengineering is the gulf between the top-level redesigned processes and the current practice of the corporation. If this gulf cannot be bridged, not only is there no clue as to the practicality of the top-level processes, but also those involved in the current corporation, who must eventually accept the new thinking, are likely not to understand, and may therefore deride, the team's proposals.

These problems can be avoided by being able to express the top-level processes in terms of the recognized activities.

Types of Process Model

Process models have been categorized into four perspectives (*Process Modelling*, Curtis, Kellner and Over, 1992):

- *Functional*, showing what activities are being undertaken in a process and the information that flows between the activities.
- *Organizational*, showing where within the organization the activities are performed.
- *Informational*, showing the data entities involved in a process and their interrelationships.
- *Behavioral*, showing how activities interact in the process – the timing, conditional paths, and iteration of activities.

Our concern is chiefly with the functional perspective. Once it is understood, it is relatively simple to annotate it with the organizational details. The informational perspective is naturally of interest in the design of information systems, though it is not of direct interest in organizational design. The behavioral perspective is in some ways the most sophisticated model but is less relevant to organizational design because:

- It is usually only necessary to understand the broad sweep of a process in preparation for its improvement, as opposed to its detailed operation.
- The behavioral aspects can vary according to interpretation by individuals (unlike the activities and data flows, which are constant). Any process model may, therefore, only represent a single interpretation of the process.

We now review the specific techniques available for creating process models, concluding with a detailed description of a functional decomposition method.

There are generally no shortages of such techniques available, some of which are paper based, while others are supported by software tools. We describe the type of tools that can be used and conclude with a preferred option.

Critical path networks. Project management is the field where the use of graph models to represent the links between activities necessary to meet a final goal is most established. The method is known as critical path analysis and several individual network techniques have been developed. They include:

- *Activity-on-arrow networks*, in which the intermediate states of the system are represented by nodes. Activities cause movement between the states and are represented by arrows.
- *Activity-on-node networks*, where the nodes represent the activities themselves, and the arrows show the links between the activities.
- *PERT charts*, a more comprehensive form of a model, which can be used to show the effect on the overall program of the statistical variation in execution times of individual activities.

Flow-charting techniques. The use of flow charts to understand processes, particularly information-related processes and computer applications, is well established. These general flow-charting techniques can also be used to represent processes and highlight decision-making points.

Simulation packages. These software packages carry the simple representation of a system a stage further to build a model of the dynamic operation of the system. Even if this step were not required, the advantage of the packages in carrying out the simulation requires a very close definition of the properties of the activities and the relations between them.

Decomposition methods. These techniques model a system by successively decomposing a high-level summary into a lower-level description. One such technique is called $IDEF_0$; IDEF stands for ICAM Definition, where ICAM was the United States Air Force's program for Integrated Computer-Aided Manufacture. The subscript zero indicates that this is the function model, as opposed to $IDEF_1$, which models information flows, and $IDEF_2$, which is the outline of a dynamic simulation model. Of these it is $IDEF_0$ which has been most widely adopted.

$IDEF_0$ is now widely used to describe systems containing a mixture of hardware, software, and people; its use is no longer confined to the manufacturing area. The method begins with the highest level, Level 0, which for our purposes would be the process name and would show the input to and output of the process. The next level, Level 1, would show

FIGURE 3-6
Sample IDEF₀ Diagram

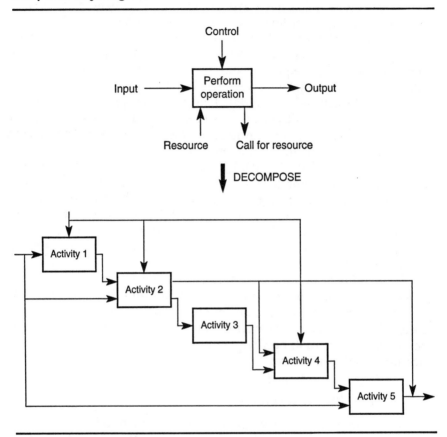

the principal activities within the process; the IDEF₀ format prefers between three and six activities per level. Each activity has a name, which is a verb, and is assigned a box. There are four parameters linked to each activity, which are assigned arrows (see Figure 3–6).

The four parameters are:

- An input to the activity, from another activity, drawn as an arrow entering the left of the box.
- An output from the activity, leading to a subsequent activity, drawn as an arrow leaving the right of the box.
- A resource consumed by the activity, drawn as an arrow entering the bottom of the box (or the reverse to show a call for resource).
- A control on the activity, drawn as an arrow entering the top of the box.

The activities are then annotated with a code and any other information that is desired, such as cost, lead time, or other nonfinancial attributes. Once the first level has been defined, the model is extended down to subsequent levels, according to the level of detail required.

The chief benefit of $IDEF_0$ is its use as a communication tool. There may be several different perceptions of how a process actually operates and to resolve these requires a succinct means of describing a process; $IDEF_0$ meets this need. However, it needs to be understood that two different people will define the details of the same process in different ways, so although $IDEF_0$ is a means of sharing an understanding and obtaining an agreement of principles, it does not force a convergence in the detailed representation of that process.

While it may appear that $IDEF_0$ is a very precise method, in fact the method does not comprehensively define a business process; for example, the conditional paths a process may take. This imprecision is a double-edged sword; it can assist the team by allowing them to concentrate only on those parts of the process model that are of relevance to the case at hand. However, it can result in endless sundry annotations to the process model.

The benefits of process modeling come from the benefits of a concise representation, universally understood. With this foundation, it becomes possible to share ideas on the improvement of a process. In Step 3, Radical Change, we explore ways in which these processes can be improved. We first, however, outline the method by which activities are linked to processes.

The Third Interview

We have described the use of face-to-face meetings to collect information on activities and their costs. This will now be continued with a further round of interviews with the same set of individuals. The purpose of these interviews is to:

- Link activities to processes.
- Trace the costs to the processes.
- Where possible, show the relationships between activities within the process, in the form of $IDEF_0$ diagrams.

A documentation pack should be produced and circulated prior to the meeting, explaining the task at hand. It will contain:

- A list of activities and their costs.
- A list of the business processes.
- An explanation of the tracing procedures to be used and the principles behind representing processes graphically.

In some cases, the linking of an activity to a process and the tracing of cost will be straightforward: it will be clear that a particular activity belongs to a particular process, and its cost can be allocated in its entirety. However, there can be complications.

The first complication may be that an activity is part of more than one process. To resolve this problem requires the identification of a tracing factor, to trace the cost. Tracing factors have already been introduced; they are quantitative bases used to allocate costs. For example, an activity "administer market research" may form part of a process called "acquire new customers" and a second called "design new products." The activity will consist mostly of staff costs, which could be traced using time-sheet data or by estimating the time spent on specific research projects. A second activity, "commission agency," consisting of agency fees, may exist, and these costs will be analyzed using the value of invoices received and how they are split between the two processes. There would be a problem, however, if there were a single activity, "market research," consisting of both types of cost, because the proportion of staff costs and agency fees spent on the two different processes may differ. If such an activity has been created, it is worthwhile to go back and split the activity.

The second complication may occur where an activity does not appear to form part of any identified process. This can occur because the list of processes was derived using a top-down approach which considered the organization's ideal activities. The list of activities was compiled using a bottom-up procedure, which sought out what was actually taking place within the organization. Approaches to dealing with activities which belong to no process vary.

One school of thought is that it is not necessary to trace all the activities and their costs to the processes, since the intention is simply to find the costs of the processes which have been identified. The author's view is that this is hazardous, since it can easily lead to processes being undercosted and to a false impression given of value for money. It is more likely that the full cost of processes will be recognized if it is the rule that all costs will be traced either to a process or to a "remainder" category which will be closely examined afterwards for value for money. This has the great advantage of providing an arithmetic check on the tracing of costs, since the sum of all the process costs and the remainder category must equal the sum of all the activity costs, which in turn must equal the cost base.

Interview Conduct

The first step is to review the allocation of activities to processes. This generally does not cause a problem as long as the nature of the processes has been understood. If all the activity relates to a single process, the allocation of cost is also simple. Where an activity is split between processes, there is a need to review the managers' choice of tracing factor.

The most interactive part of the interview is the construction of the IDEF$_0$ diagrams. The best approach is to take a pencil and paper, discuss how the activities interact, and start drawing. After the interview, the end result can be entered into a PC tool, if one is available.

TRACING COSTS TO COST OBJECTS

Cost Objects

During Step 1, External Review, the business was divided into segments. One of the criteria for the recognition of a segment was unique cost behavior; for example, special product support requirements and special customer terms.

The segments live on, but in this step they are termed *cost objects*. A cost object is the eventual destination of the various cost allocations which are employed. First, the cost base is allocated to activity centers, then to activities, and finally to cost objects; for example, products or services, customers or distribution channels. The term will be used extensively in the description of the building of cost models given below.

This is the final stage of the activity analysis and the one that delivers the most prized information—that is, the costs incurred by products or services, customers, and distribution channels. The tracing of costs-to-cost objects is invariably more difficult than the tracing of costs to processes because very few activities are carried out for a single cost object, and an extensive search for suitable tracing factors is needed, as opposed to using simple allocations.

Single or Multiple Tracing

At this stage, the question arises whether the cost base should be traced in its entirety only once or repeatedly to each cost object. To illustrate, assuming only product and customer costs were being considered, it would be possible to:

- Either trace all the activity costs to products and then trace all the activity costs again to customers,
- Or trace all the cost to either a product (if the activities were product dependent) or to a customer (if the activities were customer dependent).

The author's preference is to adopt a single tracing of costs to different types of cost elements. This appears more logical to the company's managers who are being asked to trace product-related costs to products and customer-related costs to customers. Asking the managers to relate a product-related cost to a customer would invite disbelief! Most of the overhead activities supporting the early part of the supply chain, apart from order entry, tend to be product dependent, while those near the latter end tend to be customer dependent.

A single allocation of costs does, however, require the subsequent reallocation, by the project team, of the product-related costs to customers, and vice versa. The means of doing this is explained later.

Problems occur with single allocation where there are substantial activity costs which are dependent on more than one cost object simultaneously. In this case, it is best to redefine the activity to separate out as far as possible the different components; for example, product and customer specific parts.

We will assume that there is a single allocation of the cost base. Given this, the next step is to identify the type of cost object to which each activity cost will be allocated. Typically, activity costs will be traced to:

- Product ranges, if they are product dependent; for example, purchasing, design, and product operations.
- Customer and market groups, if they are customer dependent; for example, customer service and most returns processing (excluding warranty returns).
- Distribution channels, if they are channel dependent; for example, dispatch costs.

There will be many activities which appear to relate to none of these. In this case, the default is to consider the activities as product dependent, as it simplifies the subsequent consolidation of costs.

The Fourth Interview

In an ideal case, each cost object would have a bill of activity (similar in principle to a Bill of Material) relating the consumption of support activities to the cost object. If this were the case, there would be no limit to the number of individual cost objects that could be analyzed. For example, the product costs could be calculated by summing the consumption of each activity by the product, multiplied by the unit cost of the activity. We can consider this a "bottom-up" calculation of the allocation of costs to cost objects.

If this were possible, the indirect cost could be computed in the same way that direct costs have been traditionally calculated. Unfortunately, this is rarely possible, because associating the consumption of indirect activity to each cost object is impractical.

For this reason, it is necessary to use an interview to allocate activity costs to product groups from the top down, to start with an activity cost and allocate it to a cost object on the basis of a tracing factor. The challenge is to find suitable tracing factors. Tracing factors which the author has used in the past are shown in Table 3–1.

TABLE 3–1
Tracing Factors

Tracing factor	Application
Number of:	
Customers	Customer service costs
Customer orders	Order processing
Shipments	Distribution expenses
Returns	Return processing
Brands	Brand management
Product families	Product monitoring
Purchase orders	Buying department
Production faults	Fault rectification
Production orders	Production scheduling
Batches	Production setup costs

FIGURE 3–7
Tracing Process

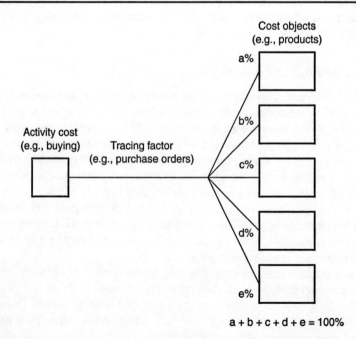

The number of different types of tracing factors is fairly small. The tracing process is illustrated in Figure 3–7. For a tracing factor to be viable, it must be a number which can be broken down by cost object; for example, the number of purchase orders would not be suitable for analyzing purchase costs for each product range if it were not possible to identify how many purchase orders related to each range.

Often, there has to be recourse to the allocation of activity cost between cost object on the basis of time. It is possible for this to be rigorous where the activities have been recorded on time sheets and properly coded. Usually this is not the case, and as a last resort the manager may have to use judgment on whether a particular product range, customer, or distribution channel takes up a certain proportion of the activity. This subjective process has two consequences:

- It is difficult to obtain repeatability of the process.
- It places an upper limit on the number of cost objects that can be analyzed, to perhaps 10 products and customers respectively; otherwise, it becomes impossible to allocate subjectively.

At the end of the interview, the project team will have sufficient information to trace costs to the relevant cost objects. These costs need a further stage of consolidation before they can be used for calculating product profitability.

Consolidation of Costs

The cost base has been allocated to different types of cost objects, according to which is the most relevant. To calculate the profitability associated with each cost object, it is necessary to reallocate the costs so the entire cost base is finally allocated to each one. For example, to calculate the customer profitability, it is necessary not only to know the customer-related costs by customer, but also the product-related costs by customer, which depends on product mix. This is illustrated in Figure 3–8.

In general, it is relatively easy to reallocate product-related costs to other cost objects. It is done on the basis of product mix (e.g., number of units per customer group), and as long as the mix of product groups by customer and distribution channel is known, the rest is arithmetic.

Allocating customer or distribution costs back to product is less simple. For example, allocating activities which were originally traced by the number of customer orders back to products using the number of units would be misleading; it is necessary to know the number of orders by product group. We usually have a limited number of factors on which to reallocate costs back to product groups:

- Number of units—the product mix.
- Number of orders.
- Number of dispatches.

FIGURE 3–8 *Cross-Allocation of Costs between Products and Customers*

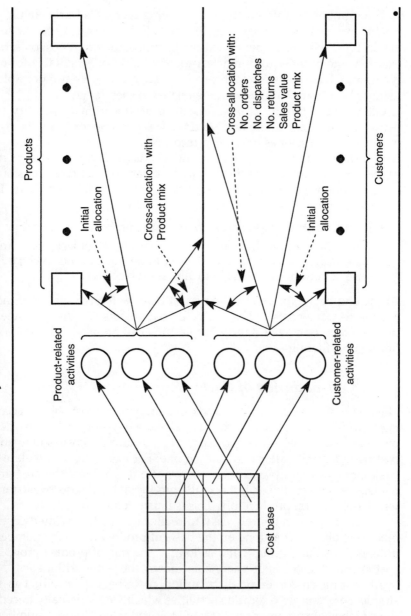

Number of returns.
- Value of the sales.

The procedure for reallocation is to select the most appropriate factor for a given activity and break down the total for the chosen factor by product group. This breakdown is then used to reallocate the activity cost back to products.

SEGMENT PROFITABILITY

Method of Calculation

The calculation of segment profitability is not a complex task. Once the company's costs have been fully allocated within each of the cost objects, each of which represents a segment—for example, a product, customer, or channel—the remaining step is to allocate the revenue to each segment. Taking product ranges as an example, the costs associated with each range will have been calculated, and once the revenue associated with each product range is also known, calculating the product profitability is simply a matter of subtracting cost from revenue. Customer and channel profitability can be calculated in a similar way.

We now discuss the typical results of calculating segment profitability and how these can be used to ensure better control of overheads.

Product Profitability

The chief benefit arising from the calculation of product profitability along activity lines is that the impact of the cost of complexity is fully understood. Typically, when costs have been absorbed on the basis of labor or machine hours, the high-volume/low-variety products have been penalized at the expense of the low volume/high variety products, since it is the former type which involve the use of a large number of direct hours but with relatively straightforward scheduling and tracking. In contrast, low-volume/high-variety products incur relatively few labor and machine hours (because of their low volume), but a large amount of effort is involved in the overhead functions to deal with the high variety. This can be a recipe for disaster: Competitors offering only the high-volume/low-variety items are more than able to compete on price when these items have a minimum selling price based on costs. The company's market share and volume inevitably shrink, provoking a vicious circle of diseconomies of scale and yet higher prices. Eventually, the company has to retreat into an array of peripheral products, and this defeat is rationalized as a victory for niche marketing!

Less typically, additional variety may involve additional direct labor or machine hours but minimal administrative effort. An example would be a manually intensive customization at the end of the production process; this could have a minimal effect on the overhead functions, with the additional cost being confined to the cost of the operators and their immediate support functions; for example, personnel. In this case, if the company used fully-absorbed costs to set minimum selling prices, the result would be that such attempts to adapt to the requirements of individual customers would be prohibitively expensive.

In both cases, the competitiveness of the company is handicapped by a lack of knowledge of the costs of the underlying activities required to provide a product or service. Inevitably, this affects pricing decisions and can lead to the company becoming uncompetitive and eventually failing.

Customer Profitability

Many companies do not produce customer profitability information. Often, the only customer-specific information that is available relates to the discounts provided to each customer. There is therefore a lack of vision on the demands particular customers or markets make on a company, either through making particular demands on the company or through necessitating particular levels of sales and marketing expenditure.

The absence of this information creates two damaging blind spots:

- There is a lack of the basic information needed for customer negotiations. For example, if an influential customer is seeking a discount, without the customer profitability information there is no way to determine if it should be granted to retain the business.
- There is an inability to construct a rational marketing strategy. For example, for most companies it is far from clear whether the small customers, who are relatively complex to service but less able to extract discounts, are more or less profitable than large customers, who demand discounts and delivery to be made in a particular form. Without profitability information, it is not possible to direct the business into the most profitable sectors.

The creation of customer profitability information enables the company to plan and negotiate far more rationally.

Channel Profitability

Channel profitability information is very similar to that calculated for customers. It would only be necessary to deal with the two segments separately if the same customer received goods though more than one channel.

Distribution costs form a large part of the cost base for many companies and in the past have been apportioned on the basis of revenue, as part of the appropriately named SAD category (sales, administration, and distribution). In fact, distribution expenses are channel specific, and tracing these costs to different channels allows decisions to be made on the future distribution strategy.

INFORMATION ASSESSMENT

Introduction

A decision needs to be made regarding the emphasis given to the information systems and technology part of this program. There is no doubt that it must form some part, since the provision of good information in a systematic way is a key part of overhead control. Beyond this minimum, however, there is a choice between emphasising the organizational aspects of a program and emphasising the systems aspect. It is assumed here that the former takes precedence and this has influenced the amount of work proposed for the information assessment. For example, when discussing the data used within the organization we have not suggested defining the relationships between data entities (the items on which data is maintained, e.g., products, customers), which would be a natural part of a customized systems design. If the reader is considering developing an information systems and technology strategy as a preliminary stage to the complete redesign of the company's systems, rather than to make some improvements to the current systems or to undertake a package selection exercise, it would be best to seek professional advice.

Having said this, the level of examination of the information systems and technology proposed in this program as a bare minimum goes far beyond that which is often undertaken when administrative control is discussed. Too often, there is a belief in "more from less," with no real idea of how savings are to be made. In practice, most of the savings will come through more effective and efficient manipulation of information (though individual investments may do little towards this end); the information aspect is therefore vital.

Level of Detail

During this step, the team has defined between 50 and 400 activities, a geometric mean of around 150. This is generally quite adequate for examining the organizational characteristics of a company and its cost behavior. It may not always be adequate, however, for examining the information requirements, where a finer level of detail could be required.

The solution is to permit an extra level of subdivision if necessary. If it is found that within an activity there are different types of work requiring different information, it is possible to define subsidiary tasks. For example, when building a cost model, it may be sufficient to define an activity "issue purchase order," but for an information model, three subsidiary tasks could be identified: identify supplier, define purchase order lines, and issue order/update systems.

It may be necessary to define up to five tasks per activity. This gives a maximum number of 2,000 tasks within the organization, which should be adequate for most purposes.

Timing of the Assessment

The project team has three options for the timing of the information assessment. The team can carry out the assessment during:

- *The first or third interviews.* These interviews are generally fairly easy to conduct, and there is a natural affinity between asking managers about the activities undertaken in their areas, or the association of these activities with processes, and assessing the information systems which support those activities and processes.
- *The second or fourth interviews.* This is less desirable, since the second and fourth interviews are usually difficult to complete because of the detailed tracing of costs to be undertaken.
- *A separate fifth interview.* This is possible, though it does have the disadvantage of a further series of meeting arrangements and the placing of an additional burden on management time.

It will be assumed below that the first route was taken, and the gathering of details on the information requirements and systems is combined with the collection of details on the activities or their association with processes. While the two tasks may be performed in tandem, it is important that the activities are clarified first, before the information issues are discussed; otherwise, the framework on which to consider the information issues will not be in place.

Structure of Assessment

The first stage is to determine the information required by managers for each activity or task; this was briefly considered in the previous step. Then the purpose was to broaden the horizons of the project team as regards the type of information which might be available. Now the task is to ask the managers what information they require, using the previous understanding as a basis for review.

Once the information requirements have been understood at a detailed level, the next step is to record the information which is actually available as well as the level of satisfaction, in terms of its accuracy, timeliness, and relevance to the activities and tasks at hand. The information is the output from the systems, produced by the processing of data, and the team will need to record the databases which are maintained within each activity center.

The systems which convert the input data into the output information consist of applications (the information conversion processes) and technologies, of which the most important elements are the platforms on which the applications operate, the hardware and operating systems. The project team will record the applications and technologies in use in each activity center.

The intention is to investigate each of the items discussed above during the interviews. Over the past decade, this approach has become an accepted way to analyze information systems and technologies and propose new strategies (though it is now being challenged by the "rapid prototyping" approaches). Another example of a planning methodology is given in a paper, "Strategic IS/IT Planning" (Hickey, 1993); here too, one of the steps is the building of IDATO architectures, where IDATO stands for information, data, applications, technology, and organization of the IT resource.

At the end of the assessment, the project team will be in a position to identify weaknesses in the systems. These weaknesses will refer not only to the ability of the systems to support the current operations, but to the prospective weaknesses as the organization changes to meet its longer-term goals. There follows the task of synthesizing a strategy which will tackle these weaknesses while protecting the existing and future investment in systems.

Information—Required and Available

The procedure for gaining an understanding of the information requirements is quite simple. Managers are asked to state their views on the information needed for each activity, and if necessary each subsidiary task and the answers must be judged critically.

Where managers declare a need for information, it is important to relate this to a decision which falls within their responsibilities; the effects of a declared absence of information can also be discussed. It is more difficult to identify where there is a lack of necessary information which may go unrecognized by managers. However during Step 1, the team previously considered the information requirements of the processes from the top. Using the understanding gained, the team is able to challenge managers on whether particular types of information would prove useful, even if their need is not currently recognized.

The project team then seeks to understand the managers' views on the information currently available. This will encompass the parameters

FIGURE 3–9
Information Gap

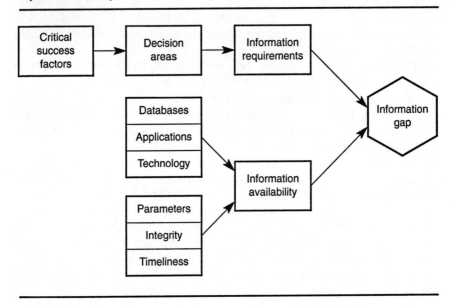

which are available, the frequency with which they are reported, and the perceived integrity of the information.

Again the managers' opinions need to be challenged. The views on the availability of information may be wrong because of a limited understanding of the systems. Complaints about the integrity of the information may be exaggerated. Therefore, the project team needs to probe the answers given.

It now becomes possible to draw up an analysis of the gap between the information needed and that which is available, as shown in Figure 3–9.

Databases

There is likely to be a variety of databases maintained in the organization, resulting in both duplication and fragmentation. It is necessary for the project team to identify the various databases, many of which may be not be computerized, which are maintained in each activity center.

Once a database has been identified, its data entities are summarized. The entities are then linked to the applications which draw upon the data.

It is also possible to relate the data and the data entities to individual activities, as has traditionally been done with data flow diagrams. However, since the salient data flows have already been recorded in the IDEF$_0$ models, this is not essential.

Applications

When discussing the information requirements, we remarked that it is simple for the manager to discuss information needs which are already met but more difficult to identify a requirement which exists but goes unrecognized. In a similar way, it is relatively easy to identify applications which are formally recognized and implemented on computing systems, but it is more difficult to deduce data processing which is informally undertaken but nonetheless forms an important part of the business.

The first step is to record those applications which are formally recognized, extending this where necessary to include manual systems. The next stage is to deduce the less formal processing of data, which may merit a more formal application in the future (e.g., the maintenance of a list of approved suppliers, reflecting recent performance, which may be undertaken informally but could merit a special database application in the future).

Once the applications have been identified, the next step is to link their use to particular activities or tasks.

Technologies

Recording the technologies in use is usually a fairly mechanical task which involves listing the hardware (both processing and storage) and operating systems available to support each activity or task. This exercise should not only cover computers, but also:

- Nonelectronic technologies; for example, a sophisticated manual project monitoring and control system.
- The communications equipment in use, whether for data links, or for voice or graphic communication or storage.

While none of this is difficult, it usually reveals the wide spectrum of technology employed.

Collation of Results

At the end of this procedure, a large amount of information will have been collected on the information systems and technologies which are in use to serve particular activities or tasks. It is now necessary to begin identifying opportunities for improvement. There will normally be no shortage of such opportunities, involving:

- A shortfall in information requirements, either as a result of information being absent or of inadequate timeliness, frequency, or accuracy.
- Inconsistent or duplicated data being maintained within the organization.

- The boundaries of applications reflecting arbitrary organizational boundaries as opposed to those set by the business processes.
- Limitations in technology; for example, the absence of computerization or modern communication technology.

There is a need to identify patterns in these opportunities for improvement, so as to arrive at a condensed version of the main shortcomings of the current systems for both the current and proposed operations.

The results from this work—a record of shortcomings—will be used in Step 3, Radical Change.

IT SUPPORT TOOLS

Need for Tools

It will be apparent that a large amount of information is being produced during this program. The project team can easily become overwhelmed by detail, especially when the cost models are being built. We now discuss the various options for IT support that are available.

Spreadsheets are of course easily created and very useful for ad hoc calculations. There is a danger, however, that the information in the project will become fragmented over a series of spreadsheets, making proper control of the information difficult. This is especially the case if the information is liable to change and is recorded on more than one spreadsheet.

There are many inexpensive commercially available packages for activity-based costing, process models, information system analysis, project management, and so on. These are a great boon to productivity in their particular area of application. The drawback is that the transfer of information between the different packages may not be simple. The issue of data transfer needs to be addressed when a tool set is being chosen. Sometimes compatibility is not possible, in which case a database application may be appropriate.

Since the basic objective of the PC support tools is to store data in a structured manner and to identify links and patterns, there is some logic in constructing an application to run on a PC database system. This has the advantage that the data are integrated and can be drawn upon as required.

The disadvantage is that it takes some effort to write such an application; the skills may not be readily available. Furthermore, the work needs to be done prior to the start of the project; otherwise, the lack of PC support will be an impediment.

We now consider the use of automatic transfer of data into these tools.

Preparing for Automatic Transfer of Data

Whatever the form of the support tools which are eventually adopted, the first step is to arrange for the source data to be conditioned into a usable form. Usually, the data on the main corporate systems are held in a much greater level of detail than is required. The first step is therefore to aggregate the source data in preparation for transfer for the support tools or local systems. Either the aggregation can be a first step, to simply reduce the data volumes in preparation for transfer, or it can result in the complete aggregation of cost lines into cost elements and cost centers into activity centers. The latter course is often not adopted because it can be easier to keep the detailed database programming on the local system and away from the mainframe system; this is consistent with the use of client/server architectures to retain the "legacy systems" the company has inherited as a server, while setting up new systems, in this case for activity costing, as clients.

The transfer itself can be over a network or by means of a disk. The network solution is the more elegant; but if the disk can be produced on the site on which it is required, the disk solution is adequate.

Streamlining the Transfer Process

Once the data have been transferred onto the local system, the next step is usually to process the data further (e.g., to remove cross allocations or to aggregate the data). Ideally, this is carried out in the main activity costing application, though in some cases a preliminary spreadsheet is required. Wherever possible, the use of spreadsheets to condition data in transfers between applications should be avoided because it creates version control problems and complicates the transfer process.

However, spreadsheets can prove useful in collating and verifying data that have been manually input. Although much of the input data will be loaded across automatically, some will have to be loaded manually. It can be inconvenient to tie up the main application for this purpose, particularly if it is single-user; in these circumstances the data can be manually input and checked in a subsidiary spreadsheet and then loaded into the main application in a single action.

Setting up a Periodic Reporting System

If the data transfer processes are well designed, they can form the basis for a periodic reporting system, where the activity costing and other information are recalculated on a periodic basis and distributed to managers.

In such a system, it is important to distinguish between the dynamic and the static data. The static data will comprise the activity library, the attributes, and so on. The dynamic data will include the costs for the most recent period. Tracing factors should be dynamic, so that the activity costs reflect the changing activity levels within the company.

LIFE-CYCLE COSTING CASE STUDY

Background

The company designs, manufactures, and sells garments. This apparently simple mission in life is, in fact, extremely complex. Some of the garments are "plains," which do not vary from season to season; others are "designs," which are unique to a particular season. Many of the customers are small and deal on standard terms but can be costly to service. Some are large companies who have immense negotiating power and demand special arrangements, some of which incur cost, others of which reduce it—for example, not returning goods. Some of the garments are made in-house from purchased fabric, while other garments are purchased as finished goods. Finally, there is great variety in the business, due to the large number of combinations of garment sizes, fabric designs, and fabric colors. The result is that the business has to manage tens of thousands of stock-keeping units, and manufacture is carried out in very large numbers of small batches.

The demand this places on the company's management is heavy, and responding to this demand forms the basis of our next two case studies. This case study is concerned with the improvement of the product life cycle of the designed garment; the second case study (at the end of the next chapter) is concerned with the calculation of product and customer profitability. The foundation for both was a major activity-based costing exercise, which we describe below. First, however, we define the objectives of the present case study.

Objectives

The objectives are to identify, for designed garments:
- The key points in the life cycle at which cost is either committed or expended.
- Changes to the life cycle, with a view to shortening it.

These objectives are critical to the profitability of the whole company. We will see that a major opportunity cost relates to "clearers," which are gar-

Life-Cycle Costing Case Study

ments that have to be sold at a discount at the end of a season. If clearers are to be reduced, the costs and lead times within the life cycle need to be changed so that better decisions on design are made closer to the season during which the garments are purchased by the consumer.

Approach

Naturally, the first step is to define the product life cycle. Fortunately, this is straightforward. To ensure that the designed garments are available on time, a critical path analysis has been carried out by the company, which states what has to be done by when in order for the garments to be available on time. An abbreviated version of this is shown in Figure 3–10.

The second step is far more complex. It is to carry out the activity analysis program described in Step 2. There is no need to repeat the description of the procedure here, only to summarize the results. A total of some 180 activities was identified, though a strong Pareto curve was found, with a few activities amounting to the majority of the cost. Nonetheless, the full complement was included in the analysis to reassure the managers that the activity analysis was fully their own.

FIGURE 3–10
Product Life Cycle

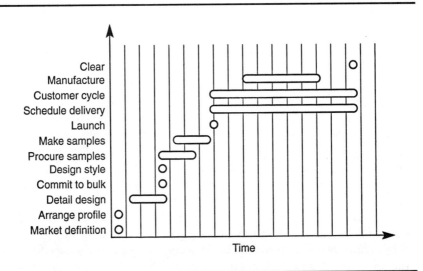

FIGURE 3-11
Profile of Accumulated Life-Cycle Cost

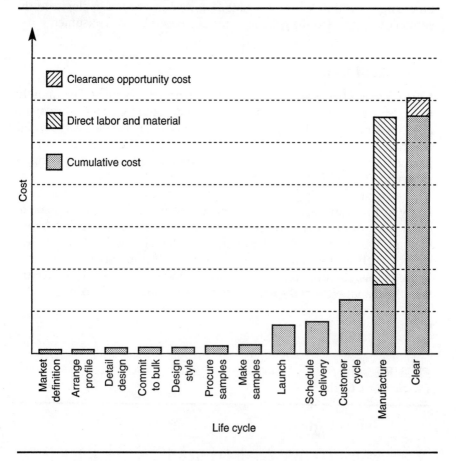

The third step is to allocate each activity to the stage in the life cycle with which it is concerned, where possible. For most of the cost, some two-thirds in this case, it is possible to associate an activity with the life cycle. For some costs, this cannot be done; for example, administration costs. Rather than attempt an apportionment, these were simply left to one side. Furthermore, some of the activities which support the life cycle of a "design" garment will also support a "plain" garment; this can be accounted for by separating out the latter costs.

Once these steps have been carried out, we can calculate the accumulation of cost during the product life cycle; this is shown in Figure 3–11. It is a common pattern, which is observed in many industries; for example, mechanical and electrical engineering.

Life-Cycle Costs

The first conclusion from Figure 3–11 is that major commitments of future expenditure, namely on the purchase of fabric, are made very early in the life cycle, when very little money has been spent, in terms of the total cost of the garment, on researching the market and designing the fabric.

Given the high opportunity cost of "clearers," shown on the right of the figure, it may be justified to considerably increase the expenditure on early market research and design to reduce the clearers. Furthermore, the manufacturing cost will also have been determined very early on, with relatively little expenditure.

There are two major conclusions for the company:

- The cost of good design is cheap when expressed as a proportion of the total life-cycle cost, and the company may wish to spend in this area for later benefit.
- The cost of bad design is high, and the quality controls on the design function are critical to profitability.

Incidentally, these conclusions are not unique to the garment industry.

Life-Cycle Timing

The timing of the life cycle is also crucial. Figure 3–12 shows the life cycle marked to illustrate when funds are committed, when orders are received, and when payment is actually made. For the company, a worse situation could hardly be imagined: Major commitment and expenditure are made on fabric months before a single order has been received; there is then a further period of several months before delivery is accepted by the customers and payment for a garment is received.

Of all these delays, it is the one between commitment to fabric and receipt of orders which is the most serious. There is a vast opportunity to forecast badly the fabric designs and the quantity of fabric needed. This may not be due to poor forecasting practice but simply because the market radically changes beyond all reasonable expectation.

Therefore, the objective for this company is to move from a "buy before you sell" situation, to a "sell before you buy." This is not out of the question, due to the long interval between orders being taken and delivery being expected.

Segmenting the Product Life Cycle

A single life cycle, defined by the critical path analysis, has been defined for the whole product range. This simplifies the operation of the business but needs to change. There will always be some parts of the product

FIGURE 3-12
Financial Commitment

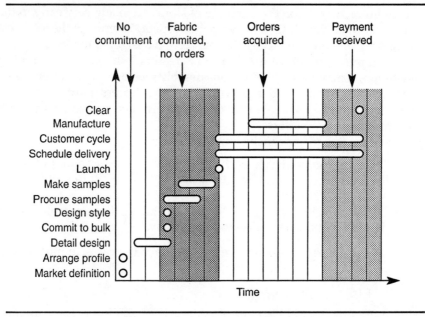

range, the unique part, which will have to be individually designed and fabric ordered in advance. Much of the design range is, however, far from unique. It either uses fabrics which are relatively conventional, or it uses yarns of a standard color and composition. The company therefore has the option to divide its life cycle into three parts:

- A life cycle along the lines of current practice.
- A life cycle which uses standard fabric designs. An order is then placed upon the supplier for the appropriate quantity once the initial orders for the garment using this design have been taken.
- A life cycle which uses standard yarns but which are woven into unique fabric designs. An order is placed for weaving capacity, but the use of this prebooked capacity is left open until initial orders for garments have been taken.

The product life cycle also has an impact on the manufacturing strategy. One reason for the early ordering of fabric is to receive it long before delivery of the garments is expected. In this way, the manufacturing demand for the season can be spread evenly across half the year, even though the delivery to the retailers is concentrated in a small proportion of the year. The exercise in segmenting the life cycle must therefore go hand in hand with the specification of the manufacturing strategy. This itself is a complex area with several variables, including:

- Whether to subcontract manufacture of the garments or to buy in work from other manufacturers who wish to subcontract.
- The phasing of the manufacture of the "plains" and the "designs" in the factory.
- Whether to use the factory for short runs, offering high responsiveness, or for high-volume/low-variety work to minimize costs.

This manufacturing strategy work cannot be carried out in isolation. It must be done with awareness of the manufacturing capabilities of both suppliers and competitors.

Conclusion

The life-cycle analysis has suggested that the fundamental operating cycles of the company be radically altered. Not only should the design function be better resourced, controlled, and equipped, but the approach to the procurement of fabric should be radically changed.

The effect of these changes will also affect the relationship the company has with its suppliers. At the moment, it deals at arm's length and specifies its requirements uniquely and independently, but if it is to start using fabrics designed elsewhere and yarns specified by others and to ask weavers to hold open capacity for fabric designs yet to be specified, it will need to build closer relationships with its suppliers.

Chapter Four

Radical Change

To every thing there is a season and a time to every purpose under the heaven. A time to be born, and a time to die; a time to plant and a time to pluck up that which is planted . . .

ECCLESIASTES 3:1, 2

INTRODUCTION

Objectives

The objective of Step 3, Radical Change is to exploit the understanding provided by the combination of Step 1, External Review and Step 2, Activity Analysis. The emphasis is on identifying the priorities for change, generating ideas for process improvement, and defining gains in the area of cost, lead time, and quality. To these are added improvements deduced from analyzing the attributes and drivers of the organization and the potential for rationalization of segments of the business; we also consider the effectiveness of the information systems and the organizational structure.

At the end of this step, the terms of reference are defined for a small number of task forces to carry forward the work once the project team has completed its work.

Deliverables

During this stage of the work, illustrated in Figure 4–1, the project team will provide:

- Priorities for comprehensive change to the processes of the organization.
- Ideas for improvements to these processes and models of the processes on which the proposed changes can be tested.
- An analysis of the attributes and drivers to generate additional ideas for improvement.

Introduction

FIGURE 4–1
Step 3: Radical Change

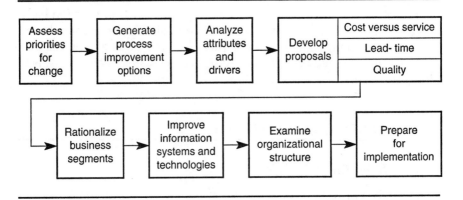

- Proposals for:
    New trade-offs between cost and lead time.
    Shortened lead times within processes.
    Improvements in quality within processes.
- Options for the rationalization of certain business segments; for example, products, customers, or distribution channels.
- Plans for the improvement of the information systems and technologies.
- Changes to improve the organizational structure.
- Fully consulted management and fully briefed task forces in preparation for implementation.

Issues

The key to this step is the comprehensiveness or breadth of the change being considered. Most improvements to corporations are undertaken locally or within departments because their area of application is limited to the span of control of the manager initiating the change; we consider this type of change in the next step of the program. In this step, however, we consider the wider possibilities. Compared to local change, radical change tends to be:

- More comprehensive, in that it requires a greater degree of change in the way the organization operates.
- More rewarding, in that it delivers a greater improvement in performance or reduction in cost; for example, factor of 10 improvements in lead time are not unknown.

This step, therefore, counters the temptation to consider the existing structure as a fixture and to confine increases in performance to improving the current arrangement. It needs to be considered whether a radical approach would yield benefits and whether an overhead function has to be done in a particular way or even done at all. The recommendations will include changing the business processes and rationalizing the business so that the need for certain activities, or scales of activities, is no longer present.

ASSESSING PRIORITIES

Need for Priorities

The need to prioritize is a consequence of success. If there were only a small number of opportunities for improvement, all of them could be put into effect. In practice, there will be limitations because the number of potential improvements will be too great for the project team to examine and the organization to absorb.

Given that it is impractical to deal with every possibility, we need guidelines on how to select priorities for improvement, from the various avenues of investigation into information systems processes and organization which could be developed in this step. We now outline how these priorities are to be decided.

Setting Priorities

The first influence on setting priorities was considered during Step 1, External Review. There are two relevant conditions.

- The shortfall between the required and the actual performance.
- The degree to which the shortfall affects the performance of the business.

During Step 1, the major processes were defined on the basis of their importance to the business. For each of these processes, the performance customers expect and the value they place on it being met were also examined. The project team, therefore, now knows if some processes merit special attention because they are both important and performance needs to improve.

The second influence on setting priorities was examined in Step 2, Activity Analysis. Information was collected on both the general cost drivers and the attributes of activities, with the intention of identifying common themes. Both can be used to identify opportunities for improvement across the organization:

- Cost drivers show general influences on the level of cost throughout the company.
- Attributes, which are defined by the project team, show common features; for example, the relevance of a quality issue.

By summing the total cost of all the activities for which a particular cost driver or attribute is relevant, the significance of the parameter can be assessed.

There will, of course, be a great deal of overlap between opportunities identified from the two sources. Many of the shortfalls in performance seen by customers will arise from problems identified from the attribute/driver analysis. At this point, a decision has to be made whether to view the problem from a process or a driver-and-attribute perspective. The choice depends on whether a particular issue affects a particular process; if a single process is affected, a process approach is the more focused.

Summary of Priorities

The priorities for action need to be agreed on with the senior management before proceeding. There should not to be too many priorities; the intention is to finally arrive at no more than five simultaneous initiatives, which is the limit an organization can absorb.

Once the priorities are established, the search for improvements can begin. It is possible that in some cases no improvement can be found. In the others, however, the analysis is carried through to the point where a task force can be set up to implement the improvement once the project team has finished.

PROCESS IMPROVEMENT

Idea Generation

We have already alluded to the fact that change which affects the whole organization is likely to be more radical and result in greater reward. This begs the question of from where these radical ideas are expected to arise. Here we see an opportunity to transfer expertise and techniques from the area of product design to process design.

The first step is to identify the sources of new ideas:

- *Individuals within the company.* Many staff will no doubt have accumulated years of dissatisfaction with the way the company's operations make their lives difficult. These ideas represent an internal view of improvement.

- *Customers.* They can be a very useful source of ideas, since they bear the brunt of any problems. The project team will have already canvassed the customers on their requirements, and this can be extended to their views on how requirements can be met by a change in operations.
- *Suppliers.* These can occasionally offer useful ideas on how to integrate their operations with those of the organization. Much of the emphasis on partnership sourcing is concerned with this topic.
- *The press.* Regular reading of the business press reveals reports on how other companies have achieved success or of new systems and technologies that are becoming available.
- *Competitors.* These are a natural source of ideas perhaps gleaned from ex-employees.

The second step is to agree on the forum in which the new ideas can be canvassed. One obvious route is to set up a short meeting with the originator of the idea. This is excellent for examining the idea because its substance can be carefully picked over during a dialogue; this is far more effective than relying on reports of new ideas where only one-way communication is possible.

Brainstorming sessions also have a role; their advantage is that many ideas can be generated by individuals bouncing ideas off each other and combining them. The disadvantage is the natural disorder of the event. However, on no account should this be countered since it will destroy the spontaneity of the meeting on which its success depends! Once the meeting is ended, the ideas need to be explored further.

At this stage, the level of documentation and bureaucracy needs to be kept controlled to the minimum necessary to assure the quality of the work. Most of the best ideas will arise from informal meeting of minds.

Assessment

A careful balance has to be struck between generating radical new ideas and ensuring they are practical. If the balance is not met, there will be either a startling set of ideas which cannot be implemented or a rather dull set of proposals which closely resemble current practice. To avoid the latter, two steps are necessary:

- Idea generation needs to be separated from idea assessment. Early assessment stifles creativity as potential contributors see ideas being knocked down.
- Idea assessment should be postponed until the full results from the external and internal analyses are known. This is assured with the proposed program because these tasks are undertaken in the first two steps. It needs to be stressed, however, that pressure to deliver early solutions will result in these solutions being relatively conservative.

Process Improvement

Nonetheless, eventually an assessment of the ideas is essential. To be useful, this assessment needs to develop the ideas as opposed to criticizing them. One technique that has a long pedigree in the design field is the use of peer group review. The roles which are relevant to designing new processes are:

- The project team which has now collated its proposals for change.
- The steering group whose purpose is to comment on the new processes.
- A person to chair the meetings who should not have any vested interest in the discussion and, therefore, should not be the project manager. An ideal candidate is the chief executive of the company. An absolutely necessary skill is to be able to steer the discussion constructively so as to enhance the original proposals.

The meetings should last no more than a few hours, and a follow-up meeting should be arranged to occur within a few days, when the recommended changes will be examined. In this way, the iterative process of developing the ideas can operate as rapidly as possible.

Carts and Horses

When it comes to implementing process improvements, a choice will have to be made between:

- Pursuing the ideal solution and designing the tools to support that solution.
- Researching the market for the tools which are available and molding the processes to use them.

The first course of action may seem the natural course, namely putting the horse before the cart. However, in the real world the horse often takes second place. The reason is the high cost of customized vehicles, namely the customized information and distribution systems needed to support an individual process design.

Even major organizations—for example, large utilities—can come to regret customized system development. The costs of ensuring that the system is kept abreast of modern developments can be exorbitant when the IT is not amortized across many installations. The "packaged solution" is now accepted as at least the first step for systems as diverse as general ledgers and manufacturing resource planning. It may also be the last step—the company accepts its procedures will match the needs of the package completely, or alternatively some degree of custom development is accepted as inevitable. The extent of this development has to be controlled. If it is too great, the potential for upgradeability will be destroyed.

Therefore, any search for improvements to a process has to take account of the standard systems on the market. These standard systems may be confined to the processing of information or irvolve physical processing; for example, physical distribution systems.

This issue is not confined to the application of packaged systems. More generally, there is the question of whether the business ought to drive technology or the other way around. Posed in this form, there seems only one answer: The business issues should determine which technologies are adopted. In practice, however, many improvements in business operations are made by observing the emerging technologies and asking How can I apply this? either to an existing business or to a new business. So, for example, the fax machine and the portable steros were products created by searching for new purposes for the available technologies.

Matters become even more complicated when the company has the resources to develop the technology. The technology development then becomes one part of the corporate strategy, and decisions need to be made on whether to incur the costs associated with maintaining a technological lead or to apply the technology developed by others. Either route is viable; but if the decision is made to develop a technological lead, the management of this process is key.

In summary, when seeking process improvement, one eye has to be kept on the business itself and the other on the systems or technologies which are available off the shelf or for an economical cost of development.

Idea Generation—Summary

Any program to seek radical change will fail if new ideas are not forthcoming. To succeed, there needs to be:

- A forum for the generation of ideas.
- A means of assessment of those ideas that does not interfere with the idea generation.
- A recognition of the availability of off-the-shelf solutions.

These influences are summarized in Figure 4–2. We now consider specific ways in which the ideas for improvement can be developed.

Specific Types of Improvement

Generally, a process may fall short of required performance in three ways:

- *Cost and service levels.* The costs involved in operating the process do not justify the value of the services delivered in terms of the customer—there is a need to strike the best trade-off between cost and customer service.
- *Time.* The time taken within the process is too long to satisfy the requirements of the customer.
- *Quality.* The quality of the product or service delivered is impaired.

FIGURE 4–2
Idea Generation Process

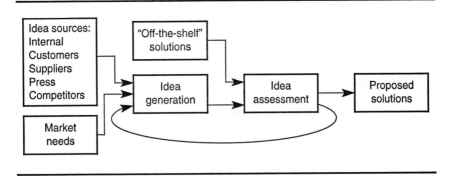

Quite often, these problems are interrelated. For example, a quality problem can give rise to unnecessary iterations within a process, which result in lengthy lead time and unnecessary cost.

Focusing Attention

It is instructive to take the $IDEF_0$ process model, which has decomposed the processes to their constituent activities, and annotate the model with the activity costs, lead times, and a measure of quality (perhaps quality cost or failure rates). An example is given in Figure 4–3 for the supply chain management process.

This immediately helps focus attention on where within the process effort should be concentrated. So, for example, with the supply chain management process, it may be that accepting orders is a relatively inexpensive activity compared to the clerical or manual tasks involved in their execution, but it can take an undue length of time. If the emphasis is on cost reduction, the order-taking activity may merit only scant attention (except if it gave rise to a quality cost elsewhere); however, if the object is lead-time reduction, then a detailed analysis is justified. For manufacturing companies, the sales office is often an area where substantial reductions in processing time can be achieved at minimal cost compared to investments required elsewhere; for example, equipping sales representatives with personal computers and modems for daily direct entry of orders is far cheaper than installing flexible manufacturing technology to reduce set up times on the shop floor.

The advantage of examining cost, timeliness, and quality in the process is that attention is focused in the locality where the most can be gained—on the Pareto principle, that 80 percent of the benefit will be gained in 20 percent of activities.

FIGURE 4-3
Process Diagram

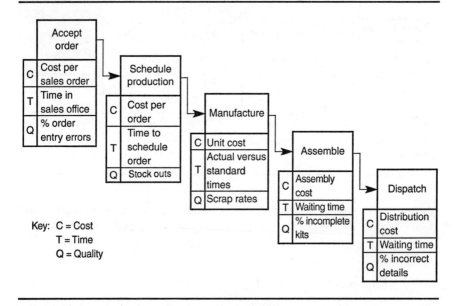

Detailed Process Models

Once the areas which merit the closest attention have been established, it becomes worthwhile to develop the process models to a closer level of detail in these areas. The purpose of the detailed process modeling is to:

- Define what is undertaken in a concise and unambiguous way.
- Act as a medium for communicating when discussing potential improvements.
- Provide a means of modeling the effects of possible changes.

The process modeling can be done simply by carrying out the $IDEF_0$ decompositions to a lower level of detail. There are alternatives, however. We have already commented that although $IDEF_0$ is a useful tool for describing mixed systems, it does not capture all the information on a process, for example, the decision points within a process, so it may be useful to adopt a different method for the detailed process models. Some alternatives were outlined in the previous chapter; for example, flowcharting or simulation. We now consider a futher method.

FIGURE 4-4
String Diagram for Clerical Functions

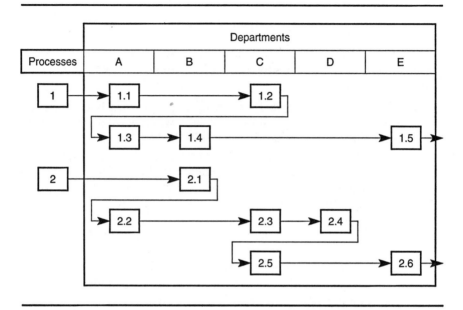

String Diagrams

One technique for simplifying process flow has been taken directly from a work study method used to improve physical distribution. This is the string diagram, which is illustrated in Figure 4-4, where the progress of an item during manufacture and distribution is charted on a peg board using a piece of string. Unidirectional flow over a short distance is evidence of a good organization of the process; a plate of spaghetti is evidence of quite the reverse!

In a similar way, it is possible to plot the process flow as it moves from department to department and back. In general, numerous crossings of boundaries should be avoided because:

- There is often a cost, delay, and risk of error associated with the transfer as the process moves from one system to another.
- There is a loss of accountability as more managers become involved in the process. Where there is failure, the cause can be obscured in a fog of complexity.

The process flow, which may involve physical movement, information flow, and authorization is plotted on a chart. Different departments are distinguished either by the use of different locations or in some other way, such as the use of color or cross-hatching. Unnecessary crossings of departmental boundaries become apparent, and opportunities for streamlining the processes can be investigated.

Process Simplification

Whatever method is employed, an immediate advantage of the graphic representation is that possible simplifications become apparent. These may arise from:

- *Elimination of duplicated activities.* If the process is complicated, duplication is quite possible, especially where it involves the checking of information which has been checked before.
- *Avoiding generating unnecessary information.* Especially where paper forms are involved, there is a huge inertia in changing data collection procedures. Information may have been collected in the past to support a procedure which is no longer carried out.
- *Avoiding unnecessary decision points.* In most flow diagrams, there are conditional points, where the route taken within the process depends on a piece of information. The conditional paths can be unnecessarily complex, and this offers the chance for simplification.
- *Moving from a serial process to a parallel process.* The direct benefit of the change is lead-time reduction but there are ancillary benefits, namely a simplification of process iterations and enhanced quality as relevant information becomes available to participants more quickly. This is one principle behind concurrent engineering.
- *Combining or separating process flows.* In some cases, similar processes exist side by side, and it would be possible to combine these, perhaps with the addition of some conditional tests, to achieve economies of scale. In other cases, separation of processes is called for; this is particularly the case where the same process is being used to support both high-volume/low-variety and low-volume/high-variety flows. The process complexity needed to support the latter type of work can result in unnecessary cost when the process is used for the former type.
- *Avoidance of unnecessary movement.* Sometimes this is physical movement; in other cases, it involves data crossing departmental boundaries.

Once the options for improvement have been identified, using the approaches described above, the next step is to test their practicality. We now describe how this may be done.

Quality Function Deployment

We now consider a technique to link the internal operations of the process with the needs of the customer, since in simplifying processes there is a need to judge which activities are relevant to meeting the customers' needs and which are not. In this way a value is attached to an activity.

This is a crucial point often missed. It is common to distinguish between high-value and low-value activities. Sometimes the distinction is obvious, but in other cases an activity only acquires value though being part of a process which serves a customer. There is therefore a need to associate a part of a process—an activity, or a characteristic of a process with the customers' requirements—so as to judge the relative importance of those parts and characteristics.

This is a familiar problem. In product design, there is the need to relate the physical features of the product, such as its weight, power consumption and features, with the needs of the customers. If this is not done, the efforts of the design engineers will be unappreciated by the eventual customer. There is a clear parallel with the specification and design of process where there is a similar requirement to connect the internal and the external view.

A tool which has demonstrated some success in the product design area has the name of Quality Function Deployment. It originated in Japan and has also been developed under the banner of the House of Quality; a detailed account is provided in *The House of Quality* (Hauser and Clausing, 1988). The heart of the House of Quality is a matrix, as shown in Figure 4–5: The method is a way of compressing diverse information into a small space in a way that is easily understandable and attractive to those who receive it.

The sides of the matrix are a statement of the customer requirements and the values which the customer expects and actually receives; this information was gathered in Step 1, External Review. The top of the matrix lists the internal characteristics of the product (or process); at the bottom is a measurement of the characteristic, comparing the product (or processes) under development with its rivals. Finally a roof is added, which consists of a matrix showing the interdependency, both positive and negative, between the different internal characteristics.

We therefore have a means of being able to relate the internal characteristics of the process to the external requirements of the customer. A proposal to introduce parallel processing to reduce lead time, to restrict the variety of work being undertaken, to move to electronic media, or any other change can be examined and discussed using the House of Quality. The strength of the method is its ability to display information in a form that is accessible to all and thereby encourages debate.

Process Testing

Finally, before proposing changes to processes a view has to be taken on how the changes will be tested, since the practicalities of testing may affect the proposed solution. The alternatives are to have the changes:

FIGURE 4–5
House of Quality

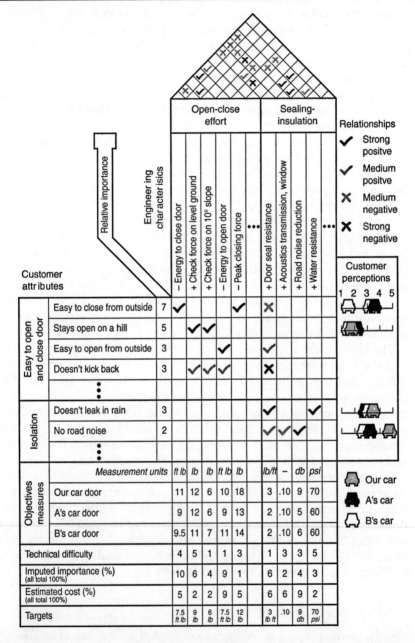

Reprinted by permission of *Harvard Business Review*. An exhibit from "House of Quality" by John R. Hauser and Don Clausing, May–June 1988.
Copyright © 1988 by the President and Fellows of Harvard College; all rights reserved.

- Implemented in one go—the "big-bang" solution.
- Implemented gradually, so that a change in one area is tested before the next change is made.
- Tested in a parallel system, which mimics the operation of the live system until there is sufficient confidence in the new system for it to assume the operational workload. At this point, the original system becomes the parallel back-up as the new system goes "live." When no doubts remain about the new system's performance, the old system is finally dropped.
- Tested in a pilot system, before adoption.
- Simulated using a computer simulation language. This has the advantage of being able to test the new proposals without affecting the organization as a whole.

The first option should only be adopted for noncritical systems—where a failure is not serious and the damage is repairable. Gradual change also has its dangers, as some parts of the company work according to the old systems and others to the new; however, if the various components of the proposed changes are relatively independent, it is possible.

The last three options are all feasible. Parallel working is the surest way to ensure the new processes work correctly, but it is expensive, hence the adoption of a pilot study in many cases. While the simulation approach can be cheaper still, there is a need for the simulation to be sufficiently realistic.

ATTRIBUTES AND DRIVERS

Application

So far, we have emphasised the process view when seeking methods to exercise tighter control over the administrative functions of the company. We now consider the use of attributes and drivers. These were introduced during Step 2, Activity Analysis, when attributes, cost drivers, and activity drivers were discussed. They are used to spot common issues or problems that may not be confined to a single process and which, while they may not merit attention if their impact on individual processes is considered, do merit action when their overall impact is understood.

Attributes

We have also explained how attributes can be used to investigate lead time or quality, mark candidates for a make-versus-buy analysis, or group the activities into certain classes. We will dicuss lead time and quality improvement later in Step 3, Radical Change and consider the make-versus-buy decision in Step 4, Focused Change. We consider here the use of attributes in linking similar activities.

If activities are in some way similar, there may be an advantage in taking this into account within the organization because problems can arise when activities with common attributes are dispersed throughout the organization. The factors to be considered when activities show common attributes other than simple centralization include:

- *Installing common monitoring mechanisms.* For example, if there are activities which have an environmental impact there may be a need to install common systems; alternatively, if there are several activities responsible for purchasing material from suppliers, this too would require some form of control.
- *Sharing information.* There can be advantage in providing links between staff carrying out similar types of activity to share expertise.
- *Common support.* Activities with the same attribute may require similar support, in terms of training or information systems.

When used in this way, attributes identify common features between activities, with a view to associating them in some way. This can be useful in the larger organization, where the diversity of operations prevents an understanding of the individual features of the activities.

Cost Drivers

The cost drivers collected in the previous step are of two sorts:

- Those specified by the project team in the knowledge that they were factors relevant to the organization.
- One or two open cost drivers, where the interviewee is invited to state the major irritations and obstacles to good performance.

These are now used to identify the relative priorities for cost reduction. Common examples include the availability or the functionality of the information systems of the company and the lack of accurate forecasting within the organization. The cost driver analysis also reveals the costs associated with complexity; common drivers include the diversity of the product or service ranges or the number of transactions that need processing, regardless of their importance to the company.

The cost drivers named by the managers are also interesting because where these factors recur they indicate areas which may merit investment to correct a shortcoming.

Summary

The analysis of the attributes and drivers provides additional insights into the ways in which performance can be improved. These are combined with the results of the process improvement analysis and are used to propose changes in the overhead functions, with a view to improving costs and service levels, lead times, or quality.

COST AND SERVICE LEVELS

Introduction

Cost reduction is often the primary objective in a program to control overheads. Nearly all of the techniques which will be described have a place in reducing costs, given a certain level of service within an activity. The current topic is more general, namely the trade-off between cost and service level within a process.

This trade-off is always of concern, either to understand the degree to which cost reductions will affect the quality of service delivered to customers or, more positively, to question whether an increase of expenditure in an area will deliver value in excess of the cost incurred.

Measurement of Value

The project team has been considering the value of activities of the company's performance in many ways, including:

- The measurement of the customers' requirements and the quantification of their needs, using conjoint analysis.
- The classification of activities using attributes such as value-added and non-value-added, or by the use of other similar categories.
- The use of Quality Function Deployment to relate the internal operations of a process to the customers' needs.

Taken together, these perspectives provide the team with a measurement of value to examine different combinations of cost and service level and to judge their attractiveness to the customer.

Constant Service Level at Lower Cost

We have already commented that different activities offer different cost versus service level trade-offs; for example, the sales office example given previously, where lead-time improvements may be particularly economical to obtain, compared to activities elsewhere in the process.

The first step is therefore to examine whether overall process cost reductions can be obtained by increasing activity costs in certain areas while decreasing them in others but still delivering the same process performance overall. This is investigated using the $IDEF_0$ process diagrams; various opportunities for switching resources from one activity to another while maintaining overall performance are considered. In this way, it may be possible to make economies without compromising service.

Changing Service Levels

If the value of a particular level of service to the customer has been quantified, it is theoretically possible to adopt a mathematical approach to optimization. The stage in the process which offers the most economical method of improving service is identified and the cost associated with increased performance—for example, in delivery lead time—is understood. This is compared with the amount a typical customer would be prepared to pay for the incremental increase in service, and an optimum level is struck. While the mathematical rigor of this approach is attractive, the number of occasions when the precision of the available information allows this approach to be undertaken is very few.

More commonly, a series of proposals for changing service levels and their associated costs is considered and the impact on the customer assessed. The assessment is based on the insights into the customer requirements gained by the methods listed earlier. Generally, there is an attempt to shift resource into those areas identified as important to the customer and away from the non-value-added activities.

The team needs a means of evaluating these proposals other than poring over them at a desk. We now describe one method which has the advantage of stimulating real dialogue, namely that of challenge groups, which bring together those responsible for a process and the recipients of its output. The recipients may either be customers or their representatives—devil's advocates, perhaps from the sales function, who can argue the customer view from knowledge of the customer requirements.

If this is the case, it is still feasible to retain a rigorous approach. The approach is designed to force choices on the relative merits of different service levels, given their costs. These choices are best made in face-to-face meetings between the managers of the activities within a process and the customers. In many companies, such contact is relatively rare; by bringing the two groups together, many ideas for improvement emerge automatically.

The cost of the different activities has already been calculated, as has their position in the process. The procedure begins by confirming from the customers or their representatives the value they place on the outputs of each activity. Once this is done it will then become possible to compare the value placed on the outputs of an activity and the costs involved in providing them. It will be possible to identify:

- *High-value, high-cost outputs.* Such activities must be provided but consume resources. The priority here is to make their provision more efficient.

- *High-value, low-cost outputs.* In such cases, the question needs to be addressed whether the service should be expanded or changed to improve its value further. Possible changes could include altering the timing of the service or its scope.
- *Low-value, low-cost outputs.* These activities need not absorb much time in the study, except to question why they are to be carried out at all.
- *Low-value, high-cost outputs.* This will be the main focus of future cost-reduction effort. Where activities fall into this category, the implication is that the organization is undertaking work that may be efficiently undertaken but which is of little use to the recipients.

Most attention will be paid to the last category, namely the activities whose outputs are of low value but high cost. In some cases, the minority, it may be that elimination of the activity is the natural response. More usually, it is the case that the activity was set up to fulfill a real need but has failed to do so, and changing the activity can either reduce its cost or improve its value. Specifically, there are choices to change the nature of the activity offered or the level of service provided.

We now describe the operation of the challenge groups.

Operation of Challenge Groups

In bringing together the managers of an activity with the recipients of its outputs, naturally there is the potential for conflict. This is not necessarily a bad thing, as long as it does not obstruct the flow of ideas. The premises behind such meetings are that:

- Many of the best ideas for improving the effectiveness of overheads will emanate not from the project team bringing an independent view (though some will), but from discussion between those who manage the activity or receive its outputs.
- Such ideas will be undiscovered because there is often a lack of discussion between such groups.

Therefore, bringing the two groups together will generate useful ideas about the potential for improvement. The prospect of this declines if the exchange becomes too adversarial. Naturally, if real external customers participate, the adversarial element must be tightly controlled.

The person chairing the meetings must either be someone senior to the internal participants or from outside the organization, who must be able to spot a potential saving as the discussion unfolds; equally, the person must not be so formidable that their presence stifles discussion.

In summary, challenge groups are a practical way of finding the relative merit of activities. The groups highlight the needs of customers, draw on the wealth of experience of the operating managers, and generate new ideas by bringing these people together. The disadvantage is that a subjective element has been introduced, and while the preconceptions and vested interests of any one individual will be filtered out by the group, prejudices held by the whole group may still prevail. Therefore, the project team should still assess the outputs independently and judge whether the presence of a support activity can really be justified by the improvement it gives to the core activities.

PROCESS LEAD-TIME REDUCTION

Importance of Lead-time

Many of the methods for process simplification outlined previously can be used for reducing lead time. Sometimes lead-time improvement is the primary issue, and we now describe methods which focus on this parameter alone.

More and more emphasis is being placed on reducing lead times, the reason being that short lead times are the key to responsiveness. If lead times are generally short, it becomes possible to:

- Benefit from faster introduction of products and services, where often the largest cost is the opportunity cost of lost revenue during the development process.
- Win orders by offering prompt delivery. This applies to both manufacturing and service sectors. In the former case, an alternative to reduced lead time would be to hold inventory, but this is very costly. To an accountant, inventory is an asset, but it can also be a liability: It represents potential obsolescence and is costly to store.
- Provide product variety through the use of short change-over times to move from the delivery of one product or service to another.

This responsiveness is often there for the asking. Low responsiveness may have arisen because low priority was attached to it, or the performance measures have emphasised other aspects of performance such as utilization of resource or cost.

Cycle-Time Reduction

The concept of cycles recurs in many forms within the organization. There is a purchasing cycle concerned with obtaining external supplies, a sales cycle concerned with selling goods and services, an operational cycle concerned with satisfying a customer's order, and a development cycle concerned with designing new products and services.

Once a process model has been built, attention can be paid to the reduction of the time it takes each cycle to execute. An indication of the scope for improvement is the ratio between the time spent working on an item (adjusted for the number of staff engaged on the work) and the elapsed time between the start and completion of the work.

$$\frac{\text{Time input/Number of staff involved}}{\text{Elapsed time}}$$

This ratio can often be very small indeed; for example, it may be that only a few minutes of work by many people is spent in actual processing, but it takes several weeks for the cycle to be finished. The remaining time is spent waiting and in storage. This ratio can rise to a value of one, whereby all staff involved work on nothing but a single task until it is completed.

Usually, this ideal situation will not be attainable. Nonetheless, some improvement can be made:

- *Identify the bottlenecks in operations.* In some cases, there is not a stable bottleneck because the location of the limiting factor is dependent on the mix of work being undertaken. In other cases, there is a single stage in the process which limits the entire rate of operation. Work backs up behind the critical stage and represents a limit on reduction in cycle time. This is justifiable if there is an uneven supply of work and a resource with limited capacity which has to operate at an even utilization. Often, though, this arises from bad planning. Backing-up of work, and hence cycle time, can be reduced through smoothing the supply of work to be handled and investing in capacity at the bottleneck stages.

- *Synchronize operations.* Frequently, buffers between sequential operations are allowed to develop because the operations do not operate in synchronization. These buffers can be removed if the successive stages in the process are tied into a common timetable; for example, specifying the tasks to take place on each stage on each part of the day on each day of the week.

- *Measure work in progress.* There is no better way to ensure that work does not flounder within a system than measuring its progress. Each stage in a process can be considered as containing a backlog of work, the number of items outstanding at the start of the period. During the period being measured, units of work will arrive and also be finished. The work outstanding at the end of the period is simply.

    Initial units + Received units − Finished units

This measure can be supplemented by others such as the maximum period any outstanding item has had to wait in the backlog. Installing such a process measuring system allows management to monitor the flow of work and immediately respond to obstructions. The author installed one such system in the order-taking, marshalling, and dispatch process of an instrumentation company; it allowed backlogs to be driven down quickly and ensured that managers became involved in the causes of backlogs—computer breakdowns, sickness, and so on.

These three steps form a natural sequence: First attend to the structural issues of limited capacity and uneven supply of work, second ensure the process works in unison, and finally monitor the performance of the system to identify problems promptly.

We now turn our attention to one area which is a major cause of excessive lead time, the problem of including unnecessary authorization procedures within the overhead functions.

Unnecessary Authorization

The inclusion of unnecessary checking and authorization of others' actions has impact in terms of cost, time, and quality. The impact on cost is obvious: Checking consumes resources and adds nothing. Ironically, excessive use of referrals to higher authority can also have a detrimental effect on quality: Those doing the work know they are not trusted and can get away with poor quality without eventual ill effect. However, it is in the area of timeliness that the effects are most felt.

When work is referred upwards or to a checking procedure, this involves stopping the task at hand and waiting for the higher authority to brief themselves on the matter and give their approval. When the times involved in transmitting the information are taken into account, the time taken to obtain approval can be longer than that necessary to carry out the work.

Authorization procedures need to be pruned to the bare minimum. Doing this requires recognition of why intervention is necessary:

- Either because a higher degree of skill has to be introduced than is available at the operator level,
- Or the scale of the consequences of error make security paramount.

In considering the first point, the question of whether additional training would remove the need for referral has to be examined. There is sometimes a tendency for managers to underestimate the abilities of employees who, given the right training, may be capable of greater responsibility and "empowered." In reducing the incidence of needless approval, the amount of work actually being corrected needs to be analyzed. If work is almost never corrected, there is clearly little need for checking. If the type of fault is concentrated in a particular area, a focused training course may be appropriate. If the faults are many and varied, there is a fundamental problem in the operation of the process. If the problems are few but varied, the problem is less tractable. A comparative analysis needs to be undertaken between allowing the errors to occur (while ensuring the full cost of bad quality is recognized), staffing the process with higher skilled operators, or continuing the approval procedures.

As regards the second point it may be more effective to ensure there is clear accountability for actions and penalties for carelessness. It is probably no coincidence that industries that offer excellent job security also seem to require an inordinate amount of checking and verification! There will always be some cases, however, where the consequences of any mistake or malpractice are so large that verification is required. A risk assessment needs to be carried out, and this is another area where the techniques which were developed in product design carry over very well into process design. One method, called Failure Mode Effect Analysis, systematically considers each possible fault, its probability, and the consequences of the failure. With this information, a rational choice can be made on the need for approvals and the threshold above which an approval is triggered.

Very often, thresholds are used in approvals procedures; if an item exceeds a threshold, usually monetary, referral upwards is required. Slight movement of these thresholds would not substantially affect the risk faced by the organization, but can dramatically affect the volume of referrals. To check for these opportunities, it is necessary to plot the distribution of the number of items against their monetary value. This can then be used to position referral thresholds so as to retain their effectiveness while reducing their cost. A side effect of this analysis is often to highlight the large number of trivial items, where the cost of processing the transaction—for example, the cost of raising a purchase order—can be far more than the cost of the item being purchased. In these cases, the answer is to introduce a second threshold—a minimum value below which a transaction is barred.

Just in Time for Clerical Operations

The group of techniques which go under the banner of Just in Time (JIT), have been remarkably successful in transforming manufacturing operations and raising Western levels of productivity to Japanese levels. Most of these techniques are equally applicable to "paper factories," and we now outline the basic principles of JIT.

The JIT principles are intended to counter a tendency among Western countries to install ever more complex scheduling, inventory holding, and quality assurance systems. These do not add value to the customer, and indeed their very size seems to make companies unresponsive. As a reaction, JIT advocates:

- *A perpetual drive to eliminate waste.* It has much in common with Total Quality Management in the way it advocates continuous improvement.

- *Reduction in inventory.* Inventory itself is regarded as a thoroughly bad thing. It is used to insulate the organization from its faults, such as unreliability, poor forecasting, and so on. The metaphor often quoted pictures the company as a boat floating on a river of inventory. If the inventory level is lowered, rocks appear; these represent the dysfunction within the organization, which are now visible and can be tackled. By progressively lowering inventory, the organization is forced to reform.
- *Synchronization of tasks.* Removal of inventory also forces successive activities to become better coordinated because inventory no longer acts as a buffer. This ensures that all those involved in the process are better informed of the purpose of their work and the external goals.
- *"Pull" scheduling.* JIT advocates that work should be pulled through a process by demand signals being passed up the process, as opposed to being "pushed" through the system by product being launched at the beginning. The implication is that work is only produced when it is needed by the next stage down the process.
- *Even flow of work.* There are many advantages that arise from an even flow of work, some of which were alluded to when discussing lead-time reduction: Work does not back up; the use of small batches allows increased responsiveness; there is a reduction in inventory; and, if there is a quality problem, this is identified immediately. The need for work to be produced in small, frequent batches encourages initiatives to reduce changeover times, which again increase the flexibility of the company.
- *Reduced setup time.* An important requirement for economical operation with small batches is a short setup time. An emphasis is therefore placed on reducing setup time to allow batch reduction to take place.
- *Simple visual controls.* Rather than attempt to schedule or model the whole operation from the center, the preference is for simple signals to be passed between operators on when work should move along the process. These are called kanbans (a term of Japanese origin). A kanban may be an empty storage place for work in progress. When the place is clear, those involved in the task upstream know to start generating work so as to fill it. A secondary advantage is that work in progress can only be stored in designated places. In paper factories, the equivalent to the kanban would be the old fashioned filing tray, though without a "pending" facility!

All of these principles are as applicable to the design of support processes as they are to manufacturing processes. The elimination of waste is transferable to all areas of activity. The relevance of the reduction of inventory to clerical operations may seem obscure, but there is a work in progress associated with clerical operations: First, this inventory has a value (e.g., the value of orders stalled in the sales office), and, second, the information in transit between successive tasks represents a lack of precision in the monitoring of the process. The synchronization of tasks is a method of avoiding this "information in transit" by the elimination of intertask buffers. Pull scheduling is another means for reducing the information in transit by releasing future work only when it can be processed. An even flow of work helps avoid unaccountability associated with work in progress. Finally, the close positioning of related clerical operations encourages the "little but often" approach, and the insistence that work in progress be confined to "kanbans" or set places ensures that supervisors know exactly the state of any backlogs.

In fact, clerical operations are much more susceptible to JIT approaches than the manufacturing operations in which JIT was developed, not least because the setup time for changing from one operation to another is usually less significant in clerical operations. The application of JIT principles can be imagined by visualizing a good and a bad office. The former is marked by a general lack of paper—in either the right or the wrong places—an orderly flow of work, and an understanding of current problems. The latter is marked by general confusion and unexplained delays. In reforming this situation the JIT techniques explained above are all relevant.

PROCESS QUALITY

Need for the Information

When an organization measures its cost of quality—the cost of bad quality—the typical result is that the cost amounts to about one-third of the total costs of the company. At first sight, this may seem unlikely, but it is supported by a study of the overhead function, "The Hidden Factory" (Miller and Vollman, 1985), which analyzed the number of transactions, and showed their composition to be, on average:

- One-sixth "balancing" transactions, matching supply to demand.
- One-sixth logistical transactions, which result in the movement of material from one location to another.
- One-third change transactions, which deal with alterations to the products and services from their previous state.
- One-third quality transactions, which ensure that actions take place as intended. This includes the audit function.

The startling conclusion of this research is the low proportion of the transactions concerned with adding value to the business of today.

Not all the cost of quality will be accounted for by the activities categorized as "waste" in the earlier attribute analysis. In some cases, the costs will be hidden with the activity costs of core and support activities.

Furthermore, there may be activities which were classified "policy," whose costs are part of the cost of quality. It is therefore necessary to collate the different costs, where necessary separating out the proportion of activity cost which has a quality aspect. This collation needs a clear definition on what constitutes a quality-related cost, which is provided below.

Measuring the cost of quality is a necessary step to its reduction. However, in itself it is not a sufficient step, since the measurement must be in a form that allows the cause rather than merely the effect of a quality problem to be identified and is linked to mechanisms for the reduction of quality problems. The cost of quality information is therefore to be used as part of a quality improvement program. Typically, the information is used to attach priorities to the various ideas for improvement and to monitor the success of the quality improvement teams. Quality improvement is of course a major topic in its own right and well covered by current material. Given that over a third of the transactions of the support functions are related to quality in one form or another, quality clearly has an important role in the control of overheads.

Calculation of Quality Costs

Quality costs are typically divided into four categories:

- *Prevention costs*, which refer to the costs of preventing poor quality from occurring; for example, assessing suppliers, monitoring of equipment, and training of staff.
- *Appraisal costs*, which refer to the costs of test and inspection; for example, sampling work to check that quality is being maintained.
- *Internal failure costs*; for example, the cost of rework or scrapped work.
- *External failure costs*; for example, the costs of warranty claims and dealing with customer complaints.

This classification has the drawback that it does not relate to the underlying causes of bad quality within a company. It does, however, have the merit of defining the broad scope of the cost of quality.

Therefore, to measure the cost of quality, four attributes are used, corresponding to the categories of quality cost given above. For each activity, the attribute is set to zero if the activity does not relate to the relevant type of quality cost and is set to one if the activity does relate. It is preferable, though more complicated, to have fractional values; so if only half an activity is related to appraisal, the relevant attribute is set to 0.5.

Once each activity has been marked in this way, the cost of quality can be calculated. Since the activities taking place in each department are known, the cost of quality in each category can also be related to department. However, this analysis will not include the cost of lost sales due to failure to satisfy customer requirements because it does not form part of the cost base; therefore, a separate estimate needs to be made of this quantity.

As well as understanding where quality problems occur, it is necessary to understand why they occurred in the first place. To do this requires analyzing the causes of bad work in a particular department and apportioning the cost of quality to the originating activity or department. The results can be startling. Most of the cost of quality occurring in activities towards the end of the supply chain is usually the result of mistakes made earlier in the process. Clearly, it is pointless insisting to the "downstream" departments that they reduce their quality-related costs if these are outside their own control.

In general, the most expensive mistake that can be made is one which is made early and allowed to exist for a long time. So the cost of an error in specification that is undetected before the delivery of a product or a service to the customer is exorbitant; whereas, the cost of a mistake by an operator which is detected soon afterwards is relatively small. The implication is that quality control needs to be the most rigorous during the initial stages of a process. Ironically, this is seldom the case. Often, the early stages are the most intangible, and it is wrongly assumed that quality control cannot be exercised.

Fish Bones and Dominoes

In tackling quality problems, it is useful to clarify how the factors and actions interrelate, both in causing a problem and as a result of a problem occurring. Two graphic techniques enable clarifications of these interdependencies to encourage debate on their solution.

The first is a fish-bone diagram, whose name is apparent from Figure 4–6; it is sometimes called an Ishikawa (after its originator) diagram. It seeks to trace the cause and effect that lie behind a particular quality problem. While it may not appear an especially profound analysis, the benefits of using these simple graphical techniques to communicate a concept to management and staff should not be underestimated.

Sometimes, the reverse analysis is useful. Rather than seeing how a combination of factors converge to cause a problem, the need is to understand how the effects of a problem in one area have a domino effect on others. This can be examined by a form of flow chart, where the effect of the initial action (e.g., correcting some documentation) is plotted out as the changes ripple through the organization. This is illustrated in Figure 4–7. Sometimes, each of the side effects can be costed and a view taken of the total cost of the initial action. Usually, the cost is greater than first imagined, since the full ramifications were not previously understood.

FIGURE 4–6
Fish-bone Diagram

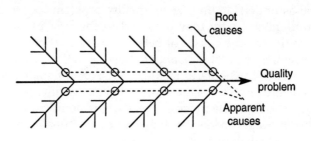

FIGURE 4–7
Domino Effect

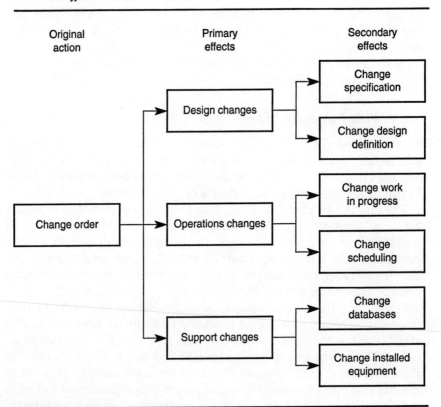

SEGMENT RATIONALIZATION

Dangers

Before discussing rationalizing segments of the business—for example, products and customers—it is worthwhile considering the dangers of too much enthusiasm in this area. It is far simpler to close down parts of a business than to create new parts, and care is needed when reducing volume (which is implicit in any rationalization exercise) that there is sufficient contribution—the difference between revenue and fixed costs—to cover the hard core of fixed costs. The key term here is *hard core*; many fixed costs are not fixed and can be eliminated if certain products or customers are abandoned. However, there will be some costs which will not go, and this needs to be recognized.

With this is mind, we first outline some of the alternatives to rationalizing the business and then describe the concept of "attributable cost," which is a better tool for considering rationalizing than the simple fixed and variable concepts alluded to above.

Alternatives to Rationalization

Before considering the deletion of products or customers, thought ought to be given to the alternatives. Some of the options include:

- *Price increases.* If a segment is unprofitable, it may be the case that the company is simply not charging the market rate, either for its products or for particular customer terms.
- *Price decreases.* Unprofitability may arise from too low a volume; and if there is a strong price elasticity in the market coupled with a high product contribution, the segment could move back into profitability with the volume increase associated with a price decrease.
- *Promotions.* This is another method of increasing volume while retaining the selling price.
- *Process improvement.* Process improvement has already been discussed, and the discussion on segment rationalization should always be postponed until the options for improving profitability have been explored.
- *Product redesign.* This is a potent weapon and is as applicable to the re-design of "products" in the service industry as it is to manufacturing. In the latter, most of the costs—the usual estimate is 80 percent—are effectively committed once the design is complete.

These avenues, and others identified by the project team, need to be explored before undertaking segment rationalization.

Attributable Costs

When considering product abandonment as a means to reducing the costs of complexity, the concept of "attributable" cost becomes very useful; this was developed over 30 years ago in a paper "The Concept of Attributable Cost" (Shillinghaw, 1963). The attributable cost of a product is that cost which would cease to be incurred if the product ceased to be produced. This is the figure which is needed to understand the net increase or decrease in profit upon the abandonment of a product.

The key point about attributable costs is that they are not additive. So, for example, if a single item from a product range were deleted, the net cost reduction would most likely be limited to the direct cost of the item. If, however, several items were deleted, the cost reduction would not only be the direct cost but may well include an element of indirect cost. Therefore, the attributable cost of an aggregation of products is at least the sum of the amount for each individual product.

Not surprisingly, calculating such costs on anything other than an ad hoc basis is difficult. It is possible, however, to survey each activity within the company and determine the degree to which its costs would fall given the deletion of ever greater aggregations of each product or customer range. Once this is done, management has a tool for "what-if" analysis on the effects of product abandonment and of losing the business of a particular customer.

Even if this sophistication is not adopted, the key point to bear in mind is that by no means will all the "product cost" cease if a product is deleted. Even if cost can be directly traced to a product through activity-based costing, for deletions of small elements of a product range staffing levels may not be able to fall. Therefore, product deletion has to be handled with great care.

Procedure

The proposals for rationalization generated as a result of this project will be adopted by a task force for further examination and possible implementation. This will undoubtedly involve discussion at the senior executive level.

It is also worth considering the procedures which need to be followed to deal with rationalization on an ongoing basis, since it is usually the failure of these ongoing mechanisms to function which leads to the need for single exercises to cut back on complexity. Any procedure will need the following elements:

- A specified forum for taking the decisions. In some cases, this is centralized into a single individual, perhaps a brand manager, and the views of others are transmitted through cost and price signals. More usually, there is a discussion among a group of people. The

membership of this group and the frequency with which it meets need to be clarified.
- The criteria on which business segments are judged to have failed. In this program, the implication is that segment profitability is used for this purpose, but there are alternatives. Examples include market share, management time, or turnover.
- A procedure for considering alternatives to deletion of a segment, on the lines of those proposed in an earlier section.

Most companies will not have such a procedure; it seems that just as baptisms are universally more popular than funerals, introducing new products or customers is more attended to than their deletion.

INFORMATION SYSTEMS AND TECHNOLOGIES

Objective

The team has now obtained two perspectives of the information systems and technologies which are relevant to the organization:
- The first, gained in Step 1, External Review was a top-down view of the information needed to effectively manage the processes, the applications which would support this, and the current and future technologies. This was done in the context of a business strategy and an understanding of the critical success factors for the organization.
- The second, gained in Step 2, Activity Analysis was a bottom-up catalog of the actual information required and provided, the data kept within the company, the applications in use, and the technologies employed. From this, was distilled a list of areas where improvement is needed.

The task now is to create a strategy for the development of the information systems and technologies, which:
- Is consistent with the business strategies of the organization.
- Exploits the opportunities provided by the market in terms of the applications and technologies which are available and being developed.
- Tackles the shortcomings in the existing systems and technologies.

The first of these items is paramount. In Step 1, we suggested the use of the five forces model to bring views on how information technology and strategy can assist in providing competitive advantage. If this has been done, there should be some initial views on how the technology and the systems are intended to evolve.

In a few such cases, the information systems and technology are the centerpiece of how the company intends to compete. Usually, this is not the case, but there will be a set of critical success factors, already defined, for which good performance is essential. For most of these factors, whether they be linked to cost, time, or quality, the use of information technology will enable this performance to be bettered.

Alignment of the business and information strategies therefore involves ensuring that proposed direction for investment in information systems and technologies will assist in meeting the critical success factors and the customer requirements. This will usually imply investing in applications and technologies that enhance the core customer-related processes.

The team will be also be constrained by the availability of managerial and financial resource. They must therefore condense their ideas into a series of projects, with stated costs and benefits, which can be considered alongside the other proposals for change. But first the information strategy must be defined.

Definition of the Information System and Technology Strategy

The team should avoid the temptation to combine immediately their knowledge of the opportunities presented by information systems and technology with their understanding of current practice within the company, to produce a set of changes. Any changes need to be consistent with a coherent plan for the development of the systems and technology. Drafting this plan is a technical task, and if no plan already exists the team would require assistance in preparing one. We first summarize the main issues which need to be considered.

Operating systems. The major issue in the field of operating systems has been the advance of open systems, which began in 1984. In theory, the principles behind open systems are *portability*, to allow applications to be moved from one platform to another; *scaleability*, to allow a system to be expanded while retaining the initial investment; and *interoperability*, to allow systems bought from various vendors to work together. In practice, this requires standards, which allow the buyer to avoid commitment to a particular supplier and enable the internal operations of a system to be transparent to the user.

For example, the Unix operating system is now an established standard for multiuser systems, and companies which have adopted it have flexibility in choosing hardware suppliers. The problem is that many different versions of Unix have evolved, and this is threatening portability between different Unix environments. In response, the industry is developing the Posix specification, to which the different vendors of Unix can tailor their operating systems (moreover, non-Unix operating systems are also being designed to suit the Posix specification). Not all standards are part of the open systems movement; for example, the MS-DOS operating system and Windows graphic user interface are *de facto* standards which nonetheless provide flexibility in the sourcing of PC hardware. While there is certainly a wide range of hardware to choose from, there are still some constraints; for example, a decision to adopt a certain operating system can contain a hidden commitment to a small range of processors. There are moves to ensure processor flexibility by defining a set of standard calls to a processor which every processor could comply with.

Although the ideal of open systems has not yet been attained, the major financial benefit is largely available: It is possible to avoid being locked into a particular hardware and held to ransom on support and licensing fees. There is substantial, but not complete, choice in the components of a platform (i.e., hardware and operating system), access to a wide range of application packages, and a reliable upgrade path.

Communications. Communications is another major area of interest in open systems. We have already touched on the reasons for the importance of communication:

- External communications allow a company to improve its competitive position; for example, by locking in customers and reducing lead times by closer links with suppliers. This is the area of Electronic Data Interchange.
- Internal communications permit a company to adopt radically different methods of organization and for staff to work more efficiently.

To communicate requires a network. External communication requires a wide area network, usually using the public network (including, where applicable, the Integrated Services Digital Network for high speed data, voice, and image transmission). Internal communication may use either a wide or a local area network. Options for each abound, and there has been a demand for common communications standards. The framework here is the Open Systems Interconnection reference model, which defines seven layers as shown in Table 4–1.

TABLE 4–1
Seven Layer Model

Level	Name	Scope
1	Physical	Specifies connectors, cables, and so on.
2	Data Link	Transfers binary data and corrects errors.
3	Network	Creates the connection and route.
4	Transport	Ensures efficient and reliable transfer of data.
5	Session	Coordinates the operation of the connection.
6	Presentation	Formats and converts.
7	Application	Provides user interface.

Some levels are more populated than others. Level 3 is well covered by standards; for example, Ethernet, TokenRing for local area networks and X.25 packet switching specification for wide area networks. At Level 7, there is X.400, for electronic mail (the "X" prefixes refer to standards developed for the public network by the CCITT). To add to the variety, it is also possible to implement a local area network using a private automatic branch exchange or a wide area network by linking these exchanges, usually by leased lines to reduce the costs of call charges.

This very brief overview illustrates the bewildering range of choices available and the need for expert assistance. However, for many companies the conditions in their industry will dictate the choice. So for example, Ford suppliers will use the Ford system and military aerospace companies will be guided by the CALS standards.

Databases. There needs to be a view on the best way to store the data within the organization. Ideally, the databases should be defined so as to ensure a "master" version of each item of data is held uniquely. This is not always the case: Sometimes data are stored separately to enable individual access by various applications; instead, there should be a common set of databases accessed by the different applications. However, not all the data need be held on a single database (e.g., there is frequently no need for the personnel records and the marketing records to be held on a single database), and a common database need not be centralized, but distributed.

Distributed databases have advantages in that they allow data to be kept and maintained near to the operations that use them. The difficulties that arise are version control (ensuring all parts of the organization are using the same versions of the data) and ensuring a reliable audit trail. Many of these problems are only now being overcome by technology. However, it may not be necessary to adopt the latest technology; in many cases the situation may not demand a genuine distributed system. For example, it may be acceptable to maintain a central database which is downloaded each day to the subsidiary operations, where it is used and updated, and then reloaded overnight.

There are also choices to be made on the principles behind the database management systems— the software through which applications read and update data. Using this intermediate software allows the design and development of the database to be undertaken independently of the many applications which may use it. In the past, database management systems were hierarchical, whereby the relations between data were defined by a series of parent/child relations. Now there is interest in relational database systems, whereby data are stored and linked by a series of tables. The technicalities matter less than the respective benefits: Hierarchical databases are less flexible but faster; the converse applies to relational databases. Therefore, the role of each database needs to be examined before selecting the best type of database management system.

Client/server architectures. Client/server architectures are a response to the inevitable change in the way organizations buy and use systems and technology. In the past, systems were highly centralized and under the tight central control of a department of technicians, needed because of the technical expertise needed to operate and develop the information infrastructure. This has now changed completely. The users of the systems can buy platforms and applications cheaply and are now able to install and operate them with the minimum of assistance. They therefore do so.

This has the advantage that separate parts of the company can become more productive and effective, but there is risk of the overall quality of information in the company declining as the systems and the databases become fragmented. This can be extremely wasteful if data has to be separately keyed into many systems and if there is inconsistency between them so time is wasted arguing over what is the "right" information.

Client/server architectures seek to resolve this problem while retaining the flexibility for users which the new technology provides. They do this by linking the "clients," typically PCs, to one or more central servers. There is a spectrum of possible client/server architectures, which we now consider.

Computing systems have three key functions: data management, the applications, and the user interface. It is possible for all functions to be centralized, as in the case where many terminals are connected to a single computer. Alternatively, some proportion of the functions can be decentralized. As a minimum, the user interface could reside on each client to display the information in an accessible way. Decentralizing further, there could be a central repository of data on the server which are accessed by the clients to run their own applications. It is also possible for the clients to hold some data and only access the server for data which are not held locally; though in this case it is preferable for servers to be able to access data held on other servers.

To create a client/server architecture there are three essential components: more than one client, one or more servers, and a network. Naturally, there are therefore thousands of possible ways of providing this. A particularly common option is for several PCs to be linked to a central file-server, which acts as the central data store, using a local area network; this provides users their own machines, while ensuring common data are used, and allows incremental expansion of the system. For large companies with an existing mainframe, a client/server approach can use the mainframe as a server with data being extracted and manipulated on client machines to meet individual circumstances. This can be preferable to attempting to update the "legacy" mainframe systems themselves to meet new needs.

Prototyping approaches. The analysis of the information systems proposed in Step 2, Activity Analysis is sometimes called the integrated systems approach, which involves a systematic analysis of the information requirements of an organization and the data, applications, and technology available to provide that information. An alternative approach is the prototyping approach, whereby a prototype solution is rapidly put together, tested, and modified. This may sound attractive, but it was the approach software always used to be developed before the software engineering came into being to avoid some of the resultant calamities (the author has been responsible for quite a few "rapid prototypes" of embedded software while working in product design, although less polite terms were used at the time – fortunately, no one died). Nonetheless, where lead time is important and error can be tolerated, the prototyping approach can be very effective. It is best applied on a local basis, however, and client/server architectures can be useful here: The prototype system can be set up as a client and the effects of any errors contained.

Prototypes are usually written in fourth generation languages (e.g., SQL, which has been adopted as a standard) or using application generator tools. These languages and tools are far easier to use than traditional computer languages. (For the curious, first generation languages refer to machine code programs, second generation to assembly language programs, and the third to the traditional high-level languages, e.g., Cobol. Because they are easier to use, it becomes possible for the users themselves to play an active part in the building of a prototype and its modification. The prototype is then frequently changed to meet the users' requirements and eventually expanded or rewritten for the final version. Occasionally, the final version may be written in a third generation language if the processing speed of the application is crucial, since applications written in fourth generation languages do tend to be slower.

Computer security. Information systems can suffer a breach of security, defined as the occurrence of a loss; the loss may be of availability, integrity, or confidentiality (*Security of Computer Based Information Systems*, V. P. Lane). A breach occurs when a threat to the system discovers a vulnerability. The range of threats is wide and includes risks to:

- *The physical system*. The least subtle threats can result in the most damaging breaches of security. The risk of fire and damage (e.g., dropping the disk) have always been present; the risks of theft are increasing as equipment becomes more portable.
- *Data*. Preventing the breaching of the security of a database is closest to the common perception of computer security; anecdotes of hackers abound, though more serious are those breaches motivated by malice or greed rather than entertainment.
- *Applications*. Corrupting the applications on a system, or the operating system itself, is usually a deliberate act. The attack can take

many forms. The last two are often created for a perverse pleasure rather than gain.

A change in the code of an application program. This is usually to obtain benefit. An ingenious example of this was a financial application altered to round all the calculations downwards and transfer the accumulated rounding errors to a particular account.

Viruses, namely strings of code inserted in the operating system which replicate for a while and then damage the systems.

Time bombs, namely programs which lie dormant until triggered.

- *Technology.* An information system is a piece of technology and represents an investment which has both a value and a cost attached to it. If it were stolen, or simply copied, it may enable others to compete without the expense of a development process of their own. There is therefore a need to protect proprietary knowledge.

Although computer security can become a highly technical subject, the risk of breaches of security can be greatly reduced by simply considering these various threats and then assessing the vulnerability of the system to each of these and how it may be reduced. These issues need to be considered at the design stage.

Voice and image. Paradoxically, while most information systems and technologies are concerned with manipulating data and text, most information is acquired and circulated using voice and image. The quality of decision making and the effectiveness and efficiency of a company can therefore be greatly improved by improving the voice and image systems.

The capabilities of telephone systems hardly need explanation, but two aspects deserve special mention:

- *Conference calls.* The most obvious benefit of substituting conference calls for meetings is the avoidance of the time and cost of travel. Less obviously, a conference call can normally be scheduled far more rapidly, and the reduction in waiting time can improve the responsiveness of the organization.
- *Voice mail.* The ability to easily record messages and access them increases the speed with which an organization can respond, especially where staff are mobile. While a reliable answering service is a boon, the systems can be developed further. They can be made interactive by allowing callers to prompt with the telephone keys and integrated with the computer systems; for example, to provide an automatic account query service.

Image-based systems have not gained such a wide acceptance. The attempt by system vendors to encourage the paperless office has foundered on doubts over the benefits, given the substantial costs involved, and the need to retain at least some paper documents for legal purposes. Also, videoconferencing has suffered from the need for participants to travel to special studios. This is now set to change as:

- Scanners become cheaper and more common, usually spurred on by the desire to capture images for graphic communication.
- Videophones able to operate on normal telephone lines become available.

The project team need to consider whether these developments are relevant to the company and can create better information flow.

Knowledge-based systems. Knowledge-based systems (or expert systems, as they are often called) may appear formidable to the lay reader. However, the managers of an organization do not need to be experts on expert systems to judge whether such systems should have a part in the information systems strategy. Instead, there is a need to consider the benefits, as opposed to the features, of these systems to the business. The systems are likely to be relevant if there is a need to:

- Either make knowledge more widely available, or perhaps available at all following the departure of a key individual,
- Or improve the speed, consistency, and accountability of repetitive but expert decision making in a way that will either improve performance or reduce costs.

If either comment is applicable, an expert system would be useful. It may not necessarily be feasible, but this is the stage to seek outside assistance.

Decision support. Decision support is relevant to a central theme of this program, namely that exercising sound control over an organization requires information. In the short term, this information then allows managers to move from the bounded rational approach to decision making, to the rational approach. More fundamentally, it may be possible to automate the decision support through the use of expert systems and to make radical changes to the organization.

The desire to introduce automation into management decision-making processes has a long and undistinguished history. The earlier optimism, which foresaw managers running a business by undertaking complex what-if analyses on management information systems, has now passed. There has been some success—for example, automatic inventory control—but there has also been much disappointment as management information systems acquired a reputation for being unwieldy and supplying information which was in limited use in running the business.

Now attention has turned to executive information systems, which condense the available information into an individually tailored form and present it in a graphic format, perhaps drawing inferences on the way by means of a knowledge-based system. Recent developments in technology—for example, client/server architectures and fourth generation languages—may lead to such systems gaining better acceptance than their predecessors, as users are able to extract information from the main systems and generate applications themselves locally.

Definition of strategy. There can be no step-by-step guide on how to develop the information systems and technology strategy itself. The reason is fundamental: A strategy, whether related to business or information, is the organization's best judgment on how it is to beat the competition. An attempt to create a strategy following a prescriptive approach will fail because competitors can easily match the strategy by copying the approach and then pull ahead by incorporating their own judgments on where the opportunities lie.

The development of the information systems and technology strategy is inherently iterative, beginning with the business position as analyzed by the SWOT analysis, examining how this is affected by the possibilities (both welcome and unwelcome) offered by the information systems and technology, and then repeating the process. In some cases, it is the possibilities presented by the information systems and technology which is the dominant influence; in others, it is the business aspects. Whatever the case, the resulting business and information technologies have to be consistent, or "aligned," as the aficionados would say.

Tactical Planning

Once the information systems and technology strategy has been developed, the next step is to apply it. There will usually be a large gap between the vision contained in the strategy and the current state of the systems and technology within the organization. This gap is broken down into a series of specific shortcomings which are matched to potential solutions.

Each of the shortcomings can be linked to an activity and, by implication, one or more processes. In this way, the relevance of the potential solutions to processes (and hence the ability to satisfy customers and meet the critical success factors) can be assessed.

The solutions which appear most promising in their ability to assist the business are examined further and an outline project plan and a cost/benefit analysis drawn up for each identified change in systems and technology.

Selection of Projects

Usually, there will be a surfeit of opportunities, which would overwhelm the financial and managerial resources of the organization if they were all implemented simultaneously. Furthermore, in addition to the information-related projects, there are the other proposals for change that are developed in the program. In choosing the projects with which to proceed, the team first separates the opportunities into two categories:

- Significant projects, involving changes to systems which will affect the whole organization. These are considered in this step, along with the changes affecting other areas.
- Small projects, often involving localized change and minimum investment. These are carried forward to Step 4, Focused Change.

The intention is to collate the various options for change so as to rank them for access to resource.

ORGANIZATIONAL STRUCTURE

Sequence

We have left the consideration of the organizational structure to the end of Step 3, Radical Change. The structure can only be put in place once the processes have been clarified and the effects of the various radical changes assessed. This is in contrast to traditional approaches, which begin with fixing the corporate structure and then work within it. We consider here three aspects of organizational design: centralization, the structural efficiency of the organization, and delineation of organizational boundaries.

We discuss the cultural impact of organizational structure in Step 5, Sustainable Improvement. In this section, we concentrate on the principles behind the design of the reporting structure itself.

Centralization

It is not only processes which can be split across many different departments; it is quite possible for individual activities to be split as well. This usually occurs when individual departments are not satisfied with the central provision of a service and choose to provide it locally. On occasion, the better responsiveness can make this worthwhile, but there are drawbacks:

- There is a lessening of control associated with the dispersal. This is especially the case when the purchasing activity is spread over several departments. In these cases, it is difficult to ensure that business is being placed with the most competitive suppliers.
- Information becomes fragmented, making coordination difficult. For example, if sales orders are accepted at multiple points there can be a lack of visibility of the business being done with a single customer, with possible deterioration in customer service.

- There is a loss of economy of scale, both as regards the organization of operations internally and in dealing with suppliers.
- There is a dilution of expertise. Some activities require a "critical mass" of personnel and skill if they are to attain acceptable standards.

While the arguments for centralizing of expertise appear to be strong, the costs associated with poor flexibility can be enormous as well. The challenge, therefore, is to gain the benefits of centralized expertise while preserving flexibility. The use of client/server networks and creating a customer service culture among the providers of central services are both important tools in achieving this.

Structural Efficiency

The two traditional measures for organizational efficiency are:

- Spans of contro—the number of staff a manager has reporting.
- Layers of management—the number of layers in the organization, from chief executive to the most junior employee in a particular area.

It is undoubtedly the case that in the past decade the pressure has been to encourage flatter organizational pyramids, by means of "delayering," which is a process as painful as it sounds and which broadens the spans of control. The driving force for this has been the economy which follows from removing levels of middle management. There have been two facilitating factors:

- Information technology, which has allowed managers greater visibility of the status of the operations, without the need for intermediaries.
- Greater willingness to allow junior employees to use their discretion and the reduction of the need for referrals upwards for authorization.

A further benefit from removing layers of middle management is an increase in the responsiveness of the organization, as the junior staff are able to act without referral and the senior staff become more in touch with the reality of the business.

It is not possible to give ideal spans of control or guidance on the number of layers. Spans of control will need to be smaller where there is a greater variety and unpredictability within a system; they may be large when there is considerable routine work to be carried out by clerical staff. However, in seeking improvement it is possible to:

- Use benchmarking techniques to identify apparent anomalies in the spans of control and number of organizational layers between the company and suitable comparators, whether internal or external.

- Examine the effects of incremental changes on a case-by-case basis. In this instance, questions are posed on the effect of specific changes to the spans of control in order to identify the precise need for managerial input and the consequences of its absence.

In this way, the project team can challenge the level of managerial support. In Step 5, we discuss the application of the principles of empowerment, which can also have an impact on the degree of managerial support which needs to be borne, and expand on the concepts of crisp and fuzzy structures.

Reporting Hierarchy

The division of the company into a reporting hierarchy of responsibility centers is an important step. It is usually observed that difficulties arise from the interfaces between different functions, and therefore the location of these interfaces is crucial. Various approaches have been tried in the past; these are outlined with their advantages and their drawbacks:

- *Functional organizations.* This is the traditional form of structure where particular skill groups or functions are identified, and departments are formed around them. It encourages functional excellence, as the staff in a single discipline are grouped together and encouraged to develop and compete. As was commented on earlier, it does, however, lower customer response, as most processes have to cross over several boundaries.

    The most extreme example of a functional structure observed by the author occurred in a small socialist republic; it is illustrated in Table 4–2. It shows a state-planned system which was able to ensure that the basic production facilities kept functioning, since each type of facility had its own ministry (e.g., ministry of agriculture, ministry of agricultural buildings, ministry of bread production), but was slow to react to change, partly because of the degree of cross-functional coordination required.

- *Project structures.* These are formed for a particular purpose, usually a project, and disbanded thereafter. This provides the advantage of the structure being designed to deliver a particular result, though has the disadvantage of the dispersal of the group and its expertise at the end of the project.

- *Matrix structures.* These are intended to combine the advantage of functional structures in the development of functional excellence and retaining the advantages of project-orientated teams. Individuals retain a functional reporting relationship, which is responsible for developing functional excellence, but are also engaged for project-related tasks. The only disadvantage is the ambiguity involved in dual reporting lines. Nonetheless this form of organization suits many types of professional organization well.

TABLE 4-2
Governance of a Small Socialist Republic

Forty-Seven Ministries to Govern Four Million People

Academy of Agricultural Science	Foreign Economic Relations
Academy of Science	Gasification
Agricultural Buildings	Internal Affairs
Agriculture	Irrigation & Water Supply
Archives	Justice
Border Policy	Labor & Training
Botanic Heritage	Land Reforms
Bread Production	Material Reserves
Broadcasting	Meteorology
Building	National Security
Building & Architecture	Nature Protection
Building Materials	Newspapers
Censorship	Oil Products
Communications	Public Health
Consumer Goods	Religious Affairs
Culture	Road & Transport
Customs	Social Security
Defense	Sport
Economic Planning	Statistics
Education	Supply
Ethnic Press	Supreme Judiciary
Fishing	Trade
Food Processing	Trade Industrial Police
	Wood & Countryside

- *Process structures.* These seek to divide managerial responsibility along process lines and, in doing so, reduce the number of interfaces that occur within a process. In adopting a process-orientated organization, an important point is to allocate responsibility so that there is unambiguous responsibility for key parameters. We raised these issues in our discussion of sample processes in Step 1, External Review.

There is, of course, no universally correct form of structure: Functional structures are appropriate where functional excellence is paramount; project structures are appropriate where each single project is a new enterprise; and matrix structures allow the dual development of skill and project focus. Process structures maximize process efficiency and, by implication, customer satisfaction, but at the expense of functional expertise.

PREPARING FOR IMPLEMENTATION

Context

During Step 3, Radical Change, there will have emerged a number of proposals for change. The proposals will usually overlap in some way. Most radical changes will also affect more than one department. There is therefore a need to:

- Bring together the overlapping ideas into a small number (no more than five) of projects.
- Carry out a cost/benefit analysis on each project and create outline project plans.
- Identify clear terms of reference for each project and nominate a task force.

The use of task forces is necessary because the proposed changes bridge the departmental structure. Proposed changes that are contained within a particular department are best managed through the line management structure, and are discussed in Step 4, Focused Change.

Work Definition

Defining the work to be undertaken needs to be carefully considered. The challenge is to avoid treating the symptoms of a problem without dealing with underlying causes and to avoid dealing with an underlying cause in a way that is oblique to the needs of the business.

One way to avoid this is to consider how any proposed program is relevant to the critical success factors of the business and how it will close the gap between the customers' requirements and the current level of performance. If the program is not directed to closing this gap, it is misdirected. The key is to identify an interrelated set of problems which contribute to a shortfall in performance in a particular area and to develop a feasible solution.

Project Planning

Once the content of the project has been set, the next step is to create an outline project plan, to check on the feasibility of the proposed programs and the interdependencies that may exist between the different actions. It is necessary to ensure that the full scope of the tasks has been understood and to form realistic estimates of elapsed time for these tasks. Once this has been done, an outline project plan can be drawn up. At this stage, the intention is not to create a detailed project control document; this is done in Step 5, Sustainable Improvement once approval is granted. The intention is to enable the plan to be explained to the task force members and for them to accept it as plausible and commit to its success.

Business Case

Once a cohesive group of actions has been identified, it is necessary to subject each change to a cost/benefit analysis. This does not need to be particularly complicated. Often a convoluted assessment process can obscure the fact that the information upon which the assessment is based is relatively speculative. With this in mind, most of the effort needs to be concentrated on forming realistic estimates of the costs and benefits themselves and the risks attached to both these categories; only once the basics are understood should the finer points, such as the time-phasing of the cash flows, be considered.

Risk is another important dimension to the business case. It has several dimensions:

- The probability of a mishap occurring, which increases rapidly with the number of parties involved.
- The consequences of a mishap, which can vary between the insignificant and the catastrophic.
- The drain on the resources of the organization. Adequate resources may not be available, which increases the probability of failure; or even if they are available, their diversion to implement the change may increase the risk of mishap elsewhere.

Once the risk has been assessed in this way, a judgment can be made whether the return provided by the proposed change (as defined by the cost/benefit analysis) justifies the risk entailed.

This analysis can then be appended to the project plan for the change, ready for submission to the senior management for approval in Step 5.

We now discuss the selection of the task forces to carry forward each major change.

Staffing of Task Forces

The next step is to choose a leader for each of the task forces. (The topic is discussed further under Building Change Management Teams in Chapter 6.) It can be a difficult choice: The leader must have a thorough, and recognized, understanding of the topic. However, it is also essential that the leader not be an established protagonist in the area. These two requirements can be contradictory; often the most knowledgeable people are those with an established position. Nonetheless, the task force will be unable to draw cooperation from the organization if its leader is partisan; therefore, someone must be selected who will be trusted not to pursue a personal or departmental agenda.

Furthermore, the leader needs to act in the role of arbitrator, as opposed to an originator or shaper of ideas. The key to success is to develop a working team, and this cannot be achieved if the nominated leader begins to domineer. This begs the question of whether a leader is required at all; in the author's view, this is definitely preferable, because once the project moves into the implementation phase, the company has to hold an individual accountable for achievement.

As regards the members of the task forces, the guiding principle is to achieve breadth of membership. Not only does this ensure a good range of skills are available to the task force, but it helps achieve acceptance among the company through wide involvement.

Information Systems Task Force

In nearly all cases, there will be a need to set up a task force specifically to steer through improvements in the information systems. One part of their terms of reference is to ensure that the activity-based analysis carried out in Step 2, Activity Analysis is kept up to date. Another part of their work will involve the coordination and planning of the information systems initiatives which were identified.

The latter may seem the natural province of the management information systems or computer department. Unfortunately, this function can often be introspective and interpret its role in terms of data processing as opposed to providing management information. For the latter role to be played requires an understanding of the business priorities. Therefore, there is a role for the task force in setting the agenda for the development of the information systems department, working with them in implementing the priority developments and monitoring the results.

Briefing of Task Forces

The stage is now set for the briefing of the task forces. The members need to be told of the proposed program and its objectives and taken through the outline project plan. Most likely, they will have their own comments to add, and this should be encouraged because it increases both the sense of ownership of the plan and accountability for the results.

Once the task force is broadly content with the project plan, the plan is ready to be presented for approval, in Step 5, Sustainable Improvement.

CUSTOMER AND PRODUCT PROFITABILITY CASE STUDY

Introduction

The previous case study recounted how a garment manufacturer calculated its life-cycle costs. The same company also wished to calculate the profitability of its customers and products. For reasons alluded to before, the exercise was particularly complex because the company sells to customers with varying powers to negotiate special terms and manufactures both "design" garments and "plain" garments, which require different activities to support them.

Objectives

The purpose in calculating the profitability of the customers and the products is to guide:

- The marketing strategy of the company and to prioritize the market sectors it should develop.
- The product strategy of the company and in particular the pricing policies it should adopt.

These are crucial areas for all companies. In many cases, however, decisions are made on the basis of no information, which is the usual case where customer profitability is concerned, or inaccurate information, which is the case where the calculation of product costs involve substantial apportionment.

Approach

The activity costs were calculated during the exercise to establish the lifecycle costs of the company. The calculation of the profitability of the products and the customers follows the approach defined in Step 2, Activity Analysis. The major practical task in implementing this approach is the selection of tracing factors along the lines described in that chapter.

Once the activity costs are traced to products and customers, there is also the need to reallocate the product costs to customers and vice versa. The product costs are allocated to customers by means of the product mix which the customers buy. Customer costs are allocated to customers by means of a limited number of cross-allocation factors, also as described in Step 2. Once this is done, the full product cost and the full customer cost is known and can be deducted from the revenue for the product or customer.

The final part of the analysis was to measure the growth or decline of each product, in order to guide the product strategies of the company.

Customer Profitability

The customer profitability is shown in Figure 4–8; the graph shows the profitability of significant individual customers and a general category of small independent customers. The first conclusion is that the profitability of the individual customers is not volume dependent; small

FIGURE 4–8
Customer Profitability

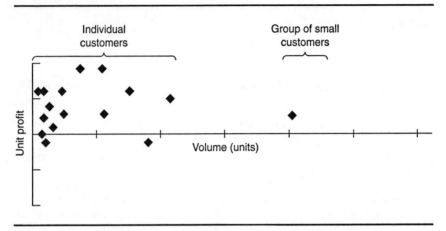

individual customers can be more or less profitable than large individual customers. The profitability depends both on the discounts extracted by the customers in negotiations and the special demands the customer makes on the company.

The second conclusion is that the general category of very small customers, who deal on standard terms, has only middling profitability due to the costs of supplying many small orders. This conclusion was surprising to the senior management, who were painfully aware of the ability of the large customers to extract discounts but who were unaware of the costs of servicing the very small customer on standard terms.

The company is also now able to modify its customer terms to those customers or sectors which are less profitable.

Product Profitability

A comparison of product costs calculated according to a standard costing system and an activity-based costing system is shown in Figure 4–9. It can be seen that the product costs differ widely. The standard costing systems have overestimated the costs of the plain garments by not accounting for the lower costs associated with their support. This has a major implication for pricing strategy because the company is experiencing strong price competition for these products and it is now apparent margins can be maintained even with a price reduction.

For design garments, the activity-based costs are both higher and lower than the standard costs. The relationship becomes apparent in

FIGURE 4-9
Product Family Costs

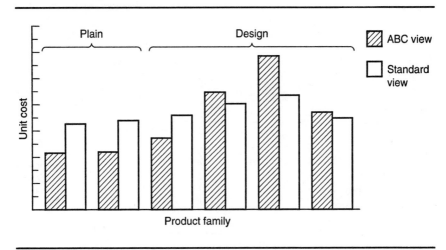

FIGURE 4-10
Unit Profit Versus Volume

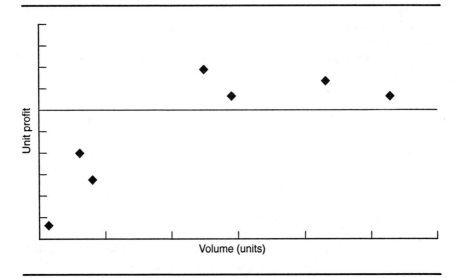

Figure 4-10. It can be seen that product profitability is highly volume dependent. There are many costs which are incurred once a product family is created, and if the volume is insufficient the product family will be unprofitable.

FIGURE 4–11
Portfolio Analysis

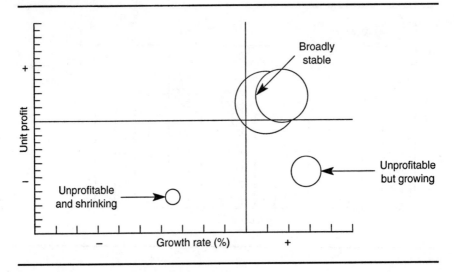

A further view is given in Figure 4–11, where we consider the growth rate of the product families. Some unprofitable families with only a small volume are growing, so their continuance in the product portfolio is justifiable in the expectation that as the volume increases they will become profitable. One family with low volume is, however, shrinking and is likely to become even less profitable in the future. It is therefore a candidate for product deletion.

Production Cost

Many of the differences between the standard cost and the activity-based cost relate to differences in the tracing of administrative overhead. However, these differences also reach back to the production functions.

Generally, the activity-based costing view favors those product families which combine high volume and a large batch size with a small number of production orders and a small number of individual stockkeeping units. The production overhead cost for these garments is far lower due to the lower complexity of manufacture.

Conclusion

The calculation of the customer and product profitability has given a new direction to the company's marketing strategy and shown the need to examine the product portfolio.

Chapter Five

Focused Change

... a living dog is better than a dead lion.

ECCLESIASTES 9:4

INTRODUCTION

Objectives

The project team will identify improvements in the control of overhead activity by making localized changes to the support functions—within an activity center. The purpose is to improve the three components of value for money:

- The effectiveness of the activities, or the degree to which the outputs of each activity are aligned with what is required.
- The efficiency with which the activities are undertaken.
- The economy with which resources are procured for activities.

Deliverables

During this step, illustrated in Figure 5–1, the project team will:

- Increase effectiveness of support and policy activities.
- Identify efficiency improvements and match resources to workload, as well as establishing the ongoing rate of possible performance improvement.
- Identify the scope for cost reduction through more economical procurement practices for staff and materials.
- Identify opportunities for exerting better control of support functions through the introduction of market forces.
- Apply information systems and technology.
- Prepare for implementation of the changes.

FIGURE 5–1
Step 4: Focused Change

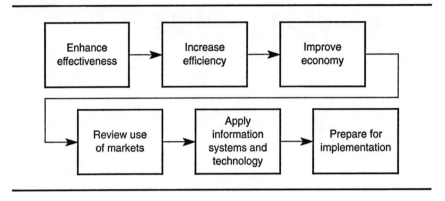

Issues

It is helpful to have a framework in which to place the various techniques and to understand their relationship. One such structure is the "value for money" audit approach. The term *value for money* refers first to a numerator and then to a denominator. Therefore a review is first made of whether the right things are being done from the customers' point of view (whether the activities are valuable) and then whether they are being done efficiently and economically. The approach began in the public sector and was developed to examine and enhance the quality of service operations. It has been summarized in a booklet entitled *Value for Money Audit* (Pickwell, 1980). While there is an accepted framework and terminology, the approach does not extend to a detailed methodology. We have, however, suggested a set of techniques which fit this framework and can be used to improve value for money.

The framework begins with a clarification of the goals of the organization and then deals with its hallmark, the "three Es," namely economy, efficiency, and effectiveness, whose meanings were defined at the start of this chapter. The usual approach to the audit is to begin with an examination of the inputs and outputs of the activities and then to consider their relevance to the goals of the organization, in parallel with an examination of the procedures and systems used to control the operations. It suits our purpose, however, first to consider methods to enhance effectiveness and then to deal with efficiency and economy in that order. We will discuss reporting systems in Step 5, Sustainable Improvement.

While it would be possible to force all the available techniques into these categories, there is one important area which merits separate treatment. This is outsourcing, and it follows on from the discussion of economy in the procurement of resources. This refers to the growing

Introduction

practice of subcontracting out whole areas of activity and trimming back the corporation to a small core; it is equally applicable in the public and the private sector.

Links to Step 3, Radical Change

Many of the techniques described in Step 3, Radical Change will be equally relevant here. In the previous step, we considered the major processes and ways to make them more effective in the eyes of the customers and to make them more efficient and economical through the analysis of cost drivers and other methods.

This is exactly our objective here, but we are seeking more localized improvement and will be concentrating on those activities which are not part of the key processes. The sense of *déjà vu* will be strongest when considering the effectiveness of the activities. This implies putting some value on the output of the activities and considering their worth to the customer. This, of course was the central theme in Step 3.

There will also be some ideas for improvement generated in the earlier step which will have been marked for consideration in this step; for example, enhancements to the information systems which only affect a localized area.

Differing Emphases

It is commonly heard that too much management attention is spent on examining the efficiency of operations and not enough is spent on considering their effectiveness, with the result that people become "busy fools." The right emphasis depends on the type of activity.

The different types of activity were discussed in Step 2, Activity Analysis. A four-part classification of core, support, policy, and waste was suggested. The use of these classifications can show if there are too many activities which do not supply value to the customer and allow different activities to be treated in different ways.

Core activities are the essential minimum. Core activities are improved through better efficiency, since their effectiveness is already assured. There would also be concern if the cost incurred in core activities is relatively small since these are the activities which are mandatory to the supply of a product or a service to the customer; if they are a small proportion of the whole, there is obviously the threat from competitors who concentrate only on the bare essentials.

Support activities have been defined as those which facilitate the core activities. While this may appear to cast them in a positive light, support activities can be of differing values to the organization or its customers. It is in this area that the major questions on the effectiveness of different activities are raised.

Policy activities are not dependent on a level of output but have been incurred through decisions made within the company or outside; for example, the costs involved in producing audited accounts for a private company is a legal obligation, but the decision on the level of research and development expenditure is a corporate decision. In the long term though, most of these costs are discretionary: If externally imposed obligations are too costly, the organization can choose to locate to an area where such costs are lower, and if it does not it will have to compete at a disadvantage against organizations who are in these areas. Setting policy expenditure is partially concerned with effectiveness but is also influenced by the strategic direction of the company.

Waste represents expenditure which is no good for anyone. This is of course a rich opportunity for improvement. By reducing waste, in fact by making it a cultural theme, the biggest savings of all can be made. This is the source of interest in topics such as "total quality," which we consider in Step 5, Sustainable Improvement.

EXAMINATION OF EFFECTIVENESS

Value of Support Activities

We have defined effectiveness to be how appropriate the outputs of the activity are to the goals of an organization, which for commercial organizations will encompass the need to satisfy customers. Implicit in such a definition is the concept of value: It is necessary that the outputs of the activity are valuable to those who receive them. We have already discussed the measurement of the value of activities within processes which satisfy customer requirements. It is also possible to examine the value of isolated activities, as long as the activity has an identifiable output which is used by identifiable recipients.

When an activity is considered in this way, the value placed on it can be:

- Treated as a binary choice—an activity is considered to be of value or not. This is appropriate for only the simplest decisions. This information may already have been collected during Step 2, Activity Analysis.
- Ranked or scored by the recipients of its outputs according to their value relative to the outputs of other activities.
- Measured as the amount someone is prepared to pay for the output. This is difficult; even if the output can be quantified, which often is not the case, a market price cannot develop where there is a limited number of suppliers or customers for the output. Indeed, there is often only a single supplier or customer.

Whichever method is used, the objective is to make some estimate of the numerator of the "value for money" expression. The denominator is, of course, the cost; the activity costs have been calculated during Step 2. It may be possible to extend this by calculating the cost per unit of output.

Initial Elimination

Very often, the information on how much is being spent on each activity is sufficient to generate some initiatives for cost reduction, without further sophisticated analysis by the project team. This is especially the case where activity costs have not been calculated previously. The project team may believe savings can occur where there is:

- Agreement that an expenditure on a particular activity is simply not appropriate for the business. Taking an example, one organization was surprised by the amount of money being spent on "project appraisal." Upon further investigation, it became apparent that a far higher number of projects were being appraised than it was possible to implement. A pre-selection procedure was then put in place, so as to ensure that only the best of the proposed projects went forward to full appraisal. The high expenditure had not been apparent previously because the expenditure was dispersed across several departments.
- Realization that the resources spent on a particular activity do not translate into tangible output. For example, if a new product has not been developed for years and the product development cost is exorbitant, questions may well be asked on the value of the activity.
- Recognition that a large but dispersed expenditure can be reduced. For example, the cost of arranging and paying for travel and entertainment is often dispersed and is not always traced by the costing systems. Once the amount spent is recognized, the potential for saving by coordinated procurement becomes apparent.
- A cost/benefit analysis which indicates a support activity should be withdrawn because of insufficient benefit. If costs and benefits can be quantified, the support activity can be subject to a cost/benefit test: Would the costs of the core activities rise by a greater or lesser amount than the support cost, if the support activity were to be removed? For example, is it preferable to maintain a substantial personnel department, or have line managers fit personnel duties into their daily timetable?

The first step is to discuss these views with the line manager responsible for a particular activity center. If there is agreement that savings can be made, then the next step is to create a cost/benefit analysis and outline a project plan. If there is not agreement, the proposal needs to be discussed more widely. One method of achieving this is to set up challenge groups which will discuss ways of improving value for money.

Value-for-Money Challenge Groups

The use of challenge groups was described in Step 3, Radical Change. At that time, they were used to investigate changing service levels within key processes and the likely impact on customer satisfaction. They are also very useful in this step where the purpose is to bring together the providers and users of internal services—the managers of activities and the recipients of the outputs of those activities. The objective is to generate options for improving value for money, either through increasing value by focusing the activities on the internal customer's requirements or by reducing costs through the elimination of the lower value outputs.

The four combinations of value and cost remain the same; it is worth reminding ourselves of these and the necessary actions:

- High-value, high-cost outputs, which need to be made more efficient.
- High-value, low-cost outputs, which may be increased in scope or frequency.
- Low-value, low-cost outputs, which are not important.
- Low-value, high-cost outputs, which are where the major opportunities for saving arise.

If cost reduction is an explicit objective, it is also useful to start with a series of hypothetical cost levels, perhaps representing increases or decreases of 10, 20, and 30 percent of the total cost of the support services. The targets are used to allow those involved to visualize what the support structures would be for different levels of expenditure and to force choices to be made between particular services.

Many such challenge groups can be held. The project team needs to document the discussion, noting points of agreement and disagreement. There is then a major collation task to bring together changes which the team believe are feasible; this should be done in conjunction with the steering group because it is essential to carry the organization along with the proposed ideas. The final decisions on which savings to adopt can only be made at the highest level within the company, either with the chief executive personally or with the board of directors acting collectively.

Controlling Policy Expenditure

All expenditure in the policy category is controllable, but of course some may be more easily changed than others. To take the extreme referred to earlier, the expenditure on meeting regulatory requirements may seem obligatory, but there is the choice of moving to areas where regulation is less severe or costly. For practical purposes, however, there will be some costs, such as the above, where the change required to avoid them is so immense that it is not realistic.

Other costs are incurred on a wholly discretionary basis, and the question arises of whether this discretion has been exercised wisely. An important influence is the overall strategy of the organization, examined in Step 1, External Review, which gives the foundation on which to examine policy expenditure. In examining this expenditure, the basic questions that need to be asked are What are the benefits? and How do these benefits relate to our objectives? We now discuss the common areas of policy expenditure.

Development is perhaps the most important element of policy expenditure, where profit is forgone today for the prospect of future benefit. The most obvious examples are research and development, and product design. Unfortunately, such activities are often undertaken in an undirected way at an arbitrary level (perhaps some proportion of turnover) and viewed as an expensive overhead rather than the foundation of the future corporation; when this is the case, these budgets are often the first to be cut. The way to avoid this is to treat development expenditure as a series of projects or tasks, each with its own expenditure and with its own deliverables and time frames. Once this project-orientated approach is adopted it becomes possible to:

- Carry out an appraisal for each project to find out if it is beneficial financially.
- Monitor the delivery of items against time frames. This at least ensures something is delivered in a regular pattern, rather than the situation where every project will deliver something sometime in the future.
- Review the original assumptions for subsequent changes in the company and its environment.

For organizations that carry out development work on a regular basis, all this should be contained within existing procedures. However, in many organizations, these basic controls are often unapplied, especially the last item.

A recent case study illustrates the point. This was provided in a paper "Creating Project Plans to Focus Product Development" (Wheelwright & Clark, 1992), which described the situation at a high-technology company whose product lead was declining, not through inadequate resource being directed at product development, but because the resource was badly directed. In particular:

- There were far more ongoing product development projects than could be completed in the necessary time.
- Engineers were reshuffled between projects according to the latest crisis.
- Engineers were not focused on the needs of the business, but on projects that were of interest to the engineers or the marketing department. There was no formal system for authorizing and terminating projects.

- Engineers spent around half their time on work not related to development projects.

The response was to install the project controls listed above and to create an overall product portfolio plan to coordinate the development effort. Wheelwright & Clark suggest classifying individual projects as *derivative* (minor change to an existing line), *breakthrough* (major fundamental change to previous practice), *platform* (significant change to create a new product line), and *research and development*. The projects can be pursued in-house or by means of *alliances and partnerships*, which are methods of increasing the total resource being directed at product development. This classification enables the management to ensure their selected projects (which should not be too numerous) possess the right balance; for example, if all the projects were classified as either derivative or breakthrough, this would be a poor balance.

Marketing expenditure also benefits from close examination. The old adage that half the marketing expenditure is wasted, but no one knows which half, may be accurate but it is hardly satisfactory. It is necessary to examine if any expenditure has actually increased sales. Any reply to the effect that this is impossible should meet with the response that the expenditure will be suspended to see if there is any difference. To take one example, the author was once involved in the evaluation of the marketing expenditure of energy utilities, where very large advertising budgets are justified on the grounds of increasing sales. On further investigation, it appeared that the sale of energy, adjusted for weather, followed gross domestic product and seemed unrelated to the advertising budget. This anecdote is provided to encourage the project team to ask simple questions and demand simple answers: Even the largest of marketing budgets can be founded on conjecture.

Community support is another common area of expenditure. Small amounts of expenditure given to local causes can generate benefit and goodwill that seems far out of proportion to the amount donated. Beyond these small amounts, however, the gains are questionable, and it can be argued that organizations should attend to their primary purpose and use their resources accordingly.

Of course, before the project was started, discussions similar to those outlined above will have taken place to justify the policy expenditure being incurred in the first place. However, there remains a role for the project team to collate information on expenditure so that priorities can be attached to each item and decisions on whether to continue it can be made at the corporate level. This avoids the funding of numerous pet projects within different parts of the organization.

EFFICIENCY IMPROVEMENTS

Introduction

So far, we have considered the effectiveness of activities—whether activities are directed to meeting the organization's objectives. For support and policy activities, this is the first stage and often the one which yields the greatest savings. Having ascertained that an activity does serve a useful purpose, the next stage is to consider whether it can be done more efficiently.

We begin by reconsidering the activity drivers which determine the amount of work which has to take place. This leads to a discussion on the matching of resource to workload, namely setting staffing levels in a realistic way, and to a discussion of experience curves, which can be used to project rates of improvement.

Drivers

We have already considered the use of cost drivers in Step 3, Radical Change. They were particularly relevant to this step because they indicated influences on cost which affected the whole company, perhaps justifying investment to remedy the problem. When examining improvements at the activity level, it is more useful to consider the more specific activity drivers.

Activity drivers have been defined as measures which are proportional to the amount of work carried out. Ideally, they are related to the input of work to a department, though if this is not possible they may measure the amount of output produced. Activity drivers have two contributions to the improvement of efficiency within an organization:

- By identifying what creates work, it becomes possible to see how to reduce it.
- It becomes feasible to scale the resources for each activity in a rational way.

The second point is discussed below.

Workload Modeling with Standard Times

Workload modeling is a relatively mature discipline. It has been the cornerstone of estimating and scheduling of industrial operations for over a century. More recently, it has been applied to the measurement of repetitive clerical operations.

In this traditional form, the approach has entailed breaking down a task into its constituent tasks, applying standard times to each of these tasks, and calculating a work rate, given various allowances for rest times. The approach has received mixed views from both managers and those to whom it has been applied. From the view of the employees, the method can be used to reduce a task to the minimum series of mechanistic components and then ensure that these are carried out at the required rate, thereby creating monotonous employment. On the other hand, the existence of detailed task descriptions and standard times acts as a barrier to those who might make arbitrary demands for increased production. Managers welcome the existence of clear information on the work being carried out since it enhances control. However, the existence of formal task descriptions and timings does limit their capacity to implement quickly any improvements they may have identified subsequent to the standards being set.

The advantages and disadvantages of these systems differ according to whether workload is rising or falling. If workload is rising, staff will often take on the additional work without an increase in resource, unless of course standard times exist which prove that more staff are required! If workload is falling, the effects are often well disguised for fear of redundancy. In these circumstances, standard times can be useful for identifying where there is spare capacity.

Despite these different perceptions of standard times, if we are concerned with searching for better ways of controlling overheads, there is no doubt that detailed information on activities is better than no information. With this in mind, we now discuss the review of existing standard time systems which may have been installed to control the overhead functions.

In calculating standard times, the first stage is to examine the component tasks of the activity and consider whether they are necessary. Some simplification may be possible using the process modeling techniques described in Step 3, Radical Change. Simplification could also be achieved by applying the techniques of work-study to improve efficiency at this detailed level; these techniques are well established, and those interested in them will find them covered in specialist texts. Even if a previous work study has been carried out, it is worthwhile revisiting this area because further opportunities for saving regularly appear through improvements in technology.

The second stage is to examine critically the standard times themselves. Two issues need to be considered:

- *The absolute amount of time allocated.* If it is possible to draw comparisons with other organizations on the times taken for specific tasks, a view can be taken on whether the allotted times are realistic. This is quite unusual; even small differences between different circumstances—causing, say, a 10 percent difference in the amount of time required—can render the comparison useless. In making such a comparison there is an adage "Don't separate the numbers from the

people." In other words, make sure that when external comparisons are being made, this is backed up by personal experience of the comparator organizations.
- *The trend in performance*. It is a matter of fact that productivity continues to increase with time (assuming other factors such as product variety stay constant). This can arise from the increased use of capital equipment, better working methods, or experience-curve effects (which are discussed below). If the standard times have not shown an improvement over the years, this must be justified. One reason may be that the work involves a set of tasks requiring minimal learning, but even here better support equipment can make a contribution to improved productivity.

In summary, the use of standard times in workload models is very well established. It is now becoming less useful as more flexibility is expected from staff and the tasks become less well-defined. There remains a role, however, for the use of standard times for repetitive work.

Workload Modeling with Linear Regression

So far, the discussion on workload modeling has been confined to the case where the tasks involved in an activity have been very closely defined and measured. There are many support activities where the tasks are indefinable, but the activity drivers are identifiable; for example, customer support activity costs may be proportional to the number of customers being supported. Often, there will be more than one activity driver, so in the previous example the activity cost may be proportional to both the number of customers and the number of products. Although the activity drivers are understood, the tasks involved in the activity may be too vague to allow the use of standard times; for example, answering the telephone and making investigations.

In such cases, it is still possible to compare relative resource levels where the same activity takes place in many places across the organization; this is common in large, dispersed organizations where there are many similar branches; for example, in retail organizations. The technique which can be used to good effect is multiple linear regression, which is a technique for obtaining the relationship between a number of input variables, in this case the activity drivers, and an output variable, such as the activity cost or staffing levels. Rather than provide any further explanation of the theory of regression techniques, the best guidance is to obtain the manual for any common spreadsheet, where instructions on how to carry out regressions will be given.

The output from the regression analysis will be a set of coefficients relating the observed resource level to the levels of activity drivers.

There will also be a correlation coefficient, indicating how good a relationship actually exists. Rather than study the coefficients which are obscure for all but the most determined, the best course is to compare the actual level of resource with that projected from the regression analysis. Too large a difference between actual and projected resources suggest that the activity drivers have been wrongly identified; if there is an ideal match, this suggests that resources are evenly distributed. Where there is a generally good match but with some exceptions, this suggests that there are some anomalies in resource levels. When anomalies such as these are identified, the next step is to investigate them for special circumstances, rather than automatically adjust the resource level on the basis of a mathematical model.

Although the technique is useful for comparing staffing levels across large organizations and is relatively quick to perform, its main disadvantage is that it can only identify relative disparities and does not examine whether the absolute levels of resource are appropriate. This cannot be done without the use of standard times or costs, and this itself requires a definition of the tasks required to carry out an activity.

Experience Curves and Volume Effects

In the discussion below, we assume that the basic principles of experience curves are understood, namely that the time taken to carry out a particular activity decreases with each repetition. An experience curve is characterized by a factor, typically between 60 and 85 percent; an example of an 80 percent curve is given in Figure 5–2, whereby unit costs falls by 20 percent for every doubling of cumulative production. Experience curves are a valuable method of predicting the future costs for an operation, especially when there is some information on the costs of a pilot operation available.

Although experience curves had their origins in production, they apply neither to products nor services, but to activities. The ability to distinguish where particular activities lie on an experience curve for particular activities becomes important when a new product or service which is partially based on a previous model is launched. The new operations can expect to experience greater improvements with time than traditional operations. Distinguishing between the costs of the new and traditional activities when making projections of future costs is straightforward if the product or service costs have been prepared on an activity basis.

Given constant technology and investment, the rate of improvements slows. However, in practice, improvement in both these areas ensures that improvement is continual. Economic statistics and independent research suggest a continual improvement in both white-collar and blue-collar productivity, though the latter grows at a faster rate because of the direct impact of capital investment. We now discuss the rates of improvement which can be expected.

FIGURE 5-2
Experience Curve (80%)

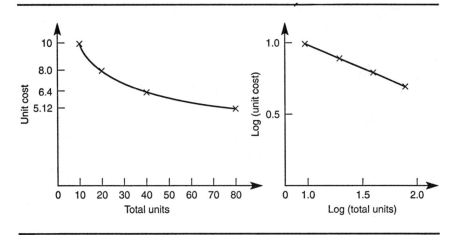

The evidence on white-collar productivity improvement is mixed. Since white-collar workers are mostly involved in the creation and manipulation of knowledge, it would be reasonable to expect productivity to rise at the greatest rate where there has been investment in information technology. In fact, this causal link is not observed. Despite this, we nonetheless see continual improvement in clerical productivity.

An extensive study of the rate of clerical productivity has been made in the United States under the auspices of the Federal Government Productivity Measurement Program. We show below figures for a 15-year period, from 1967 to 1982. It provides average rates of improvement in particular sectors for the period and a trend line of improvement for the whole sample.

Table 5-1 shows the wide range in the rates of improvement achieved over the 15-year period. Generally, the most rapid advances are made where there is a technological advance which affects the area (e.g., communications), and there is no advance (or even a backward step) where technology cannot make a significant impact (e.g., legal and judicial activities). Between the extremes, we see a spectrum of improvement lying broadly between zero and 4 percent per annum. The average for the sample over the period 1967 to 1982 is 1.5 percent per annum.

A 1.5 percent annual productivity improvement is also assumed when setting operating budgets in the civil service of the United Kingdom. However, larger annual improvements in productivity, between 2 percent and 3 percent, are assumed when a function moves from the public to the private sector, to account for the latent productivity gains which are assumed to exist.

TABLE 5–1
Annual Rates of Change of Productivity over Study Period

Function	Annual Change (%)
Communications	11.8
Library services	5.0
General support services	4.6
Finance and accounting	3.8
Personnel investigations	3.6
Records management	3.6
Buildings and grounds maintenance	3.5
Loans and grants	3.5
Procurement	3.1
Specialized manufacturing	3.1
Traffic management	2.9
Transportation	2.8
Regulation—rule-making and licensing	2.7
Social services and benefits	2.3
Regulation—compliance & enforcement	2.2
Education and training	2.0
Supply and inventory control	1.7
Personnel management	1.6
Audit of operations	1.4
Postal service	1.3
Natural resources and environmental management	1.2
Equipment maintenance	0.8
Information services	0.5
Military base services	0.3
Medical services	0.1
Legal and judicial activities	-0.2
Printing and duplication	-0.7
Electric power production and distribution	-1.5
Average for sample	1.5

Productivity gains are not always obtained at a steady pace. Table 5–2 shows the annual improvement rates in the Productivity Measurement Program sample; a cyclical pattern can be observed, with small gains in some years being compensated for by larger gains in others.

By comparison, blue-collar productivity has risen at a faster rate, possibly because of the more reliable links between capital investment and the increase in productivity.

TABLE 5-2
Annual Gain in Productivity for 1968 to 1982

Year	1968	1969	1970	1971	1972	1973	1974	1975	1976	1977	1978	1979	1980	1981	1982
Gain, %	1.1	2.4	0.5	1.6	0.6	2.8	-0.5	1.5	1.7	2.9	1.7	0.6	2.1	2.4	1.3

FIGURE 5-3
Growth in Staff Productivity of OECD Members

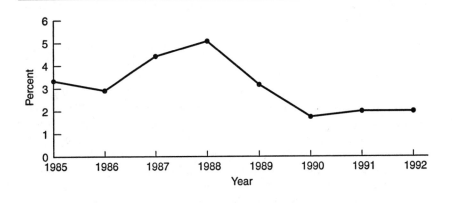

Source: OECD, *Annual Review 1993*.

Overall, manufacturing staff productivity rises at a greater rate because of the impact of capital investment on manual productivity. The annual rise in productivity, measured as the change in volume of production over the change in manufacturing employment, for the OECD countries is shown below in Figure 5-3.

Despite the fact that economic cycles are far from synchronized across the OECD membership, it can be seen that rates of improvement vary widely, between 5.2 percent per annum and 1.8 percent per annum; the average is 3.1 percent. Within the membership, average rates of improvement also vary widely, with an inverse correlation between the size of the productivity increase and degree of development of the industrial base; for example, the rates of productivity increase in Japan, Germany, the United States, the United Kingdom, and Ireland are 1.5 percent. 2.6 percent, 3.4 percent, 4.4 percent, and 7.6 percent respectively. Examining the low Japanese figure, we see that in 1992, productivity *fell* by a massive 6.7 percent as manufacturers continued to hire as output dropped. This raises two important issues:

- Japanese manufacturers are clearly not as influenced by short-term pressures as are their Western counterparts, for whom it would be unthinkable to continue recruiting during falling output on the grounds that the company will be able to draw on the new employee's skills once the recession is over.
- There is a difference between corporate and national productivity. Japanese corporate productivity may have fallen by 6.7 percent in a year, but the nation has low unemployment: a rate of 2.5 percent in 1993 compared to an OECD average of 8.5 percent. In other OECD countries, corporate productivity may rise by laying off workers, but this does not improve the national situation in the short term: The staff are simply sitting at home doing nothing.

More generally, the lack of correlation between productivity growth, as measured in terms of output per head as opposed to added-value, and manufacturing prowess raises questions on the usefulness of productivity growth as a measure, common though it is. In contrast, the rate of growth of Japanese added-value per employee for the period 1980 to 1989 was 5.6 percent, the highest of the OECD countries, suggesting that this yardstick shows better correlation with general manufacturing performance.

In conclusion, the trends of learning curves for both white and blue-collar workers need to be understood. They also apply to formulating the business strategy, which was the foundation for the work in Step 1, External Review: Substantial learning is a barrier to entry by new competitors into a market, and a decision can be made to price a new product to gain large market share and maximize learning opportunities and therefore to be ready to compete on a cost leadership basis against subsequent entrants.

Scale Effects

In making comparisons of the resource levels of activities in similar circumstances, the issues of scale always impinge. Many comparisons are made on a unit basis, and the unit parameters are often scale dependent. In examining the behavior of unit cost, it is often useful to separate out the pure volume dependencies and those dependencies which relate to the rate of production.

The first category, volume dependencies, would consist of costs such as development costs and setup costs which need to be made regardless of the volume of production. The effect of higher volumes is simply to amortize these costs over a larger number of items. Learning, or experience, is a further volume effect, and this has already been discussed.

The second category, rate dependencies, is more complex. There are some economies of scale which depend on rate of operations, relating to:

- The spreading of a time-based overhead over a facility which is able to operate at a higher throughput.
- The justification of increased capital equipment to make overhead operations more efficient.

There may also be diseconomies of scale, perhaps associated with organizational complexity or through pushing up prices of purchased services. The most common situation is that there are initial economies of scale, but these taper off and there is no net benefit for subsequent increases in rate of production.

When organizing processes, the lesson is always to evaluate the processes with the volume in mind. In many cases, the effect of economies of scale may affect the viability of the entire project. For example, there is little point in proceeding with a process whose economic scale in terms of both rate and volume is so large that the financial and organizational resources of the company would be inadequate. In such a case, after initial success at a small scale, a larger competitor would move in and obtain lower unit costs simply by achieving economies of scale not available to the initial entrant.

ECONOMY

Scope of Resources

The final element of the three Es is Economy, which refers to the cost-effective acquisition of resource, which we have divided below into staff and purchased material or services.

Staff Costs

During Step 2, Activity Analysis, the project team will have calculated for each activity:

- Staff costs, split between direct and indirect staff.
- Number of staff, split by category.

These data provide the basic information needed to calculate unit salary costs. The resulting figures, with the management group and the information systems department usually leading the field by a large margin, allow:

- Comparisons to be made with outside norms.
- Attention to be paid to the more expensive salary positions, if there is an intention to reduce human resources.

It needs to be said that controlling staff costs is not just a matter of obtaining the lowest price; nothing is truer than the adage "If you pay peanuts, you get monkeys." The most important step to controlling staff costs is the elimination of bad personnel practice. The most extreme example of this in the author's experience occurred in a manufacturing company which had the dubious distinction of turning over staff faster than it turned over stock (four and three turns per year respectively).

Good human resource management is a subject in its own right, and cannot be summarized here, though we do touch on some aspects when we discuss cultural issues in Step 5, Sustainable Improvement. Instead, we summarize the measurable signs of bad personnel management—labor turnover, sickness and absenteeism, and wasted time—and discuss the subsequent costs.

Staff turnover. The costs associated with labor turnover are immense. If we suppose that for the first six months employees are operating at half efficiency because of the need to learn the task, and for the last six months they are operating at half efficiency because they are looking for another job, if they remain for a year only, output will be half of the nominal, and if they remain for two years output will be three-quarters of the nominal. Measurement of staff turnover is best achieved through two indices

$$\frac{\text{Number of departures in the period}}{\text{Average number of employees during the period}}$$

and:

$$\frac{\text{Number of employees with } x \text{ years' service}}{\text{Average number of employees during } x \text{ years}}$$

The former ratio measures the total turnover of staff and is a measure of the recruitment and training costs being incurred through turnover. The second provides a different view, by measuring only those who have remained for a period of time, say one or two years, and is a measure of the stability of longer-serving employees who represent the skill base of the organization. When these ratios are calculated, this should be done for each activity center and class of employee. There is likely to be wide variation between different parts of the organization.

Sickness and absenteeism. The amount of absenteeism is easily measured as

$$\frac{\text{Number of days lost during the period}}{\text{Total number of days available in the period}}$$

Many compare this ratio with industry norms to identify if their own situation is satisfactory or if their organization is better than average. In fact, any absenteeism is of concern except where there is genuine illness because it implies the corporation is employing people who would rather not be there. It is not so much the time lost when a person is not at work, but how little they will be doing when they are present that is the main concern. Severe action against malingerers is associated with backward management styles, but it is fair to say that advanced companies require committed employees who do not need to be watched over and that if commitment is no longer present then neither should be the employee.

Wasted time. It is revealing for someone to take a piece of paper in their hand as a decoy and walk around the organization, counting mentally how many of the people seen are actually working, and how many are reading a newspaper, chatting, or enjoying a social telephone call. In the author's experience, this activity sampling can show the ratio of wasted time to total can sometimes exceed 50 percent, though this can soar at critical parts of the day, such as just before lunch or finishing time, with people unwilling to start a new task. This is really a function of weak management. In extreme examples, some managers strike a truce with their staff and bury themselves in their office at certain times so as to avoid the need to confront their staff.

Pay Rates

The three issues discussed above do not consider how much is being paid for the staff, but whether the money is justified given the quality of staff behavior, which is the better emphasis. Nonetheless, sometimes the level of staff benefits does become an issue, and in this case the organization needs to examine whether the remuneration for the positions is wrong.

There may have been a mistake in setting the required skills for the position. This goes back to the question of the job description, which may not have been considered formally. For example, in a purchasing department, is the "buyer" meant to set the overall purchasing policies (on matters such as number of suppliers), conduct negotiations with suppliers, or process the purchase orders? If the job has been either formally or informally overspecified, the staff costs will be too high. Conversely, sometimes important tasks are left undone because various staff interpret their job description simply as what they are able to do, and certain tasks fall in between; continuing with the previous example, one person may set purchasing policy while another processes the orders, but no one negotiates with suppliers.

Even if the job has been correctly specified, there may be an inappropriate pay rate for the required skills. This is easily settled by contacting local trade associations or relying on salary surveys.

If, after this analysis, staff costs still appear too high, relocation of some functions offers one solution. Lower pay rates can usually be obtained within in the same currency zone because of the wide variation in regional pay rates. A more radical alternative is to move to another currency zone. If this is being considered, it needs to be appreciated that the key parameter to consider is not the current level of unit wage costs, given present levels of productivity, but the projected levels of productivity relative to others in the same currency zone. This is because it is the average level of productivity within the currency zone which will determine the eventual exchange rate, and consequently the eventual unit labor cost will depend on the company's performance relative to others in the same zone. If there is a move to relocate operations, the question should be asked whether the prospective location is destined to be a high-productivity/high-wage area or the reverse and to examine the implications for the organization's own productivity levels.

Purchase Costs

The proportion of costs formed by purchased material and services will vary between businesses, but at the very least there will be an expenditure on "consumables." The purchasing of material for overhead functions is often not tightly controlled, since the amount of cost involved is not significant to any one department. This can be most evident in the purchasing of travel and accommodation, which is usually performed on an ad hoc basis where individuals make their own arrangements. The loss of potential discounts can be a major cost.

To organize the purchasing function, several issues need to be addressed:

- *Purchasing strategy.* This will dictate the views on the number of suppliers, their location, the acceptability of single sourcing, and the preference for centralization or decentralization.
- *Purchasing cycle.* This is defined later as research, specification, supplier selection, ordering, monitoring, storage, and making payment. The time spent on any phase of the sequence will of course depend on the amount of expenditure being considered. For example, the amount of time spent on researching the paperclip supply market is likely to be small; nonetheless, all the phases need to be considered, even if the consideration of some phases is brief.
- *Controls and procedures.* Managerial controls determine who is authorized to commit the organization to expenditure and how this is controlled. Procedural controls are often concerned with the avoidance of fraud. This is not an imaginary threat: Procurement is the most fertile ground for fraud within an organization.

Addressing all of these issues will form a sound foundation for the operation of a purchasing operation. Effective control of cost also requires information on:

- *Monitoring of performance.* Too often, those responsible for purchasing are allowed to take the credit for "always beating inflation," without being challenged on the fact that the price of most materials falls in real terms anyway. The monitoring of the competence of the purchasing function therefore requires the uses of indices.
- *Total acquisition cost.* It is not possible to control purchase costs using information on levels of current expenditure. When examined at a single point in time, much of the expenditure on material cost is seen to be fully committed: The point of control existed in the past when a particular piece of equipment or way of operating was decided upon. To exercise effective control, it is therefore necessary to understand the costs which will be incurred over the entire use of an item when it is purchased.

We now consider each of these five points in more detail.

Purchasing Strategy

To speak of a purchasing strategy implies there is an overall plan as to how, and from which source, materials and services are to be purchased. It might be thought that the best plan is to buy on the open market at the cheapest price, and no further sophistication is required. For a single purchase, this is the case; though where there is an ongoing requirement to buy items, it pays to consider how this requirement is to be best met.

The first step is to decide who should be responsible for purchasing. In a small organization operating from a single site, it will be possible to nominate a single individual who can be provided with the necessary support; in a larger organization, there is the option to divide responsibility on the basis of:

- *Geography.* The main advantage of local procurement of consumables is flexibility and responsiveness. If local retailers hold stock of an item, it can be obtained rapidly. As for costs, the picture is less clear. Buying centrally should allow better prices to be obtained, lower stocks to be held, and better skills to be developed, but there are also administration costs involved. The best solution can often be found in compromises, such as negotiating national contracts with a national supplier and using the supplier's distribution network for storage and delivery but permitting the use of local sources if this is economical.
- *Purchasing cycle.* The purchasing cycle is detailed in the next section, and it is feasible to divide the purchasing function along these lines. As with all such division, it promotes technical excellence in areas such as negotiation and stores control, but it fragments responsibility for particular types of material.

- *Range.* This option has the advantage of providing clear accountability for certain materials, which is a benefit. On the other hand, the individual responsible for a range now has to be a generalist.

The purchasing strategy also encompasses making decisions on the number of suppliers, which is a major issue. Very different approaches can be taken with suppliers. One approach is to maintain an arm's-length relationship and repeatedly invite competitive quotation; the other approach is to concentrate purchasing through a particular supplier in the expectation of reducing administration, and obtaining discounts and preferential service.

Finally, the stockholding policies have to be defined. While less critical for support activities, where there is usually not a major need to hold stock, the costs are nonetheless large when expressed as a proportion of the value held. Typically, stock costs an organization annually about 25 percent of its value.

Purchasing Cycle

The purchasing cycle is a familiar concept—see for example, *The Purchasing Handbook* (Ferrer, Dobbler, and Killen, 1993)—though the names given to each phase in the cycle vary. For our purposes, we have defined the purchasing cycle as comprising research, specification, supplier selection, ordering, monitoring, storage, and making payment; this is illustrated in Figure 5–4. For the common consumables, many of these stages can be given a moment's thought, however where the purchase of expensive equipment is involved, each stage must be given careful thought because, even when amortized over a number of years, the costs can be considerable. In such cases, these basic procedures need to be followed:

- *Researching the market* prior to specification can result in large savings. Even if a custom solution is inevitable, minimizing the customization will reduce costs. Depending on the formality, the research can range from a casual examination of the trade press to issuing requests to potential suppliers for a "statement of qualification."
- *Specification of the item* can proceed once an understanding of the features which are available within the marketplace has been obtained. A functional specification is a statement of what is required of the item. A technical specification is a statement of the form of the item. In principle, functional specifications should provide more opportunity for a supplier to apply their own expertise in providing a solution at minimum cost; however, it can lead to a lack of standardization in the equipment purchased. At this stage, a degree of formality is often required, particularly if there are going to be several users of the purchased equipment. This is particularly the case

FIGURE 5–4
Purchasing Cycle

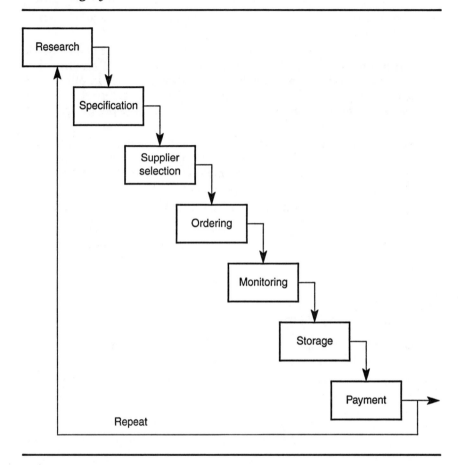

with computer systems where an unambiguous specification is mandatory to avoid the purchase of a computer system which, despite considerable customization, does not do what is required.

- *Supplier selection* starts with inviting several companies to submit tenders, perhaps through issuing a formal "invitation to tender." From the initial research, there should be a good idea of potential suppliers, which will prevent the need to contact large numbers of inappropriate companies. On receiving their responses, they should be tabulated for comparison in terms of total acquisition costs (which are discussed later), the number of nonconformances to specification, and the quality and stability of the supplier. A short-list process can be undertaken if necessary, as can visits to both the supplier and reference sites if significant expenditure is involved.

- *Ordering* is not as simple as it sounds. First, it offers the opportunity for post-tender negotiation to drive prices down further or to obtain special conditions with the chosen supplier. Second, there needs to be an understanding of the contractual terms involved.
- *Monitoring* can be a mundane task, but it should not be left to the last moment. Monitoring should not be necessary if an effort has been made to build relationships with suppliers; but in other cases it is the squeaking hinge that gets the oil. Therefore, for critical items, it pays to be attentive and to make periodic phone calls, and arrange visits to the supplier.
- *Storage* is a costly task, and we have already emphasized the importance of clear stockholding policies. Beyond that, however, the main concerns are to avoid deterioration and to ensure accessibility.
- *Payment* will conclude the normal cycle. Obviously, late payment could result in discounts being forgone and a disgruntled supplier.

The degree of formality a company wishes to adopt on its purchasing policies depends on the proportion of the total cost which material forms. For all significant expenditure, this purchasing cycle should be recognized and followed.

Controls and Procedures

Purchasing requires special care to avoid the risk of fraud. The most obvious example is a corrupt buyer who awards contracts in return for personal payment. This can be avoided by enforcing strict rules on the dealings between suppliers and buyers and dividing responsibilities within the purchasing department.

More subtle are the schemes where suppliers form cartels, either with or without the collusion of those in the buying department. Even without collusion, these can form very easily where there is a stable pattern of suppliers being invited to tender. Where the volumes of business are sufficient, there may be an agreement not to drop below a certain price, and suppliers may bid at different levels above this according to their need for the work at the time. One way to avoid this is to introduce new suppliers into the tendering process. Where this is not possible because of a limited range of supply, a further check is to examine the accounts of the suppliers. On one occasion when the author did this, it was found that the return on capital employed by one long-standing supplier amounted to a remarkable 49 percent!

Monitoring of Performance

On appointment, new purchasing managers will generally seek to justify their existence by negotiating a few plum discounts amounting to their annual salary. This, of course, is to demonstrate their worth in the short term; of more interest is the long-term performance.

However, it is difficult to measure how effective the purchasing function is. Those responsible will justify their competence by comparing this year's prices to last year's adjusted for inflation; if there is a decrease in real terms, this is taken as evidence of competence. However, in the long term, the price of materials usually does decrease relative to inflation, because of technological improvements in the manufacturing processes of suppliers, seen in the experience curves discussed earlier. This decrease is typically 2 percent per year, but for some categories can be much larger for items such as electronic office equipment.

Total Acquisition Cost

An understanding of total acquisition cost is essential for the control of bought-in overhead costs. It has two areas of application, namely:

- *The appraisal of capital purchases.* Two major components of overhead costs are usually the capital and running costs of significant purchases, such as buildings and computer systems. Many of these costs, which are virtually uncontrollable once a system has been selected, may not have been considered when the particular system was selected.
- *Make versus buy decisions.* It is important to research the full costs of both options; in particular, the costs associated with subcontracting can often be underestimated.

Total acquisition cost, which is connected to life-cycle costing, addresses these points.

In calculating total acquisition cost, one controversial point is the use of net present value techniques. These are an accepted form of accounting for costs and revenues which occur at different times. Underlying the techniques is an assumption that money available in the future is worth less than money available at the present, and for a comparison to be made the future money must be discounted. The interest rate used to discount the future receipts or payments is the cost of capital to the company. The result is that any positive or negative events in the distant future have a relatively minor effect. The clear implication that purchasing decisions ought to be focused on the short term seems to run counter to common sense. It should be borne in mind, however, that substantial price increases can be expected for the support of equipment from a supplier of troublesome equipment when there is no other source of supply. While the method is valid, it should not be used to suggest that only the immediate future matters.

In calculating a total acquisition cost, the principle is to take full account of costs. This will include:

FIGURE 5–5
Total Acquisition Cost

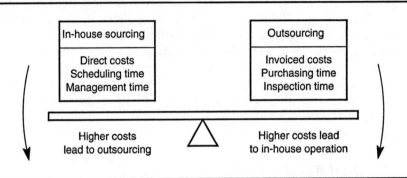

- *The initial nonrecurring cost of the item or service.* For a capital item, this nonrecurring cost may be the predominant item. Where a service is to be subcontracted, the nonrecurring cost is likely to be small, but will encompass the costs of going out to tender.
- *The ongoing recurring costs.* For a capital item, this will include the maintenance costs, which may be considerable. The scope of the recurring costs can be very broad, including the cost of buying, inspecting, and correcting the goods or services. These can add substantially to the cost of subcontracting.
- *The liquidation costs of the item or service.* These can be negative if there is a resale value or positive if there is a disposal cost for the asset or a termination fee for the service.

When buying capital equipment, once the total acquisition cost is understood, a realistic choice can be made between the various options. When subcontracting services, the total acquisition cost gives a realistic view of the additional cost which will be taken on when subcontracting; this can then be compared with the cost reductions to be expected from the cessation of in-house operations. The latter will include not only the direct costs but also the indirect support costs, which have been calculated during the activity-based costing undertaken in Step 2. This balance is illustrated in Figure 5–5.

MARKET APPROACH TO SERVICE PROVISION

Introduction

The methods described so far for controlling support activities have been largely deterministic, involving analysis and the setting of service levels

and resources from the center of an organization after data collection by the project team. There are many cases where this is not possible because:
- Either the organization is too large or complex to be analyzed in sufficient detail,
- Or sufficient authority does not exist at headquarters for resource setting to occur.

The former situation is unsatisfactory since it implies the organization is too large to be effectively controlled and by implication should be subdivided. However, the second situation is quite a common situation in public sector organizations where there has been a deliberate devolution of power, often justified on the grounds of improving the democratic process. The situation can also occur in decentralized private sector companies, where the heads of divisions, in concert, are able to resist attempts by the center to impose its will.

In such a situation, it becomes necessary to devise a means of controlling support activities which does not depend on central direction. This can be achieved by creating a market, whereby managers of one profit center have the discretion to purchase services internally or externally. In this way, a monolithic structure becomes broken up into a series of smaller independent businesses. Activities are controlled as in small companies, by managers taking decisions over a narrow range of activities under their control and being penalized by competitive forces if these decisions prove to be incorrect.

In some circumstances, a market approach may not be feasible. For a true market approach to be a viable option:
- It must be possible to specify the amount of output, or the level of service, which is being delivered; otherwise, it is not possible to know what is being purchased.
- There must be a means to exchange information and a space (not necessarily physical) to trade.
- There must be multiple suppliers or consumers of the service, preferably both.

If all these conditions are met, a market-driven approach is viable; if the last condition does not hold, it may still be possible to simulate competitive pressures by regulation of the market.

This approach has proved popular in recent times, though there are many disadvantages as well as advantages, and the adoption of a market-orientated approach to the provision of services certainly does not necessarily imply an automatic reduction in cost. These advantages and disadvantages are now discussed below. Although the use of markets is being considered here, this is to allow it to follow the discussion of the purchasing cycle; applied on a large scale, the effects are as radical as the changes discussed in Step 3, Radical Change.

The Costs and Benefits of a Market Approach

The first point to make is that the choice between a market-driven approach and a directive approach is not always obvious. This has been apparent at the national level, where for much of the twentieth century there has been debate, to put it mildly, on the best form of organization of national economies. At one end of the spectrum, there have been totally directed economies in which output was directed centrally, while at the other there have been very laissez-faire economies where there has been minimal central direction, except for the provision of such functions as the armed forces (though this is a relatively recent phenomenon, until recently these were firmly based in the private sector). This debate seems now to have reached a conclusion, albeit an unclear one, in which the most successful economies are those which allow the operation of a market in some areas (e.g., the provision of goods and services) but retain central direction in others (e.g., through industrial and energy policy).

At the more mundane level of the provision of support services, the situation is just as complex, and it is important to choose between a market approach or a directed approach on pragmatic grounds rather than on dogma. There are now enough recorded cases both of "market-failure" and the failure of directive systems to make it clear that there is no assured solution.

The disadvantages of a market approach include:

- The duplication of activity between competing organizations.
- The potential loss of economies of scale overall. However, where an activity is already fragmented, subcontracting allows greater economies of scale from specialist suppliers.
- Additional activities, such as the need to generate price lists, or pay for advertising or other forms of promotion.
- The administration of the market place, whether in electronic or physical form.

There is also a loss of top-level control and oversight. As more services are subcontracted, the management's view of the entire range of activity on which they depend becomes restricted.

Set against this there are certainly some advantages of the market approach, especially:

- Greater flexibility in responding to new needs.
- Higher staff motivation as they can link the provision of a better service to the growth of their own organization and increased personal reward.

If a market driven approach is considered viable for controlling some of the support services, there is a choice of creating an internal market or simply trading on an external market. The use of an internal market is less radical, but the company has to carefully consider whether the extra cost associated with the market is worth the likely savings, especially as it is very difficult to create a genuine market internally. It may be the only choice if the organization is unwilling to allow an activity to leave the organization; this may arise because the activity may involve a strategically important skill or there may be a substantial risk associated with them, since the act of subcontracting does imply a lessening of direct control.

Setting Prices

We have already outlined the basic requirements for a market to operate. Perhaps the most fundamental is that the unit of output, or the level of service associated with it, is measurable. This equally applies to internal markets as to external markets.

Where there is a quantifiable output, it becomes possible to produce unit prices and collect payment for each item delivered. For example, this can often be done for computing departments, where the department will charge a price for a particular operation or for a unit of processor resource consumed. Another very common example of such charging is for training provision, where each course will have an attendance charge associated with it.

In deciding the transfer price, the first question that arises is whether prices will be set following the negotiation of a price between the provider and the recipient, or on the basis of a cost-based formula. Negotiation of transfer prices forms an uncertain middle ground in the control of overhead costs. If staff are under a manager's control, the manager can control their efficiency; if a material or a service is to be purchased on the external market, the efficiency of the service provision is disciplined by the market, and the quantity purchased is under the manager's discretion. When services are purchased through transfer prices, the costs are out of reach of both means of control. While provider and recipient may go through the motions of negotiations, they have the character of a phony war.

The negotiations become more real if there is more than one source of supply. Occasionally, more than one source of supply will exist internally; though, if this is not the case, the option can be created to go on to the outside market if lower prices can be obtained. Sometimes, this is prohibited, however, and there is a directive to use in-house resource.

It is not always possible to identify individual items of output. However, it is usually still possible to measure the level of service, defined in terms of its timeliness or quality and perhaps even make the cost charged for the service depend on this. These measurements are encapsulated in a "service-level agreement," which is a formal agreement by one part of an organization on the level of service it will provide to another. Service-level agreements are an important part of the drive to break up large monoliths into smaller elements which can be held accountable.

Service-level Agreements

Service-level agreements offer an opportunity to clarify the responsibilities in a monolithic support structure without resorting to the creation of a full market. The approach recognizes that activities are carried out for the benefit of the recipients of their outputs, which may sound like a truism, but which can appear radical in some circles. These relationships between the providers and recipients of a service are identified, and the level of service formalized into service-level agreements.

Compared to the adoption of internal markets, these agreements have the advantage of avoiding the administration, and the costs, involved in setting prices and trading. On the other hand, the agreements cannot usually reward success and penalize failure; if the provider of a service fails to meet an agreement, the consequences are rarely oblivion, as is the case for unsuccessful companies. Furthermore, unlike a market, they are not dynamic: They only capture the level of service, as negotiated with the customer, at a particular time. This falls far short of a market situation, which delivers a response to a customer demand, albeit at a negotiated price, which shifts according to the changing need of the customer.

Nonetheless, the introduction of service-level agreements does provide two advantages at relatively little cost:

- They can create a shift in attitude in those providing a service, from an inward looking approach where the providers of a service judge themselves on their own standards, to considering the requirements of those who receive the service. To describe an activity as "inward looking" is not to condemn it entirely; those who operate activities in this way often place great emphasis on technical excellence, although without particular consideration as to how the results of their effort affect the organization as a whole. In practice, it is the application of an expertise that gives it worth, so, for example, technically excellent management accounts or research and development are of little use if they have no value to those who have access to them. The existence of a service-level agreement reminds staff why they are there.
- The process of setting up a service-level agreement also provides an opportunity to understand who is receiving a service and what they expect. While this may have been understood when an activity started, as time goes on the original purpose can be forgotten and staff continue a routine out of precedent.

In creating service-level agreements, managers should only be held accountable for items under their control. This may be an obvious point, but given the degree of interdependency in support activities, it is a major restriction on providing service-level guarantees.

Outsourcing

In introducing market-driven principles into administrative control, there is the option to make use of external as well as internal markets to exert control over support activities, in other words to subcontract out some activities. We have already discussed the purchasing of materials and services required to support the business processes. We now consider a wider issue, that of subcontracting much of the processes themselves. The use of the word *process*, defined as a series of activities which link together to satisfy a customer requirement, is significant. The intention is for the subcontractor to take over a structured set of activities, in fact a substantial or complete part of a business process. This approach is proving particularly popular in the public sector, where there is a move to reduce the public sector function to a core policy-making organization and devolve the execution of tasks to the private sector.

The benefits of outsourcing are:

- Access to a fresh set of skills which may improve the efficiency of the operation.
- The potential for economies of scale by subcontracting to a specialist. These economies of scale may arise from the ability to justify specialized capital equipment.
- The ability to reduce reserve capacity to cope with peaks in demand because there may be the option to carry out the activity in tandem with activities having different, perhaps opposite, demand patterns.
- The ability to devise specialized reward systems, suitable for a particular type of activity, to motivate the workforce.

As with the operation of internal markets, there are, however, costs associated with outsourcing of overhead activities.

A recommended procedure is outlined below. It is simply an adaptation of the standard purchasing cycle we have already described.

Research. The first step is to research both the market and the organization itself to determine possible candidates for subcontracting. There are two basic requirements that have to be met for outsourcing to be effective, which are similar to those necessary for internal markets to be effective:

- The service to be provided must be measurable.
- A market must exist for the service.

Using these criteria, it is possible to survey the various activities carried out by the organization and identify potential candidates for outsourcing. Each potential candidate needs to be subject to a cost/benefit test to estimate the likely benefits from outsourcing and the costs associated with the process, including any substantial risks.

Output specification. The second step is to specify the outputs, or services, which the activities provide, in sufficient detail to allow performance to be measured. Any dependencies the activities may have on the organization as a whole also need to be clarified. These are, in effect, inputs to the activities from the organization, and in drafting a contract, provision has to be made for recognizing these inputs and making sure they are of adequate quality. In some cases, the interdependencies between the activities to be subcontracted and those which will remain within the corporation are so complex as to make subcontracting impractical. The specification of the outputs of the activities and the inputs to be received from the organization need to be formalized in a requirement specification.

Supplier selection. The third stage is the selection of the supplier. This will generally be by means of a tender, requiring the issue of an invitation to tender, responding to questions and the evaluation of tenders which are received. The key here is consistency of information and approach. Any variation can lead to bidders essentially tendering for different pieces of work, with the possibility of a low bid being accepted but with the subcontractor being under the illusion that less is required than is actually expected. The evaluation of rival bids should be done in a systematic way, allowing the assessment of the quality of the response not to be affected by the price. The evaluation should also cover the managerial and financial stability of the supplier. Visits to reference sites can also shed illumination on a supplier's actual performance. At the end of this process, a preferred supplier should be identified, along with any special points requiring further attention.

Post-tender negotiation. The fourth stage involves post-tender negotiation culminating in the signing of contracts. The post-tender negotiation is intended to remedy any weakness in the approach adopted by the preferred supplier. The contracts themselves should ensure there are incentives for the subcontractor to perform in a way consistent with the aims of the organization and that there are penalties for nonconformance that are significant enough to represent a risk to the subcontractor.

Contract monitoring. The final stage is of course monitoring of the contract. At the most basic level, this is to ensure that the subcontractor simply meets the minimum requirements. The intention, however, should be to make the exchanges mutually beneficial. Many improvements in service level will not be simply a matter of tighter control; they will arise from applying the principles of partnership sourcing to link and coordinate the activities of the supplier and the customer. These can only arise if there is a spirit of cooperation. Furthermore, the contract should provide for a reward to the supplier for successful cooperation, allowing the supplier to recover any increased short-term costs.

Partnership Sourcing

The concepts of partnership sourcing originated in the manufacturing sector, where it has been observed that those countries which encourage cooperation between companies in a sector, including a company and its suppliers between which an adversarial relationship often exists, outperform those in which companies deal on an arm's-length basis. The benefits are also applicable to the service sector and, for the buying organization, include:

- Access to the expertise of the supplier in molding the specification of the services to the advantage of both parties.
- Economies through the sharing of information on operations schedules, allowing for better capacity utilization.
- Avoidance of the costs of inspection as confidence is gained in the supplier's ability to control its own processes.

There are also advantages for the supplier, most notably the prospect of a stable relationship with a customer intent on assisting the supplier improving its operations.

Of course, many managers already instinctively appreciate the advantages of dealing with a small number of reliable suppliers, who are keen to suggest improvements and to accommodate particular requirements, as opposed to relying on arm's-length bargaining with a multitude of adversaries.

INFORMATION SYSTEMS AND TECHNOLOGY

Objective

During Step 3, Radical Change, a list of potential improvements to the information systems and technology was drawn up and a cost/benefit case developed. Some of these will involve a change to the information systems which will affect the whole company and need to be supervised by the task force responsible for the information systems. Others will have a narrower scope and can be supervised by the managers of the affected areas. Once they are accepted by the appropriate manager, they can be passed up for approval of funds, which is obtained in Step 5, Sustainable Improvement. In practice, the advantage of many of the changes involving localized improvements to the information systems and technology is that the investment required is small compared to the saving and therefore approval is often automatic.

We now discuss how these localized improvements to the information systems and technologies can assist in improving effectiveness, efficiency and economy.

Effectiveness

Information systems and technology help match the services provided to those the customer requires. First, they allow a proper definition of the items, perhaps through direct entry of the requirements at a remote terminal. Second, the ability to carry out on-line scheduling allows the provider of the goods or services to make firm commitments for the timing of delivery. Finally, communication networks allow coordination of the delivery of the goods or services to the location required. In summary, computing and communication assist in providing an internal or external customer with what is wanted, when it is expected, and where it is required.

In many cases, the deliverable is information and electronic data interchange avoids the reentry of information and the delays and imprecision this causes.

Efficiency

Improvement in efficiency is the area most typically associated with installing information technology. The automation of repetitive clerical tasks was one of the first applications of computing. While there will always be opportunities for additional efficiency improvements as the cost of processing power decreases, many of the substantial gains are only possible through applying the technology in an integrated fashion.

Localized installation of technology tends not to raise internal efficiency as it creates "islands of automation," which are efficient in themselves but which still require clerical effort to operate at the interfaces. The implication is that in seeking efficiency improvements, as much attention needs to be paid to the interfaces of the activity to be automated as to the activity itself. However, in doing this, the change will frequently cease to be localized and will require coordinated change across the organization.

The previous comments apply to increasing the internal efficiency of an activity. The other aspect is the use of systems and technology to increase the efficiency of those under a manager's control, say through better scheduling of resource. This is akin to making the company more effective in its operations and are feasible even where the systems and technology are installed locally.

Economy

The economy with which resources are procured depends on the ability to execute the purchasing cycle outlined earlier. Information systems and technology can assist in each phase of the cycle; it can provide wider market research, specifications more closely matched to requirements, a more rigorous supplier selection program, the use of electronic data interchange for ordering, closer monitoring, better inventory control of stored items, and properly timed payments. Further savings can arise through better forecasting and scheduling, in order to avoid short lead-time ordering which is usually relatively expensive and the costs of carrying excess inventory arising from overordering.

Many of these benefits cannot be implemented in a localized fashion. In particular, electronic data interchange and inventory control are topics which impinge on functions outside the purchasing function. This should not discourage effort in this area, however, since purchase costs frequently amount to half of the total costs of the company. Assuming a company is operating on a 10 percent margin, to increase its profit by half either requires a 50 percent increase in sales or a 10 percent decrease in purchase costs. The consensus is that the second course of action is far easier to achieve, especially given the application of systems and technology.

Conclusion

Many of the significant benefits of information systems and technology can only be obtained by considering the organization, or at least processes, as a whole. Nonetheless, benefits can be obtained through installing systems and technology locally, and these benefits can often be obtained relatively quickly with only a minor investment.

PREPARING FOR IMPLEMENTATION

Introduction

The project team will have been identifying various options for improvement throughout this step and now needs to collate these into outline project plans.

The changes will be localized (unlike those considered in Step 3, Radical Change), and implementation can be managed through the existing structures and systems, without recourse to separate structures such as task forces.

Project Planning

Each of the options for improvement needs to be developed by the team to the point that the tasks and time frames are known. This should be done in conjunction with the manager of the affected activity center.

Business Case

A business case should be developed for each of the proposed changes in a similar way to the exercises carried out for the major changes arising from Step 3.

Next Steps

The outline plans and their business cases are to be considered by the senior management in the project planning phase of Step 5, Sustainable Improvement. At that stage sanction is given for any expenditure involved and the corporate plans recast to account for the expected benefits.

ORGANIZATIONAL EFFICIENCY CASE STUDY

Background

The organization is engaged in the product support of major pieces of equipment. Product support is complex and requires four key skills:

- *Engineering skills*, to diagnose problems in the equipment and authorize modifications.
- *Inventory management skills*, to ensure that components are available in the right place at the right time.
- *Contract management skills*, to negotiate substantial contracts with suppliers.
- *Financial skills*, to ensure that the operation is run on budget.

In the past, these skills were undertaken within functional departments, as illustrated in Figure 5–6. This had severe problems, as the process of prod-

FIGURE 5–6
Original Organization

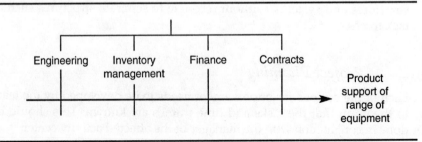

uct support of a particular subsystem involved cooperation between four separate departments. There is currently a move to create groups of staff, combining all the necessary skills, to support a particular subsystem. The exact form of these groups has to be developed. This is being done against a background of a major cost reduction being imposed on the product support organization.

Objective

The objectives of the work are to:

- Adjust staffing levels in the organization, so as to accommodate the cut in resources.
- Change the organizational structure so as to maintain service levels despite the reduction in resource.

Approach

The basic activities of the product support process are defined, and the role of the four key skills in each of these activities is determined. A model of the resource requirements of the activities then calculates the resources required for each activity. The communications between each activity and the volume of information passed is then analyzed. From these two analyses, an efficient organization structure is then derived.

Identification of Activity Drivers

There are four broad categories of activity, which reflect the required skills defined above. Each of these has its own driver of cost. An understanding of these drivers is essential to the setting of resource levels. The activity drivers vary by the type of skill involved:

- *Planned engineering tasks*. The maintenance policies for the subsystem are reviewed with a view to preventing breakdown. This varies with the number of items, but each item can make very different demands on engineering time.
- *Unplanned engineering tasks*. The engineer responds to faults being reported. Each fault report takes a different amount of time to resolve, but in general the time taken to resolve faults is proportional to their number.
- *Inventory control tasks*. The resource requirement varies with the number of items being managed. These items fall into two categories: those low-cost items whose inventory levels are automatically managed and high-cost items requiring individual attention.
- *Financial and administration tasks*. These are diverse, though mostly proportional to the complexity of the business, which in turn is reflected by the number of people employed.

- *Contract-related tasks.* The resource required depends on the number and value of contracts being issued.

These activity drivers are now used for resource modeling.

Resource Modeling

The modeling of the planned engineering tasks requires identifying the items within each subsystem to be supported. This planned engineering input is then classified into bands according to the time required annually per item. While appearing straightforward, the difficulty is that in the past this work has often not been carried out because of shortage of resource, and therefore there are no available records to support the classification. With this in mind, the bands have to be fairly coarse; nonetheless, the method provides a means of estimating the resource required for the task. In the future, during the design of the subsystem, a more precise estimate of the planned engineering time is needed for product support to be made.

The modeling of the unplanned, or reactive, engineering time presents more of a problem. Ideally, the reliability of the subsystem requiring support could be estimated, along with the time needed to respond to each type of fault, thereby allowing the requirement for resource to be made for each subsystem. In practice, this information is simply not available. As an alternative, the outputs of the reactive engineering work are measured for each subsystem, in terms of the instructions issued and their type. This is then used in a multiple regression to find the correlation between volume of output and the resources employed. The correlation is good, but the measures have two limitations:

- The resulting measures relating type of instruction and the resource requirements are relative only. They can only indicate apparent over- or underresource for particular subsystems.
- By only measuring the output from the function, the method is unable to detect if engineers are generating unnecessary work—if an area was overresourced it is possible that to stay busy there is unnecessary intervention and generation of instructions.

The resources required for planned and unplanned engineering resource are then combined and used to redistribute engineering resource across the subsystems to be supported. Since the unplanned work is largely not carried out, at present the total resource requirements amount to more than is available, and the levels will need to be trimmed back.

Inventory control is exercised through groups dedicated to particular subsystems. When the number of high and low value items is plotted on a graph, we see a curve representing the natural boundary of supervisory control, as shown in Figure 5–7; a supervisor can supervise either a

FIGURE 5–7
Boundary of Supervisory Control

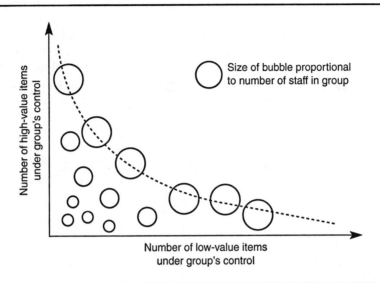

large number of low-value items or a large (but lesser) number of high-value items, but not both. There are, however, a number of groups which do not justify a section leader and are candidates for merger. The next step is to carry out a multiple regression, relating the number of clerks under a supervisor to the number of high- and low-value items being managed by the groups. The correlation is good and shows that high-value items require over 10 times the resource required for low-value items and gives an estimate of the resource required for both. When combined with the previous analysis on the limits on supervisory control, we can also deduce the natural span of control of a supervisor in this organization.

The organization employs relatively few finance staff, so resource modeling is less critical in this area. A simple approach is therefore used, and the average ratio of finance and administration staff to total staff complement is found. This will be used to apportion these staff across the organization, subject to resource constraints.

The number of contracts staff required for each subsystem is estimated according to the number of contracts being issued. Allowance is also made for the value of the material being purchased, so that staff are not ineffectively deployed to deal with large numbers of low-value contracts.

It will be apparent that most of the resource modeling is directed towards equitably allocating resource according to need, as opposed to deriving the required resource from first principles. This is satisfactory in the context of a major cost reduction: Even if an ideal staffing level is derived it is scarcely relevant if the staff will not be available to meet it. The final stage of the resource modeling is therefore to adjust the resource levels needed for each subsystem to fit the total workforce which will be available following the staff reduction. A key issue is to balance the need for additional resources for planned engineering work against additional reductions elsewhere; the increase in planned engineering resources is essentially a policy decision and this is done on a judgmental, not analytic, basis.

Lower Organizational Structure

Once the resource levels have been set across the organization, it becomes possible to consider the organizational structure. The aim is to integrate the four skills around particular subsystems.

For inventory control, the basic operating unit has already been defined: a supervisor in charge of several clerks. The scope of their responsibility is set by identifying subsystems with the appropriate number of high- and low-value items which can fulfil the working capacity of the clerks.

These subsystems will have an engineering workload associated with their planned and unplanned maintenance, which defines the number of engineers required. The engineers will report to an engineering manager. The number of engineering managers required depends on the number of technical decisions which must be referred upwards for approval, which in turn depends on the technical complexity of the subsystems, as opposed to the volume of the maintenance workload. In practice, this leads to relatively narrower spans of control.

The inventory control and the engineering units need to work closely together and are situated in the same area. The inventory control staff are much more numerous than the engineering staff, and there is a need for an additional tier of management, with several supervisors reporting to an inventory control manager. This provides a structure as shown in Figure 5–8. Each inventory control unit is associated with an engineering unit and is responsible for a particular subsystem, which can now be supported without interdepartmental communication.

The department head can be drawn from either the inventory control or the engineering routes, since at this level the work is of a general managerial nature. The departmental head is responsible for the product support of an entire system.

Higher Organizational Structure

The financial, administration, and contracts staff are less numerous, and it is therefore only practical to integrate them with the other skills at the

FIGURE 5-8
Lower Organizational Structure

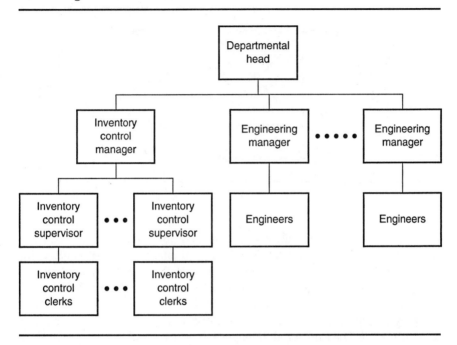

senior management level. The higher organizational structure is shown in Figure 5-9. Several departmental heads report to a divisional head, who is also responsible for a contracts department and the finance and administration staff.

FIGURE 5-9
Organizational Structure

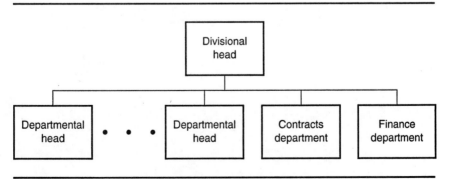

FIGURE 5–10
Contacts Analysis

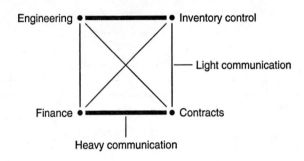

Although these staff are not closely integrated with those with the inventory control and engineering skills, communication analysis, illustrated in Figure 5–10, shows this to be acceptable. In terms of volume, the most significant communication is between the inventory control and engineering staff, who are now closely linked, and between finance and contracts, who can be located together. The divisional manager is now entirely responsible for the product support of the systems in major pieces of equipment. The divisional manager has access to all the necessary skills for this support and can be held fully accountable for performance.

Conclusion

The new structure is far better suited to effective product support. Responsibility for the support of a piece of equipment is now concentrated in a single individual who has the necessary skills at his or her disposal. The groups of staff who need to communicate are situated together and can now speak to each other without the need for formal and slow interdepartmental communication.

The conclusions from this product support case study are equally applicable to organizing for concurrent engineering.

Chapter Six

Sustainable Improvement

All the rivers run into the sea; yet the sea is not full;

ECCLESIASTES 1:7

INTRODUCTION

Objectives

The objective of the final step is to ensure that the improvements in the project-orientated phase of the work can be implemented and sustained. This is one of the most difficult aspects of the whole program and first requires the creation of a project management structure. We then consider corporate culture and the company's performance measures which are the biggest influences on management behavior. This leads into a definition of the management reporting systems required by the organization.

Finally, we consider "total quality." This is a very broad topic and one whose issues are notoriously intangible. However, this should not dissuade the project team. The ways in which staff relate to each other and the attitudes they have to their work have tremendous influence on sustainable improvement. It is also an excellent topic on which to conclude because it brings together many of the issues raised by activity-based management techniques.

Deliverables

During this final step, illustrated in Figure 6–1, the project team will produce:
- A project control system for ensuring the progress of the improvements.
- Proposals to change the organizational culture.
- A review of the performance measures used by the company.
- Proposals for enhanced reporting systems.
- A framework for implementing a total quality program.

FIGURE 6–1
Step 5: Sustainable Advantage

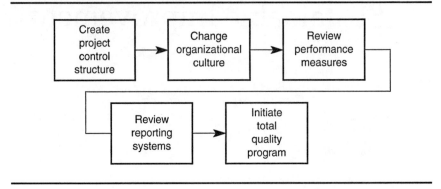

Issues

Earlier we referred to the advantages of a project-based approach, namely its ability to deliver reliable results in a short period of time. The disadvantage of the sheer speed and intensiveness of the approach is that the project team can usually move ahead of the organization.

There should not be an intellectual gap if proper use has been made of the steering group both to guide the team in the most practical approach and to inform them of the thinking of the project team. However, there is likely to be a gap in attitudes and an appreciation of what is achievable. This is the largest obstacle; if it is not tackled, there is the danger that when the team is disbanded at the end of program the organization will breathe a collective sigh of relief and lapse back into the familiar way of doing business.

PROJECT MANAGEMENT

Obtaining Authorization

By this stage, the project team will have identified many potential initiatives for change:

- The terms of reference several task forces created, during Step 3, Radical Change to tackle projects of major importance.
- Many smaller projects defined in Step 4, Focused Change, which are to be managed through the line management structure of the company.

Each of these projects will have an outline project plan and an associated business case. Many of the projects will be independent—the risks, costs, and benefits of one project will not alter if any other project is adopted. Some will be dependent and in this case, aggregated business cases will have be drawn up for the various permutations of feasible projects.

Once this is done, the senior management of the company can then begin examining the projects to confirm or withhold authorization. The first step is to exclude those projects (or combinations) which are judged unattractive because the ratio of benefit to cost is not justified given the risks involved. This judgment may be supported by sophisticated capital appraisal and risk assessment techniques, if necessary.

The remaining projects are nominally beneficial. They should be grouped into three categories:

- Those which are mandatory if the company is to remain in business. For example, if most of the company's customers are demanding a level of service and can go elsewhere for it, it must be delivered. Either the costs must be borne, or operations must cease.
- Those which require minimal funds or management time to implement.
- Those which are optional and are competing for funds and managerial time.

The first two categories can be authorized without further analysis. The projects in the final category are analyzed for their demands on scarce resource. Capital rationing analysis may play a part here, although equally important will be discussion with the affected task force members and managers to gauge their confidence in being able to bring all the changes about.

At the end of this process, each of the project plans will have been accepted (the preferred option, of course), rejected, or modified. The modified plans are reworked.

There is now formal authorization to proceed with an agreed-on set of projects, and the detailed project planning can begin.

Overview of Project and Change Management

Successful project and change management requires diverse skills. There is a need to:

- Maintain a wide perspective of the various changes taking place, so as to place differing priorities on projects.
- Pay attention to detail and possess an almost obsessive desire to meet targets.
- Inspire the staff to welcome change and avoid the "fud" problem: fear, uncertainty, and doubt. Even without fud, change is not welcomed by those who have not experienced it for some years, and this must be recognized and tackled.

In particular, it is important not to delve into detail without first obtaining an overview of the whole change program and identifying any dependencies that may exist between the various individual projects.

To obtain proper coordination, it is necessary to collate the various outline project plans so that any dependencies between the various actions can be understood; this includes the changes to be made under both Step 3 and Step 4. Once the outline plans have been collated, the next step is to apply a work breakdown structure (discussed below) to the approved schemes for change. The structure should be split according to the terms of reference of the various task forces (for Step 3 projects) and the organizational structure (for Step 4 projects).

Once the breakdown structure has been established, it is necessary to continue the decomposition until there is a detailed project plan for every occasion where there is intended to be a change in activity, either in cost, time, or quality. The detailed plans will be amplifications of the earlier outline plans but recognizing any interdependencies that have become apparent. In this way, the entire sum of change proposed for the company can be accounted for at the activity level, and nothing will have fallen through the net.

Work Breakdown Structure

Good control is assisted by identifying a clear structure to the work. The principle is to take a large, complicated task, namely the program, and break it down into smaller, less complicated parts.

Each of these parts can be further decomposed and the process repeated until a hierarchy of small projects has been identified. This hierarchy is called the "work breakdown structure"; some structures are better than others. The mark of a good structure is the relative independence of elements of work on the same level. Generally, the work can be broken down by different parameters: for example, time, geographic area, and use of resources. In this case, the division will reflect the task force and management structure. An example of a work breakdown structure is given in Figure 6–2.

The breakdown proceeds to a project plan which relates the individual activities together by means of a network, which we now discuss.

Critical Path Network

The first step in detailed project planning is to define every task necessary for the completion of the project, along with its duration and

FIGURE 6–2
Work Breakdown Structure

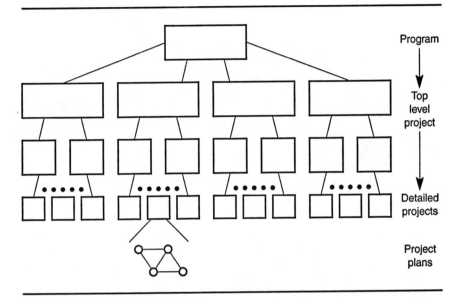

resource requirements. This can be difficult but nonetheless does more to guarantee a successful conclusion than any subsequent act.

There are always many dependencies between tasks, and understanding these dependencies is a crucial element of project control. A very useful tool in identifying the dependencies is the critical path network. There are two types; "activity on arrow" and "activity on node"; we will deal with the latter though the choice between the two is finely balanced. The various tasks are set down, and the conditions between them are drawn in. The most common condition is that one task cannot begin until another is finished, though other conditions are that a task cannot begin until another has begun or a task cannot finish until another has finished. Once the network is complete, it is then possible to define a "critical path."

The critical path is the sequence of tasks that determines the minimum time within which the project can be completed. Any delay on the critical path will cause a delay to the project. A delay elsewhere will not cause a delay in the project until it reaches a certain level. This level is called the "slack" or "float" in an activity.

Once the network has been defined, resources can be scheduled and a series of control documents produced; for example, bar charts for project monitoring.

Parameters to Monitor

Once the critical path of a project plan has been defined, the next stage is to summarize the:

- Actual resource consumption.
- Completion dates of activities.
- Major milestones, which will show if the project is on schedule.

The last item is the key to monitoring the project. Significant steps in the project are identified, and these can then be used for central monitoring of the overall progress of the project. For the Step 3 projects, the plans are for the benefit of the relevant task force; for the Step 4 projects, the plans are used by the manager of the appropriate activity center.

Finally, there is a need to recast the corporate financial budgets and plans to account for the effects of implementing the proposed plans.

Monitoring Function

The form of project monitoring selected can vary. As a minimum, a small monitoring authority can be created, which holds copies of the project plans for each action and the recast of financial targets. The function then simply monitors the progress and, when it is slipping, notifies the chief executive of the problem. Full responsibility for enacting the plans rests either with the task forces (for Step 3 changes) or with the line management structure (for Step 4 changes). This has the advantage of minimizing the disturbance to the normal reporting relations; however, if progress is slow, the monitoring authority cannot act directly to remedy this.

The alternative is to set up a monitoring authority with executive power, effectively a chief executive's department, which can intervene where progress is not being made. This will have the effect of enhancing the ability of the company to force through change but at the expense of potentially disrupting the normal operation of the business. The choice between the two will depend on the urgency for change.

Change Management

So far the discussion of change has concentrated on the "hard" side of project management, namely the identification of activities and their dependencies, establishing critical path networks and so forth. There is also a "soft" side, which can be equally important. We highlight here the main issues to be tackled in creating change in organizations.

First, the "vision thing," as President Bush memorably called it, is crucial. There must be a simple, clear vision so that staff can see a guiding purpose for the change which is occurring. It may be to beat a competitor; one Japanese car company reputedly had as their corporate goal to "kill Porsche," and interestingly their cars resemble those of their named rival. Alternatively, the vision is expressed as a set of values; this is particularly the case with the younger, more dynamic industries where the management and staff share a vision of creating a unique type of company. Whatever the form of the vision, it can be useful to describe it in pictures as well as words, as pictures tend to be far more memorable than words alone.

Second, the simple vision needs to be supported by goals and clear objectives, which in turn cascade down into strategies for achievement, plans, and finally tasks.

Third, a large emphasis needs to be placed on communication. This would appear to be simple to achieve, though it is surprising how often there is utter failure! Good communication can take many forms:

- *The memorandum.* This is the least imaginative and is often used with a pompous introduction: It has come to my attention or To whom it may concern; it is a dry and one-way form of communication, which is unlikely to carry conviction; however, it is better than nothing.
- *The pep talk.* This at least gives the speaker a chance to express the message in a form best suited to the audience and to gauge the audience response. If the speaker is considered trustworthy, the message will also carry some conviction. Nonetheless, these events are usually treated with some cynicism by staff.
- *The pow-wow.* Here there is genuine two-way communication. Staff are invited to speak or even own the event. The higher the sense of ownership and openness, the more effective the event will be. These events do however place demands on the managers; they will have to deal with staff on a first among equals basis, while not falling back on rank.

These methods can be supplemented, if the money is available, by communication programs, newsletters, and social events; all help build relationships and a common understanding. When studies are made of how information is passed within organizations, it emerges that relatively little is passed through the formal channels. Most information is exchanged in informal ways, perhaps in a corridor or, more congenially, in a dining room or canteen. The midday meal provides an excellent opportunity for communication; the significance of rank tends to decline, and comments can be exchanged more freely.

Fourth, there is involvement which goes a step further than communication. Here the staff are given the opportunity to influence their future. Not only will they have a far higher sense of ownership of the plans, but also the plans are likely to be improved. Despite the efforts of the project team to canvass as wide an opinion as possible in creating the proposed plans, there will still be opportunities for improvement. This is where the real payoffs of good change management occur, where staff realize that all is not a sham and that their views are being taken into account.

Finally, there is the issue of cultural change. It is usually the case that some cultural change is required. It is far easier to bring about if staff are being treated in a way that assumes that it already has occurred. For example, if there is a reluctance to take initiative, this can only be remedied by allowing initiatives to be recognized and encouraged. We later discuss the topic of organizational culture in detail.

Training

The last word on change management should be on training. The most successful motivation program will achieve nothing if the staff are simply unable to function in their new roles.

When realistic estimates are made for training to bring about change, they can be surprisingly high. For example, a rule of thumb for implementing a Manufacturing Resource Planning system is that equal amounts of money should be set aside for the hardware, the software, the outside consultancy, and the training. Any implementation plan without an adequate sum for the last item will fail.

ORGANIZATIONAL CULTURE

Context

In the previous steps of the program, we have touched upon the organizational and informational aspects of controlling companies. We discussed the different options for the business—functional or process methods—and considered various measures of organizational efficiency. The responsibility for key parameters within a process has also been considered.

There is no doubt that having a sensible internal structure—which is efficient, is orientated towards satisfying customers, and provides clear responsibility for important decisions—is useful. However, it is only the lesser part of the task of building an effective corporation. Most people can recall examples of outstanding performance being delivered despite corporate structures, simply because the managers and staff worked well. Alternatively, the most sensible corporate structure cannot compensate for a poor internal culture.

We now consider the internal culture of organizations, starting with a review of the ways in which organizations have been considered in the past.

Rational Organizational Theory

The earliest organizational theory is now termed the "Rational school" and the foundation was laid in *The Principles of Scientific Management* (Taylor, 1911). An engineer by training, he adopted a very mechanistic view of the organization. He advocated a very close definition of the tasks to be carried out, so as to separate out the intellectual discretion from the execution of the work. In this way, the operator's task was to be purely mechanistic. The manager's task was also defined by sets of rules and guidelines, so as to identify the best way of operating the company.

Although Taylor's views have become unpopular, the underlying assumptions are still dominant. In gaining control over a situation, most managers will automatically define the tasks to be carried out, allocate responsibility, set up reporting lines, and create monitoring mechanisms. They will have created an organizational machine. This approach has the advantage that it ensures coordination and avoids dependence on particular individuals, but it can deny the opportunity for the individual to make a personal contribution, which may be valuable.

The Rational approach was developed further in *Economy and Society* (Weber, 1947), in which the author expounded on the advantages of bureaucracy. He identified three systems of authority; the rational/legal, the traditional, and the charismatic; of these he considered the first method to be by far the most efficient and the keystone of the success of modern societies. The embodiment of the rational/legal system is bureaucracy, which he saw as thoroughly beneficial, particularly in the way it separated the post from the individual who occupied it for a transitory period, since this detachment allowed decisions to be made within rational rules unhindered by human frailty.

Although bureaucracy is now a detractive term, most people still expect managers and administrators to operate in a way that is bureaucratic in many respects. A manager is expected to avoid personal prejudices and make a decision according to an accepted approach; people look for consistency in a way actions are taken, even if the staff in the posts change.

In summary therefore, we see a paradox surrounding the rational theories. Their limitations are recognized, but they still form the basis for most management behavior.

Human Relations Organizational Theory

Staff are not simply rational creatures motivated by economic gain; their behavior is also governed by their social and psychological needs. Few would deny this; for the manager, however, the alternative approach offers little practical guidance, apart from "Don't forget they are people."

In doing so, and recognizing there are influences on staff behavior other than the purely economic, there are two aspects which need to be considered: individual motivation and the effect of groups.

The best-known analysis of individual needs is the hierarchy given in *A Theory of Human Motivation* (Maslow, 1943). However, the concept of a hierarchy—consisting of physiological needs, a sense of security, social needs, the need for esteem, and finally self-actualization—has been challenged. There are many examples where individuals place the need for esteem over the need for socializing, or even the need for self-actualization over the need for security.

An alternative classification of human needs was provided in *The Achieving Society* (McClelland, 1961). Here, three basic needs were identified: power, achievement, and affiliation. This is highly applicable to the workplace. When working with a group of people, it can be useful to draw a triangle with the three parameters at the vertices and place individuals within the triangle according to the balance of their needs; different balances will lead to a given change being viewed quite differently.

Finally, this balance of needs will depend on the age of an individual. Various studies (typically of men) have sought to classify the different stages of adult life and their different priorities, generally noting a move from the need to strive and prove oneself in the twenties, to become established in the thirties, to acquire authority in the forties, and to reassess thereafter. A particular organizational change will be received differently by those in different stages of development.

The difficulty of accommodating this diversity of noneconomic needs of individuals is perhaps the reason many managers resort to purely economic means of motivation. However, there is one occasion when economic incentives cannot be solely relied upon: This is when teams are being formed. Teams will be of central importance to the change process; not only are the task forces required to function effectively as teams, but staff may well be put together into new groupings, either on a permanent basis or to develop particular changes further.

This was examined in *Team Roles at Work* (Belbin, 1993) where nine team roles were identified: the Chairman, the Company Worker, the Completer/Finisher, the Monitor/Evaluator, the "Plant" (an ideas man), the Resource Investigator, the Shaper, the Specialist, and the Team Worker. Although some are glamorous, such as the "Plant" and some are not, such as the conservative Company Worker, the conclusion was that for a team to work well, it had to be balanced; in particular it was found that teams with two or more "Plants" fared no better than teams with none. In forming teams, where there is a choice of members, it is useful to consider whether all the necessary roles are being fulfilled in some way.

Furthermore, teams can have a tendency to assume an identity of their own which can override that of their members. Sometimes, this can be beneficial, and managers can seek to encourage it, by arranging social events or having special clothes produced for members to enhance the group identity. The only danger is that this group identity can then obscure individual judgment, so independent assessment of the team becomes essential.

Finally, it is worth bearing in mind that nearly all the staff who come to work will have a private life that probably will not be passive. The staff could be running sports teams, organizing political parties, or raising funds for charity. All this requires initiative and competence, which are qualities that are available to the employer. While this may sound simple enough, it is the area of interpersonal skills which seems to represent the chief area of weakness in many managers. Managers usually rise to their post through an ability to master the technical side of the job and are often very task-orientated. When it comes to managing staff, however, they often apply this task-orientated "product" approach (as opposed to process-orientated "people" approach), which can antagonize and demotivate their staff. The distinction between product and people approaches to management was made in *The Managerial Grid* (Blake and Mouton, 1964), where they also advocated a "team" approach to gain the best of both approaches.

Building Change Management Teams

We have already touched on how teams operate when discussing human relations organizational theory and how teams can be analyzed using Belbin's nine defined roles. We now consider the use of teams in the change management process. The prime teams will be the task forces set up as part of this program, though the need will arise for other teams to be created on an ad hoc basis; for example, to tackle a particular quality problem.

The virtues of teamwork are now seldom questioned: The need for teamwork is often preached by those who conspicuously fail to practice it, and any manager stuck for ideas can safely enthuse on the benefits of teams and how they represent the way forward. Before swimming with the tide, it is worthwhile to answer a few basic questions on the topic:

- *Why is a team needed?* There are two main reasons for forming a team:

    Complexity. Simple tasks are within the capabilities of an individual; larger tasks are not within the capabilities of an individual, but nonetheless the decision making can be concentrated at a single point. As the task expands, however, decision making, as well as execution, must be shared between many, and a team is needed.

    Consensus. If several people are to be affected by a change, involving them in the change process will encourage the change to be accepted.

    A team should never be created for its own sake; compared to individuals, they are usually slower and less accountable.

- *Does the corporate culture permit a team to form?* For teams to operate, there have to exist certain qualities, most notably openness and an ability to trust others. These qualities are rarely present throughout any organization but it is possible to create islands of teamwork. For example, the designers may be able to function as a team, while the members of the main board are out for themselves. For this to be feasible, however, an area has to be self-contained and communication funneled through a leader who can play by one set of rules in the organization at large and encourage a very different set for those working to him.

- *How is a team built?* The fundamental characteristic of a team is a sense of common purpose. Second, there is a belief by the members that this purpose is best served by working together rather than individually, sacrificing personal gain if necessary. These are necessary but not sufficient conditions for a team to exist. There are many occasions when these conditions hold, but teams do not form. There is also a need for personal relationships, often arising from the "storming, forming, performing" process which gives rise to teams. This can be encouraged by maximizing the need for individuals to work with and depend on each other; a common working area is also a great asset.
- *How should the team operate?* It is wasteful for a team to tackle all their tasks collectively. The most effective approach is for the team to generate the tasks to solve a particular problem and each member to work on a selection of those ideas individually. The eventual outcome is then assessed collectively and further tasks generated, to be worked on individually again. In this way, the advantages of group assessment and ownership can be retained, while allowing parallel working between individual team members.
- *How is a team and its members motivated?* It is essential that the team is rewarded for group, as opposed to individual, performance. Rewards can take many forms. Some are provided externally; for example, financial gains or recognition. Some are internally generated; for example, a sense of worth or usefulness.
- *Does a team need a leader?* In general, teams do not need leaders, but it helps. A leader, if skilled, can help draw out contributions from the more retiring members and move the team forward; where the team must meet standards set externally, the team leader can also be held accountable for performance. This last point is crucial where change is being managed and, in these cases, a team leader must be considered essential. Where a team does not wish to accept an externally appointed leader, one option is for the group to elect its own leader. If the individual enjoys the respect of their colleagues, this can be a very effective solution.

The Environment

While the Rational and Human Relations approaches to controlling and motivating were very different, they had one element in common, namely they treated the company as a closed system. The implication is that the company is in control of its own fate; by designing either procedural or social systems in which its staff operate, it will obtain the desired results.

Other theories stress that the corporation is not self-contained but exists in an environment. The environment is all-important. It is the source of staff, materials, and customers. It will regulate the company either formally through legal means or through informal social norms. It will generate the technologies which affect the company. Therefore, the company must be recognized as an open system.

This is consistent with the modern corporate view that companies need to be outward facing and not introspective. It is also very realistic. There are very few Western companies now that are fortresses, so strong as to dictate to the environment and not vice versa.

Within this open-systems approach, a contingency theory has been developed, in which the design of an organization is viewed as dependent on its own environment. There is no longer a view that a single structure is suitable for all companies. We now discuss some of the influences on corporate structure which the project team may wish to consider.

Design of Organization

The appropriate form of organization was explored in *Designing Organisations A Decision Making Perspective* (Butler, 1991), where the author defined the Principle of Requisite Decision Making Capability as an organization needs to design a structure of the requisite capacity; that is, one sufficiently crisp to minimize decision-making costs and sufficiently fuzzy to achieve adaptability.

The implication is that crisp structures, with clear roles and rules are associated with low decision-making capacity. The effect of rules is to reduce discretion and to mechanize decision-making processes; in effect, the decision will have already been made by the individual who defined the decision-making procedures. This has the great advantage of economy; in the past low-paid clerks could be used to act in critical areas because the procedures were clear cut. Nowadays, the clerks themselves may not be necessary because the processing could either be undertaken by conventional computer systems or artificial intelligence. However, crisp structures are not adaptable and require clearly defined objectives and clearly defined means to satisfy those objectives. They do not function well in ambiguous or complex environments.

Fuzzy structures, which permit greater discretion, have a higher decision-making capacity. Decision making tends to be more interactive and collective, and the process can tolerate ambiguity in both objectives and the means of achieving them. There are costs associated with this, however.

Butler also makes the point that the culture within the company is dependent on the balance between crispness and fuzziness. Crisp structures tend to encourage only a narrow range of ideas and opinions, are very efficiency-orientated, and hold individuals responsible for shortcomings. On the other hand, fuzzy structures permit a far broader range of differing opinion, are more concerned with the appropriateness of policies, and are mutually supportive. These differences are often apparent in moving from the production facility of a company, with its very crisp structures, to its corporate strategy unit, with its emphasis on fuzzy decision making.

Empowerment and Information Technology

We are now in a position to consider the implications of empowerment and the major impact information technology has in this area. Following the Principle of Requisite Decision Making Capability, the aim is to design as crisp a structure as is feasible given the ambiguity, complexity, and uncertainty of the environment in which a particular activity or process must operate. This, of course, is following the Rational school of organizational design, but accepting that there will be many cases where the fully rational approach to decision making is not possible; in these cases a decision-making approach which can accommodate imprecision becomes necessary.

The effect of the five-step program itself should be to increase the overall level of crispness and rational decision making that is possible within the company because the level of information and understanding of the company and its processes will be far higher than when the program started.

Where crispness is possible then information technology is applied to automate the tasks; as indicated earlier, this can now be carried out to a far greater degree than previously. There is now relatively little need for staff to carry out repetitious clerical or manual tasks. The remaining posts will therefore have a degree of fuzziness associated with them, which is currently beyond the ability of technology to automate. These are then filled with staff who all have some degree of decision-making authority. They have, in effect, been empowered. They will remain so until technology advances to automate their decision making, and then they will become redundant.

When these ideas are applied to companies, there is automatically a need for cultural change. As was noted in the previous subsection, the culture in fuzzy structures differs from those in crisp structures. There will continue to be a shift in culture and staff relations away from that proposed by the Rational or Taylorist organization design.

The paradox is that empowerment is not only the antithesis of Taylor's methods, but is the result of Taylor's methods, when all the low decision-making elements of the structure have been automated.

Implications for Management

The emergence of a smaller empowered workforce has serious implications for the management of a company. These are most evident where a traditional company is being forced to adopt new technology in order to survive. While the workforce is changing, the management may not be. If this is the case, problems normally arise. The newer type of worker can soon resent the attitudes of the old guard management, leading to high labor turnover.

Sometimes, the old guard anticipate the problems and refuse to change. Perhaps the most extreme example of this at the national level was in Romania, where the national industrial plan for the 21st century of the old communist government did not have any reference to electronics factories, only steelworks and the like. An advanced workforce would have implied a degree of national cultural change which could not be contemplated by the government. The government fell apart, as will any other corporation where the management chooses not to adapt to the environment because the implications are too dreadful.

The ability of the company to change its management style ultimately rests with the chief executive. Even if a sole voice, the chief executive has the unique ability to initiate change single-handedly. However, if the chief executive does not see the need for change, progress will be difficult since the elements who are reactionary to change will always be able to appeal to the top to maintain the status quo.

Once commitment from the chief executive has been obtained, the next stage is to begin the training and development programs. These should begin with management, though as time progresses they should encompass all the staff. In changing the culture within the company, which is a key part of many Total Quality programs which are discussed at the end of this chapter, training and education will be a significant expenditure. This expenditure should include not only the time of staff, but also the engagement of professional trainers.

The effectiveness of this investment can be monitored through the use of surveys of staff attitudes, to identify where change is being achieved and where attitudes remain an obstacle to change.

PERFORMANCE MEASURES

Past Failure

We have already referred to the adage "What you measure is what you get." Most staff and managers are acutely aware of the few parameters on which they are measured. They are likely to concentrate on appearing good on paper, especially if there is an unsympathetic management style.

For this reason, the choice of performance measures a company chooses is critical. In the past, there has been well-justified criticism of the performance measures which companies have adopted, or been forced to adopt. The main criticisms are:

- *Short-term measures predominate over long-term measures.* This seems to be a national, as opposed to an international, problem. Countries which use the banking system to discipline the efficiency of managers, such as Germany or Japan, seem to be able to take a longer view; those which use the stock market to ensure good corporate performance, such as the United States and the United Kingdom, are forced into short-term decisions. The relative performance of the two systems speaks for itself, and the cause is obvious. In the U.S. and U.K., it would be a foolhardy chief executive who cut dividends to increase inward investment: It would be a case of fattening the goose while simultaneously lowering the price.
- *Proxies predominate over reality.* The real corporate issues—for example, the product leadership over rivals, the delivery reliability, and the level of customer satisfaction—are ignored. In their place, is the language of earnings per share and return on capital; the senior managers, therefore, operate the business one step removed from reality. The irony is that these financial measures are themselves easily manipulated by skilled practitioners and are not a reliable guide. The dangers of the overuse of proxies were highlighted in *Management Rediscovered* (Curtis, 1990).
- *Efficiency measures predominate over effectiveness measures.* While it is sometimes possible to derive measures which show the efficiency with which operations are carried out, the measures neither address the relevance of the activities to the customers of the company, nor consider the quality of the work carried out. This can be a real hazard if efficiency measures are crudely applied; it is relatively easy to appear efficient under simplistic performance measures if the quality and relevance of the output is ignored.
- *Economy measures predominate over efficiency measures.* It is often not possible to measure the efficiency of conversion of input into output. In this situation, the measures simply record the amount of resource expended in particular areas. Most variance analysis of fixed costs is of this form, noting over- or under-expenditure compared to the budget. By this stage in the five-step program, this should be less of an issue, because there will at least be an appreciation of the relationship between the input of resource and the output of activities.
- *Functional measures predominate over customer-related measures.* Senior managers frame measures for their juniors which are orientated around the functional performance of their department, as opposed to meeting the needs of customers.

The classic cases of inappropriate performance measures come to a spectacular climax in the manufacturing sector. The most common case is where the factory manager is given a *short-term measure* and a *financial proxy* to follow, say, overhead recovery. Recovery of overhead requires sheer throughput, without regard to whether the operations are *effective* in meeting the needs of customers. While the efficiency of the manual labor and the raw material utilization will have been measured, the same cannot be said for the significant support functions, where the only tracking is of the *economy* of support expenditure. The manufacturing managers are likely to insist on *functional measures* such as high utilization of labor and machinery from their subordinates to deliver the throughput, with the result that batch sizes will be extended and the production orders "cherry-picked" for those most likely to provide good functional performance.

The net result is that the manufacturing operation will be pursuing an agenda which will no doubt result in good overhead recovery. What the customer thinks of it all is a different matter.

Designing New Performance Measures

We have outlined the hazards of poor performance measures. More constructively, there is a need to design better ones. The basic information needed to do this has already been acquired by the project team.

The critical success factors have been identified, and these have been translated into specific, measurable requirements. Given an understanding of the external performance parameters and of the process which delivers this performance, one set of internal performance measures becomes immediately apparent. The internal measures for each activity in the process can simply be the external parameters broken down into several parts. The simplest example to visualize, shown in Figure 6–3, is lead time. If lead time is an important factor and the delivery process is linear, it is straightforward to stipulate the minimum waiting times and lead times necessary to meet the customers' requirements. In practice, there may be unforeseen iterations and delays; while these make a simple sequential model unsuitable for predictive purposes, it does not negate the use of lead time as a performance measure. Whatever the internal problems with meeting a given lead time, if lead time is a customer requirement then it remains a relevant performance measure for each activity in the supply chain.

The concept of process measures can also be applied to cost and quality. The costing of the activities within a process is particularly useful. As noted above, many performance measures only reflect resource consumption, without addressing the efficiency of conversion. If the activity costs can be correlated with the existing level of activity, it is possible to use the activity costs as a performance measure. The understanding of the current levels of an activity is also of use in setting budgets, and lies behind the principle of activity-based budgeting.

In measuring quality within a process, it is crucial to identify the source of a problem and measure the incidence of faults and their cost, rather than measuring the effects at a point which may be far removed from where the problem occurred.

FIGURE 6–3
Process Performance Measures

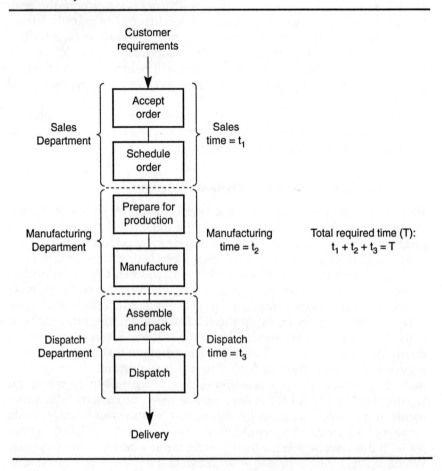

Not all performance measures will be process measures where an external measure for a process has been disaggregated into components for each activity. There will also be measures that relate to the critical success factors. For example, a technological company may need to acquire and retain first-class research staff. This does not depend on a single process, but nonetheless measurement is important and might include the proportion of graduates with first-class degrees recruited, the proportion of job offers declined, and the average employment period. Alternatively, for many companies market share is important, not least because studies show that high margins and return on capital are only achieved by those with significant market share; although it does not depend on a single process, market share also needs to be measured.

The measures will also have to reflect how the company is meeting the needs of its owners. The measures used to assess this have already been considered in Step 1, External Review. The owners are likely to be interested in the value of their asset. The two main influences are the level of earnings and the level of dividends. The level of earnings influences the share price through the price earnings ratio, which in turn depends on the level of perceived risk to the earnings. The level of dividends is particularly relevant to minority shareholders, and the share price can be valued as the dividend level divided by the rate of return less the dividend growth rate. The rate of return associated with the share is dependent on the risk attached to the dividends and the prevailing level of interest rates. While it is incontestable that companies need to make a profit and to pay dividends, there remains a tension between short-term and long-term performance; it is possible to increase dividends, and sometimes earnings, in the short term by lowering inward investment but at the expense of long-term performance.

Another very common measure is "return on capital employed" (ROCE), popular with divisionalized companies because of the ability it offers to compare alternative uses of capital and its pivotal role in much of the theory of financial management. The problem with ROCE as a performance measure is that it discourages capital investment by both lowering the numerator and increasing the denominator of the measure. Whatever its theoretical attractions, if it is applied to companies which are undercapitalized, as many U.S. and U.K. companies are, and it discourages additional investment, it is not a particularly good performance measure. An alternative is residual income, which deducts a capital charge from the earnings of the company; this has the advantage of encouraging all investments whose earnings exceed their finance charges.

A Hierarchy of Measures

There is a need for a hierarchy of measures. Even if all the measures originate from a consideration of the critical success factors, some of them are appropriate to the top level of the organization, others to the middle managers and others to supervisors and junior staff.

The three levels relate to:

- *Strategic direction.* In the private sector, such measures may include market share, customer satisfaction, key staff retention, earnings, and dividends. In the public sector, it will be necessary to measure how the organization is meeting its basic objectives. In both cases, the purpose of the measures is to indicate to the senior management the areas in which the company is succeeding or failing.

- *Processes.* These measures are used by middle management to indicate the degree to which customers or other stakeholders are being satisfied or disappointed, on a day-by-day basis. The process measures indicating cost, timeliness, and quality are all relevant here.
- *Activities.* These measures are used by junior managers who may lack the opportunity to judge how their performance affects the process as a whole. Concentrating instead on the internal operations of the company, the managers require measures of the effectiveness, efficiency, and economy of the activities they control. Measures here may include defect detailed costs, cycle, and queuing times.

The challenge is to ensure that:

- There are no gaps in the performance measure framework, whereby higher level measures are not supported by measures at a lower level. If this happens, the junior managers may not be working towards a higher level aim.
- The measures in use at the different levels remain consistent. If this is not the case, managers will be pulling in different directions.

The last point is difficult to achieve. We now discuss how there is often a natural tension between the performance measures used in different departments.

Tension between Different Measures

In the absence of a process-based organizational structure, the different functions of the company will usually be pulling in opposite directions. To illustrate, in the finance sector, there will be a tension between:

- The marketing of lending services, where the emphasis will be on simplifying the procedures for loans to be granted and widening the lending base.
- The management of credit risk, with the emphasis on thorough examination of a borrower and the exclusion of those who present a bad risk.

In the manufacturing sector, there will usually be a tension between:

- Sales and marketing, which will generally be seeking maximum availability of product, flexibility of distribution, and variety of design. Providing these will increase the costs of inventory holding, distribution, and manufacturing, respectively.
- Manufacturing and distribution, which seek stability of schedule and low variety, coupled with high volume to provide the advantages of long batches with minimal setup times and substantial inventory which acts as a buffer against uncertainty. This will tend to lower the flexibility offered to customers.

FIGURE 6-4
Performance Measure Compromise

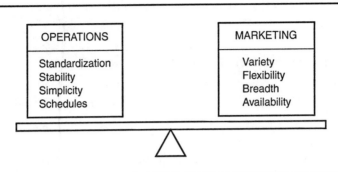

The compromises required are illustrated in Figure 6-4, and are a feature of a functional organization, where managers are concerned with only part of the overall process. If both a functional structure and the functional performance measures are retained, the resulting tension needs to be recognized. Once this is done, any differences can be actively managed at the top level within the company.

MANAGEMENT INFORMATION SYSTEMS

Maintaining Program Information

The five-step program itself has been highly information intensive; deriving the information necessary to bring the organization under control will have been a significant part of the workload of the project team. It is now necessary to make arrangements for the routine collection of data to provide the enhanced management information after the project has concluded. Implementation of this will be the responsibility of the information systems task force.

There are two possible ways to achieve this:

- Automate the data collection for the calculation of activity costs by streamlining the processes which collect the information from the ledger and other systems before transferring it into the database application, perhaps using a client/server architecture.
- Modify the main information systems, to include the enhanced functionality.

The first option is easier to achieve and allows greater flexibility in changing the system in the future and is, therefore, often preferred. The second option may provide for a more efficient system in the long run if the information requirements are unlikely to change.

We now discuss the issues to be considered in maintaining the corporate systems themselves.

System Structure and Output

The structure of the systems needs to match the structure of the business, which by now has been well researched. The team will have defined:

- The major business segments, most notably products and customer groups.
- The major activity centers, which themselves may be divided geographically.
- The major processes and their component activities.

This division of the business developed during the five-step program should be used for the main management information systems.

The output from the systems necessary for decision support were recorded during Step 2, Activity Analysis, and proposals to change the systems to meet these requirements have already been encapsulated in the project plans for developing the information systems. The systems will be used for planning, budgeting, and monitoring, which are of course crucial to the longer-term control of the company. We now discuss these in more detail.

Planning Systems

The ability to plan and forecast is one of the most basic business disciplines. It is the difference between having to react to daily events and being prepared. Most difficulties can be overcome given enough notice; in the rare cases where this is not possible, then at least an exit from an untenable situation, while minimizing losses, can be made.

It is a relatively mature field, indeed some would say its heyday is now past. In the 60s and 70s, corporate planning was highly developed: Large central staffs would produce analyses of alternative scenarios, and strategic investment and divestment would be made on their basis. This form of planning has gone into decline along with the companies that performed it. It was noticed that companies which thrived were those who directed their energies into being good at what they did.

Nonetheless, a more focused form of planning is still necessary. It begins with the strategic planning, producing on an ongoing basis the type of information used in Step 1, External Review. This does not require a large staff; instead, it requires the senior executives to devote some of their time away from the short-term issues. For this reason, it is best if the long-term strategic planning is kept distinct in time and

Management Information Systems

process from the detailed planning. Consequently, the strategic planning process usually does not have an immediate impact on the management accounting systems.

However, once the strategic planning is complete, it is necessary to ensure that it is consistent with detailed planning. The time horizon for the latter varies, though two to three years is typical. There is a choice whether to have a new plan issued annually or adopt a rolling forecast, whereby after each period, a quarter of a year say, a new period is added to the end of the plan. A rolling plan is undoubtedly the more developed planning method, but there is a cost associated with it. The detailed planning is best conducted within the framework used for the other management information; it should use the same classification.

Sometimes, there is a distinction between the financial plan for the forthcoming year and the annual budget, which is the main control mechanism of the company. These usually arise out of timing differences; there is no fundamental reason why the two plans should differ, given they are covering the same topic and time horizon. We now discuss the budgeting procedure itself.

Budgeting

We finally arrive at the procedure most people associate with administrative control. As often performed, it has been seen as irrelevant to the directing of the overhead activities towards adding value to the business. Nonetheless, it is certainly still relevant for the short-term control of organizations. Given that this topic is so well covered in other management texts, we will concentrate here on the more recent developments in the area.

The quest in budgeting has to be to relate the funds allocated to a department to the quantity of work carried out and the relevance of the work to the corporate objectives. "Zero-based budgeting" sought to overcome the setting of budgets on a historical basis, by a detailed bottom-up reexamination of the needs for each activity; this was intended to replace a more subjective top-down approach, where judgments were made on the relative importance of areas of the business and funds allocated accordingly.

This five-step program has also laid the foundation for a rational setting of budgets. The basic activities within each activity center have been identified and a view obtained of whether costs are genuinely fixed, proportional to volume, or proportional to transactions. This is the basic information needed to conduct an activity-based budgeting exercise. This is related to variable budgeting, which is well established; activity-based budgeting is simply the extension of variable budgeting to encompass many activity drivers as opposed to a single variable.

The key to activity-based budgeting is to ensure consistency between the financial plans and the various operating plans which deal with the physical side of the business, and the assumptions made on the throughput of work and the expected productivity levels. In carrying out activity-based budgeting, it is necessary for the management information systems to integrate the financial and physical projections.

Once the planning process is clear, the data requirements to support planning and forecasting out to the desired horizons will become apparent. Usually, more data are required to support the detailed short-term plans and forecasts than those for the longer term.

Monitoring

The monitoring of the company performance inevitably creates heavy demands for input data. It is necessary to:

- Identify costs as they are incurred, classifying them as revenue or capital costs.
- Allocate costs; this allocation will almost certainly be a multiple allocation because:

    The costs must be allocated to the lowest level of detail within the system and then "rolled-up" for summary at a higher level, in several dimensions; for example, to calculate the costs of activity centers, the costs of a product line, and the costs of a customer.

    Indirect costs may require reallocation; for example, telephone costs may have been recorded as a single item within the system, but would require reallocating to different cost centers.

- Allocate income to the various activity centers, products, and customers.
- Record the relevant nonfinancial parameters, both for use as performance measures and for possible use as allocation parameters.

The allocations are not simply a matter of arithmetic; implicit within them are policy decisions; for example, on the costing of spare capacity.

The ledger systems which record much of this information are the hub of the organization's information systems. Nearly all companies will already possess such a system; and if a replacement is being considered, a packaged solution would probably be the natural choice.

The usual reason for contemplating a replacement of the ledgers at all is the lack of flexibility in reporting, especially as regards the multiple roll-up of costs and income so as to provide multiple views on costs and profitability. The prospect of replacing the ledger systems, or even modifying them, is often ruled out on the grounds of cost. In these cases, the use of a PC database application with automated links to the main system has attractions. Where there is a move to replace the ledger systems, those using fourth generation languages and relational database technology are often preferred, because they offer the prospect of retaining flexibility and permitting changes to be made in the future while retaining the initial investment.

TOTAL QUALITY

Introduction

The improvement of quality within both the manufacturing and service sectors has been pursued with zeal in the past decade. Industries have been facing intense competition, much of it on a global level, and higher quality has been seen as one of the key areas of competitive advantage. Much of the competition has come from Japanese companies, whose reputation for quality has not relied on any grand innovation but on the patient application of quality measurement techniques developed in the West and an attitude that quality is paramount.

In the service sector, quality is equally important; the customer comes in contact with the provider of a service and obviously the ability to rectify faults before they affect the customer is much reduced. Not surprisingly, there is an emphasis on preventing errors before they occur.

Over time, opinions on quality have also tended to evolve. They began with a prosaic view, namely good quality is defined as conforming to specifications. Now the view is more philosophical, where quality is defined as the absence of waste, of getting it right first time and being, in short, perfect. These are not contradictory: The first view recognizes that customer requirements are paramount and the company should be aiming to meet them; the second view states that poor quality amounts to waste, which benefits neither the organization nor its customers.

Framework

The main philosophy underpinning the drive to improve quality, Total Quality Management (TQM), espouses the view that a company must identify and serve its customers. There is a great deal of literature on TQM: Rather than duplicate this, we summarize the main points, illustrated in Figure 6–5:

- An identification of the internal and external customers of the corporation and how the activities of the company serve these.
- A definition of the internal functions.
- An estimation of the total cost incurred by poor quality within the organization, namely the "cost of quality."
- The justification of a program to reduce this amount, given its size, which is typically 30 percent of total cost.
- The use of this information to identify quality improvement programs.
- The creation of quality-improvement teams.
- The use of the quality-improvement teams to implement change in the organization as a whole and to monitor performance.
- The setting up of a quality management system.

FIGURE 6-5
Total Quality Management (TQM)

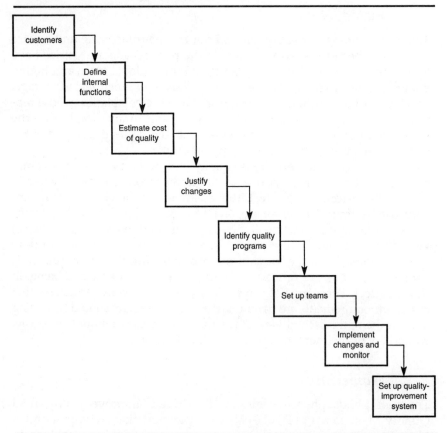

Great emphasis is placed on the management of change within the organization and especially on achieving a shift in attitudes. While this sense of priority is correct, it is also important not to neglect the quantitative aspects of total quality; without good quality costs, not only will the wrong priorities be set for the quality improvements program, but the subsequent monitoring will not be effective.

Relevance of the Program to Total Quality

Building on the five-step program to bring about a total quality culture within the company is straightforward, since the program has been totally compatible with the basic tenets of total quality. The common factors include:

Total Quality

- Attaching a priority to understanding the needs of the customers, whether internal or external. Much of Step 1, External Review was concerned with this point.
- Understanding how the organization currently operates to serve customers and how it fails. This was the emphasis of Step 2, Activity Analysis; in quality programs the contents of this step may be called function analysis.
- Obtaining the staff's ideas for improvement, which was considered in Step 3, Radical Change and Step 4, Focused Change through challenge groups.

Therefore, much of the work already undertaken has a natural place in a quality program. This relation is shown in Figure 6–6. It can be seen that the main item not yet covered is the creation of a quality management system, which we now discuss.

Quality Management System

There are very practical reasons for setting up a quality management system. During the five-step program substantial changes will have been initiated; there is a need to define systematically the new state of affairs. Weaknesses in controls and procedures may well have been evident; these need to be corrected. Even after the period of change, staff will leave, and there is a need for the new staff to be briefed on how the organization actually works, as opposed to relying on the flawed and parochial view that comes from the "sitting next to Nellie" approach to induction.

The quality management system seeks to overcome these problems by setting down how the company is expected to work. An important part of this account is how actions can remain traceable, so there is also an emphasis on defining the minimum level of documentation necessary to ensure that the company is functioning as it should. This need not lead to unnecessary bureaucracy; there is a proper way of carrying out the various activities, which should be defined, and the documentation is necessary to ensure that, at the main decision points, there is a record of who did what and when.

There is also provision made for sampling and internal audit. The use of sampling, or statistical process control, should not be confined to finding fault. On the contrary, the intention is that the operator should monitor the variability of the process, in order to trap problems before they become serious. In addition to this, however, there is a case for a more formal procedure to ensure that the system as a whole is being followed.

FIGURE 6–6
TQM and the Five-step Program

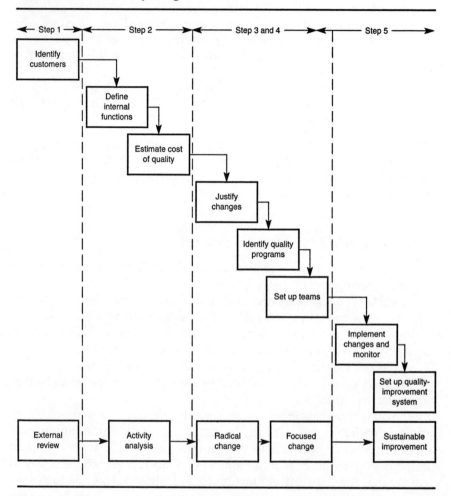

If the company undertakes to install a quality management system, it usually seeks to take credit for the achievement through applying for registration under the ISO9000 scheme. This can be a useful discipline, since it demonstrates both to the management of the company and to its customers that the quality management system conforms to best contemporary practice. It will also avoid the company having to undergo separate assessments from individual customers, as long as the customers accept the independent accreditation.

Having dealt with the procedural aspects of total quality, we now consider the less tangible aspects.

Customer Care

Much of the substance of quality within the company will not be immediately visible to outsiders; instead, the customers will gain many of their impressions in relatively superficial contacts. These contacts, while fleeting, can create lasting impressions and influence the overall perception of the company.

It is worthwhile tracing the various ways a customer will gain first-hand experience of the company and its staff and then training staff to leave a good impression at each of the points of contact. For example, the most prolific form of communication is almost certainly the telephone for most companies; therefore, it is necessary to ensure that all those who will answer the telephone do so promptly and coherently. Written material is usually the next most frequent form of contact. Given modern word-processing techniques, it is relatively simple to produce attractive material.

Finally, there is personal contact. Field sales staff rarely create problems here, since they are selected with personal appearance in mind. However, where visitors visit the company site, it could be useful to walk through their treatment and ask how it feels. One public relations agency took a high-risk approach in selling to the chairman of a company not reputed, at the time, for the courtesy of its staff. The chairman, on visiting the office was treated rudely, left for half an hour without refreshment in a dingy room. As he got up to walk out, the head of the agency appeared and announced that the chairman had just enjoyed a typical encounter with the staff of his own company!

Of all the aspects of overhead control, customer care is one of the most intangible. Apart from observing the basic courtesies, staff attitude is also important. We conclude on this point.

An Attitude of Mind

This last section apart, the tone of this book has been objective and analytical. The last words, however, need to consider attitude. When applying any of the many methods to bring a company under control, we should remember that the support functions are people. With the right spirit—of wanting to please, to achieve, to be exceptional—almost every obstacle can be overcome. A superb infrastructure plus a stolid staff will only add up to a failure.

ORGANIZATIONAL CHANGE CASE STUDY

Background

The final case study contains a useful summary of many of the techniques proposed in this program, in particular the use of market research to guide overhead cost reduction. The preliminary stages involve an activity analysis of the operations and a benchmarking exercise. This is then followed by three programs: The first is concerned with determining the customer requirements, the second reviews the organizational structure, and the third examines the value and efficiency of the operations. The program concludes with a workshop to initiate the change-management process.

The company is a regional distributor of electricity seeking to make a 15 percent reduction in its cost base over a period of five years. The change process has been proceeding well, but the company is now having difficulty meeting its financial targets.

The company covers a wide area which encompasses both rural and urban populations. Its organizational structure is shown in Figure 6–7. The customer service directorates are intended to deal with all aspects of the business which involve communication with the customer, so as to provide "customer focus." This includes fault repair of the low-voltage circuits, arranging for connection to the network, supervision of meter reading, and answering customer queries.

The engineering function is responsible for all technical functions, including the maintenance of the higher-voltage lines. The tasks of the remaining functions are self-evident from their titles.

FIGURE 6–7
Organogram

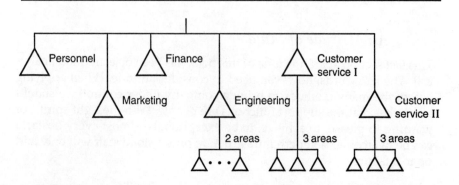

Objectives

The purpose of the exercise is to identify the obstacles to further cost reduction and to identify ways in which this cost reduction can be achieved while minimizing the impact on customer service.

A secondary objective is to ensure that any proposed program for change is consistent with a current business process reengineering program that is underway within the company, to redesign the customer-related processes. The time frames for this program are longer than those which can be accommodated for the cost-reduction exercise; nonetheless, since the two projects will run parallel, they must be consistent.

Activity Analysis

The foundation for all the work is a definition of the activities which take place in the operation of the distribution network. This is carried out through the interview of managers at headquarters and two of the areas; these two areas are then used as a proxy for the remainder. The activity analysis produces about 150 activities in order to obtain the necessary detail; to illustrate, a list of maintenance activities is given in Table 6–1.

The detail is necessary to ensure there is no ambiguity in the definition of headquarters and area activities and that the subsequent benchmarking exercises are valid.

Benchmarking

The benchmarking is carried out both on the core and on the support functions; for the former, the benchmarking gives an indication of whether efficiency improvements are possible, and for the latter whether the provision of a given level of resource is appropriate to the business. Both national and international benchmarks are used.

The national benchmarks show the maintenance activities to have far more staff than expected. The larger number of maintenance staff seems to be the result of the supervisory structure, whereby two workforces are deployed in a particular area, that is a customer service workforce and an engineering workforce.

The international benchmarks are confined to ratio analysis, which indicates that there is scope for reduction in many of the support functions. The variations are accounted for by the differing quality of systems and diverse expectations on the level of employee support that exist between different countries.

Diagnosis

First, the most serious obstacle to meeting the targets is the duplication of physical and supervisory networks which exist within the company. For

TABLE 6–1
Maintenance Activity Library

Code	Activity	Description
RM01	Repairs	Performing repairs & overhaul servicing
RM02	Operating	Performing all high voltage switching
RM03	Condition monitoring	Conditioning monitoring, e.g., oil sampling, infrared scanning
RM04	Routine substation visits	Regular visits to substations — including all readings & checking
RM05	33–132 kv lines	Line patrols & repairs
RM06	Clearing	Performing grass and tree cutting
RM07	Drafting	Maintain a graphic record of the distributor's base
RM08	Tower Maintenance	Tower maintenance, rust removal, foundation repairs
RM09	Building Maintenance	Maintenance to substations
RM10	Transport	Activities associated with transportation of transformers
RM11	Live Line	Live-line training and operating
RM12	Measurement & Control Maintenance	Fault and preventative maintenance
RM13	Transmission & Switching maintenance	Fault and preventative maintenance
RM14	Engineering investigations/monitoring	Investigating power supply problems and network performance
RM15	Maintenance planning	Scheduling maintenance and outages
RM16	Cutoffs	Cutting off customers
RM17	Protection Maintenance	Fault and preventative maintenance
RM18	11–22 kV Line	Line patrols and repairs
RM19	LV Transformer Maintenance	Fault and preventative maintenance

example, the customer service directorates maintain a series of premises. There is a network of depots, largely based in industrial estates, from which the maintenance crews for the low-voltage network operate. Near the depot, but in the commercial and retail area of town, there is a customer service center, where customers can visit. The depots and customer service centers report up to an area office. The three areas then report into a customer service directorate. There are two customer service directorates, one of which has premises outside the corporate headquarters, on a site separate from an area office but only a few hundred yards away.

Furthermore, the engineering directorate has its own physical and supervisory network. There is a need to maintain a substantial higher voltage network, and for this purpose they require their own workforce and depots, many of which are adjacent to the customer service depots but independently managed. Apart from the administrative overhead this entails, there is a further disadvantage in that each repair and maintenance workforce has to be staffed so as to deal with the peak workload in each function, with the result that excess direct labor is being carried.

Second, the company is incurring additional costs in order to provide increased access to the customer. This is the rationale for opening the customer service centers. However, these costs are being incurred without any research into the value the customer places on physical access and the use which is made of it.

Third, many staff both in the area offices and the headquarters functions are engaged in activities which have little relevance to the supply of electricity.

Proposed Plan

There is a need to recognize the difference between area activities and headquarters activities, to avoid duplication. This should also enhance customer service because, at the moment, although a customer service area office is charged with maintaining customer service, in practice much of the resource to achieve this, including maintenance of the higher voltage networks, is outside its control.

Second, there is a need to measure the actual customer requirements, to understand if the additional money being spent on enhancing the customer interface is being spent in the right way or whether it is justified at all.

Finally, there is a need to conduct a value-added and efficiency review of the activities to understand which are essential to the supply of electricity and, if they are needed, their appropriate size.

These three strands of work are shown in Figure 6–8, along with the concluding project planning stage.

FIGURE 6–8
Project Plan

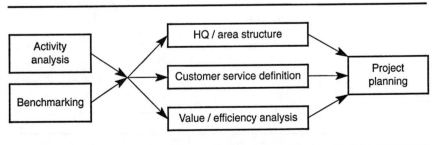

Headquarters/Area Structure

This is a critical part of the process to reduce the operating costs of the business. Each activity needs to be examined to determine whether it is properly an area activity or a headquarters activity. In applying this test there are two considerations:

- Area activities are those which require a knowledge of the locality, be it of customers, the network, or the terrain.
- Headquarters activities are those for which an integrated view is essential, or for which, given an investment in systems, there are economies of scale to be derived from centralization.

Most groups of activities fall into one category or another. Typically, we see area activities including the connection of new customers, the reading of customers' meters, the engineering work associated with connection of customers, and the physical work on the network. Headquarters functions include the billing and collection of debt; the planning of the development of the high-voltage network; and the variety of corporate functions, such as marketing, finance, and personnel.

The clear division of area and headquarters functions ensures the avoidance of duplicated supervisory networks. The area activities are placed under the control of an area manager; given the spans of control this role entails, the number of areas can be reduced from six to four.

An organizational structure which follows these principles is given in Figure 6–9. The decision to centralize the delivery of customer service is discussed below.

FIGURE 6–9
Proposed Organizational Structure

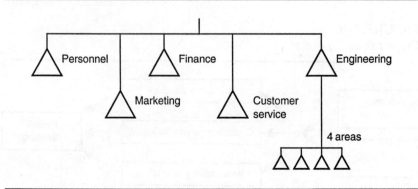

Customer Service Definition

A comprehensive market research program shows the customer service centers are not the best delivery mechanism for customer service. There are two clear market segments:

- First, customers who only use centers to pay bills, which can be easily done through a bank. For general queries, these customers prefer the phone.
- Second, customers who wish to deal face-to-face, but who have difficulty getting to the centers.

The segmentation of the market needs to be recognized and the delivery mechanisms tailored accordingly. It is proposed to close the centers and replace them with:

- A toll-free number for general queries, to address the needs of the first market segment.
- Several mobile centers which visit substantial populations of customers who cannot travel, to address the needs of the second market segment.

In this way, service is enhanced and costs are reduced.

Value-added and Efficiency Analysis

The value-added analysis is carried out in the way described in Step 2, Activity Analysis. The value-added activities comprise both those essential for the operation of the network and those services which the customer service definition shows are valued by the customer. The efficiency study draws on the benchmarking exercise to identify overstaffing in these activities.

Non-value-added activities occur to accommodate a particular policy or way of working. The purpose of the analysis is to establish the true cost behind these corporate policies and conventions. Armed with this information, it is possible to establish the cost of these policies and to justify changing them. As a result, economies are identified in the personnel and finance functions.

Project Planning

The result of this work is condensed into some 20 project plans. Each plan is a proposal for change in the following format:

0. Title
1. Definition
1.1 Description of change

1.2 Benefits of change
1.3 Justification of benefits
1.4 Constraints on change

2.   Quantification
2.1 Affected activities and their costs
2.2 Proposed activity costs
2.3 Summary of savings by activity and department
2.4 Summary of implementation costs by department

3.   Project planning
3.1 List of tasks
3.2 Timing, dependencies and responsibilities
3.3 Project plan with milestones

The purpose of the plans is to gain approval at the management board for the change. Once obtained, the plans are used to build the financial implications of the changes into the budgets and financial plans for the next year.

Relationship to Business Process Engineering

The program is fully compatible with the business process reengineering project being undertaken by the company. The establishment of the customers' requirements is an important part of the project, and the clarification of area and headquarters activities is also an essential step in the design of new processes.

Epilogue

The Three Laws of Holes

Once the five-step program is finished and the change manager embarks on the hazardous path of implementation, he might like to consider The Three Laws of Holes.

Law 1

"He that diggeth a pit will fall into it..."

Source: The Preacher, *Ecclesiastes 10:8*, circa 6th century B.C.

Law 2

"When in a hole, stop digging."

Source: Unknown, mid 20th century, A.D.

Law 3

"Nothing escapes from a black hole except by a quantum jump."

Source: Paraphrased from S. W. Hawking, *Communications in Mathematical Physics*, Volume 43, page 199, 1975 A.D.

While it is clear that the science of holes has made great advances over the millennia, the bad news is that:

- Quantum mechanics suggests there is no limit to the number of holes that may be created.
- Astrophysics suggests that the ultimate fate of life is that the universe and everything may be a black hole.

On the latter point, we conclude that it is better to travel hopefully than to arrive.

References

Belbin, M. *Team Roles at Work*. London: Butterworth-Heinemann, 1993.

Berliner, C. and J. A. Brimson. *Cost Management for Today's Advanced Manufacturing*. Boston: Harvard Business School Press, 1988.

Blake, R. R. and J. S. Moutan, *The Managerial Grid: Key Orientations for Achieving Production Through People*. Houston: Gulf, 1964.

Booth R. "Cost Leadership and Activity Analysis." *Management Accounting*, June 1992.

Brimson, J. *Activity Accounting*. New York: Wiley, 1991.

Butler, R. *Designing Organisations*. London: Routledge, 1991.

Cooper, R. and R. Kaplan. *The Design of Cost Management Systems: Text Cases and Readings*. Englewood Cliffs, NJ: Prentice Hall.

Curtis, D. *Management Rediscovered*. Homewood IL: Dow Jones-Irwin, 1990.

Curtis, W.; M. I. Kellner; and J. Over. "Process Modeling." *Communications of the ACM*, Vol. 35, no. 9 (September 1992).

Ferror, H.; D. Dobler; and K. Killen. *The Purchasing Handbook*. New York: McGraw Hill, 1993.

Fradette, M. J.; S. Nelson; and L. C. Steele. "Cost Accounting Overhaul." *Corporate Controller*, Nov–Dec. 1988.

Hauser, J. and D. Clausing. "The House of Quality." *Harvard Business Review*, May–June 1988.

Hickey, G. "Strategic IS/IT Planning" In *IT Strategy for Business*. ed. J. Peppard. London: Pitman, 1993.

Lane, V. P. *Security of Computer Based Information Systems*. London: Macmillan, 1985.

Maslow, A. H. "A Theory of Human Motivation." *Psychological Review 50*, 1943, pp. 370–96.

McLelland, D. C. *The Achieving Society*. Princeton, NJ: Van-Nostrand, 1961.

Miller, J. and T. Vollman. "The Hidden Factory." *Harvard Business Review*, Sept–Oct 1985.

Mintzberg, H. *Power in and Around Organizations*. Englewood Cliffs, NJ: Prentice Hall, 1983.

Morrow, M., ed. *Activity-based Management*. Hemel Hempstead, England: Woodhead Faulkner, 1992.

Peppard, J. "Using IT to Gain Competitive Advantage." In *IT Strategy for Business*. ed. J. Peppard. London: Pitman, 1993.

Pickwell, I. *Value for Money Audit*. London: CCAB Ltd., 1980.

References

Porter, M. *Competitive Strategy*. New York: Free Press, 1980.

Shillinghow, G. "The Concept of Attributable Cost." *Journal of Accounting Research*, Vol 1, no. 1 (Spring 1963).

Taylor, F. *The Principles of Scientific Management*. New York: Harper and Row, 1991.

Weber, M. *Economy and Society*. New York: Bechminster, 1947.

Wheelwright, S. and K. Clark. "Creating Project Plans to Focus Product Development." *Harvard Business Review*, March–April 1992.

Index

A

Absenteeism, 204–5
The Achieving Society (McClelland), 238
Activities, elimination of, 148
Activity Accounting (Brimson), 90
Activity analysis, 18, 85, 203
Activity Based Management (Morrow), 90
Activity centers, 92, 93–94
Activity costs, 106–8
  interview conduct, 108
  introduction, 106
  second interview, 107–8
Activity drivers, 111, 112
Activity map, 103–6
  activity libraries, 104–5
  collation of, 106
  first interview, 104
  interview conduct, 105–6
  introduction, 103
Activity-on-arrow networks; *see* Critical path networks
Activity-on-node networks; *see* Critical path networks
Added value, 30
Appraisal costs; *see* Quality costs
Artificial intelligence, 5
Attributes, 108–12, 151–53
  types of, 109
  use of, 108

B

Behavioral model; *see* Process model
Belbin, M., 239
Benchmarking, 57–65; *see also* Processes
  benefits of, 57–58
  case study, 75–82
  comparison issues, 61–63
  continuous, 65
  practical matters, 63–64

Benchmarking—*Cont.*
  relevance of activity-based costing, 64–65
  selection of comparable organizations, 60–61
  selection of processes, 60
  types, 58–60
Big-band solution, 151
Brainstorming, 142
Brands, managing, 71–72
Budget, 96
Bush, George, 234
Business development; *see* Processes
Business direction, 27–32
  goals, 29
  the mission, 27–29
  objectives, 29–30
  targets, 30–32
  terminology, 27
Business maintenance; *see* Processes
Business segmentation, 37–39
  distribution channels, 38
  market and customers, 37–38
  other types, 39
  principles, 37
  products and services, 39

C

Capital equipment, 212
Capital purchases, 211
Capital resources, 62
Change, pressure for, 2
Channel profitability, 124–25
Clark, K., 194
Clausing, Don, 150
Client/server architectures, 171
Communications, 169–70
Competitive rivalry, 35
Competitive Strategy (Porter), 33
Complexity, 2–3

Index

Computer security, 172–73
The Concept of Attributable Cost (Shillinghaw), 166
Conference calls, 173
Conformance to specification, 43
ConsortiumAdvanced Manufacture-International (CAM-I), 90, 91
Consumables, 101
Controls and procedures, 206, 210
Control structure, 21
Core activities, 189–90
Cost, nature of, 85–87
Cost Accounting Overhaul (Fradette et al), 90
Cost and service levels, 153–56
  changing levels, 154–55
  constant service, 153–54
  introduction, 153
  measurement of, 153
  operation of challenge groups, 155–56
Cost base, 94–103
  adjustments to the source data, 97–99
  capital requirements, 102–3
  period of analysis, 95–96
  scope of, 94–95
  source of information, 96–97
Cost centers, 92–93
Cost drivers, examples of, 111–12
Costing
  activity-based, 90–91
  full-absorption, 87–89
  marginal, 89–90
Cost Leadership and Activity Analysis (Booth), 90
Cost Management for Today's Manufacturing (Berliner & Brimson), 90
Cost objects, 118
Cost of quality, 253
Costs
  consolidation of, 121–24
  tracing, 119–21
Creating Project Plans to Focus Product Development (Wheelwright & Clark), 193
Critical path networks, 114, 232-33
Critical success factors, 39–44
  competitive position, 39–41
  cost factors, 40–41
  quality factors, 42–43

Critical success factors—*Cont.*
  timeliness factors, 41–42
  treatment in different markets, 44
Cross-charges, removing, 97
Customer, profitability, 124
Customer and product profitability, case study, 182–86
Customer development; *see* Processes
Customer requirements, 44–49
  conjoint analysis, 47–49
  identification of customer requirements, 46–47
  introduction, 44–45
Customers, 3, 35
  acquiring, 69–70
  identifying requirements of, 70
  supporting, 70–71
Customer service, 4, 43

D

Databases, 170
Decision points, avoiding unnecessary, 148
Decision support, 174–75
Decomposition methods, 114–16
Deliverables, 24–25
Delivery lead-time, 42
Depreciation, 101
Designing Organizations: A Decision Making Perspective (Butler), 241
Design leadtime, 42
The Design of Cost Management Systems: Text, Cases & Readings (Cooper & Kaplan), 90
Differential cost, 86
Direct costs, 87
Direct labor, 100
Distribution channels, 37
Dividend payment, 30
Domino effect, 163–64
Drivers, 108–12, 151–53
  cost, 152
  types of, 110–11

E

Earnings before interest and tax (EBIT), 102

Earnings per share, 30
Economy, 203–12
  controls and procedures, 210
  monitoring of performance, 210–11
  pay rates, 205–6
  purchase costs, 206–7
  purchasing cycle, 208–10
  purchasing strategy, 207–8
  staff costs, 203–5
  total acquisition cost, 211–12
Economy and Society (Weber), 237
Effectiveness, examination of, 190–94
Efficiency improvements, 195–203
  drivers, 195
  experience curves, 198–202
  introduction, 195
  scale effects, 202–3
  volume effects, 198–202
  workload modeling with linear regression, 197–98
  workload modeling with standard times, 195–97
Ethernet, 170
Experience curves, 198–202
Explanation, 105
External failure costs; *see* Quality costs
External review, 15, 16, 18, 24, 25

F

Facility expenses, 101
Federal Government Productivity Measurement Program, 199
Financial performance, 28–29
Fish-bone diagram, 163
Five-step approach, 12–23
  ancillary structures, 21–22
  business process reengineering, 22–23
  continuous improvement, 13
  controlling overheads, 16–17
  hostile environment, 21
  impetus for change, 20
  outline of steps, 15–16
  the program, 13–15
  program timing, 18–19
  project focus, 12–13
  project team, 19–20
  sequence of steps, 16
  sponsorship, 19

Fixed assets, 102
Fixed costs, 91
Flow-charting, techniques, 114
Focused change, 15, 17, 19, 230
Ford, Henry, 1
Functional model; *see* Process model

G

General ledger, 96
Global competition, 2
Gross domestic product (GDP), 6–7

H

Hauser, John R., 150
The Hidden Factory (Miller & Vollman), 161
Hierarchy of responsibility, 178–79
The House of Quality (Hauser & Clausing), 149
Human resources, 62
  managing, 73–74

I

Implementation, preparing for, 180–82
Indirect costs, 87
Indirect labor, 101
Information
  avoiding unnecessary, 148
  sharing, 152
Informational model; *see* Process model
Information assessment, 125–30
  applications, 129
  collation of results, 129–30
  databases, 128
  introduction, 125
  level of detail, 125–26
  required and available, 127–28
  structure of, 126–27
  technologies, 129
  timing of, 126
Information requirements, 65–74
  available systems and technologies, 74
  business development, 71–73
  business maintenance, 73–74
  customer development, 69–71
  need for, 65

Index

Information requirements—*Cont.*
    order fulfillment, 65–69
Information systems and technologies, 167–76, 219–21
    definition of, 167–75
    objective, 167–68
    selection of projects, 175–76
    tactical planning, 175
Information technology; *see* IT
Infrastructure, maintaining, 74
Innovation rate, 42
Integrated Services Digital Network, 169
Internal analysis, 15, 16, 26
Internal failure costs; *see* Quality costs
Inventory, supervising, 69
Investment targets, 30
Ishikawa diagram; *see* Fish-bone diagram
Issues, 25–27
IT, 35, 127, 143, 177, 199
IT support tools, 130–32
    automatic transfer of data, 131
    need for, 130
    periodic reporting system, 131–32

J

JIT, 159–61
Just in time; *see* JIT

K

Knowledge-based systems, 174

L

The Law of Diminishing Marginal Utility, 45
Lead time, 5
Level of complexity, 62
Life-cycle costing, case study, 132–37
Liquidity targets, 30
London School of Economics, 86
Long-run marginal cost, 86

M

Management information systems, 249–52
    budgeting, 251–52

Management information systems—*Cont.*
    maintaining program information, 249–50
    monitoring, 252
    planning systems, 250–51
    system structure and output, 250
Management Rediscovered (Curtis), 244
Manufacturing Resource Planning, 66–67
    system, 236
Market approach, 212–19
    costs and benefits of, 214–15
    introduction, 212–13
    outsourcing, 217–19
    partnership sourcing, 219
    setting prices, 215–16
    service-level agreements, 216
Markets, 3
    oversupply of, 1–2
Markets and customers, 37
The Material Grid (Blake & Mouton), 239
Materials, 101
    procuring, 68
Memorandum, 235
Monitoring authority, 22
Monitoring mechanisms, installing, 152
MS-DOS operating system, 168
Multiple tracing, 118–19

N

New entrants, 35

O

Open systems interconnection, reference model, 169
Operating systems, 168
Operations, 3
    identifying bottlenecks, 157
    synchronizing, 157
Operations capacity, managing, 67–68
Opportunity cost, 86
Order fulfillment; *see* Processes
Organization, 91–94
    defining the enclosed structure, 92–93
    distribution of activity centers, 93–94
    identifying the boundaries, 91–92
Organizational change, case study, 258–65

Organizational culture, 236–43
  building change management teams, 239–40
  design of organization, 241–42
  empowerment and information technology, 242
  the environment, 240–41
  human relations organizational theory, 237–39
  implications for management, 242–43
  rational organizational theory, 236–37
Organizational efficiency, case study, 222–28
Organizational model; see Process model
Organizational structure, 176–79
Outputs
  high-value, high-cost, 154
  high-value, low-cost, 155
  low-value, high-cost, 155
  low-value, low-cost, 155
Overhead functions, 187

P

Packaging, 43
Parallel back-up, 151
Parallel process, 148
Parallel system, 151
Pay rates, 205–6
The pep talk, 235
Performance, trend in, 197
Performance measures, 243–49
  designing new performance measures, 245–47
  hierarchy of measures, 247–48
  past failure, 243–45
  tension between different measures, 248–49
Performance monitoring, 207, 210–11
PERT charts; see Critical path networks
Policy activities, 189–90
Policy expenditure, controlling, 192–94
Posix specification, 168
The pow-wow, 235
Prevention costs; see Quality costs
Price decreases, 165
Price increases, 165
Principle of Requisite Decision-making Capability, 242

The Principles of Scientific Management (Taylor), 236
Priorities, 140–41
  need for, 140
  setting, 140–41
  summary of, 141
Processes, 49–57; *see also* Benchmarking
  business development, 55–56
  business maintenance, 56–57
  customer development, 54–55
  definition, 49–50
  introduction, 49
  order fulfillment, 52–53
  process identification, 50–52
  summary, 57
Process flows, 147
  combining or separating, 148
Process improvement, 141–51, 165
  assessment, 142–43
  carts and horses, 143–44
  detailed process model, 146
  focusing attention, 145–46
  idea generation, 141–42, 144
  process simplification, 148
  process testing, 149–51
  quality function deployment, 148–49
  string diagrams, 147–48
  types of, 144–45
Process lead-time reduction, 156–61
  cycle time reduction, 156–58
  importance of lead time, 156
  just in time for clerical operations, 159–61
  unnecessary authorization, 158–59
Process model, types of, 113–16
Process Modelling (Curtis, Kellner, and Over), 113
Process quality, 161–64
  calculation of quality costs, 162–63
  fish bones and dominoes, 163–64
  need for information, 161–62
Process structure, 62
Product cost, 86, 166
Product redesign, 165
Products, 3
  developing, 72–73
  planning, 71
Products/services, 37
  support, 43

Index

Product structure, 62
Profit, 30
Profitability targets, 30
Project implementation, 221–22
Project management, 230–36
  and change management, 231–32, 234-36
  critical path network, 232–33
  monitoring function, 234
  obtaining authorization, 230–31
  parameters to monitor, 234
  training, 236
  work breakdown structure, 232
Projects, classification of, 194
Promotion, 43, 165
Prototyping approaches, 171–72
Pull scheduling, 160
Purchasing cycle, 206, 208–10
The Purchasing Handbook (Ferrer, Dobbler, and Killen), 208
Purchasing strategy, 206, 207–8

Q

Quality costs, 162–63
Quality Function Deployment, 43, 149, 153
Quotations leadtime, 42

R

Radical change, 15, 17, 18–19, 36, 230
Rate dependencies, 202
Rational approach, 237
Reliability
  delivery, 43
  of the product, 43
Residual income, 31
Resource costs, apportionment of, 97
Responses, 7–12
  analysis tools, 8–9
  costing and performance systems, 9–10
  cultural change, 10–12
  outsourcing options, 12
  overview, 7–8
Return on capital, 31
Return on capital employed (ROCE), 247

S

Scanners, 174
Security of Computer Based Information Systems (Lane), 172
Segment rationalization, 165–67
  alternatives to, 165
  attributable costs, 166
  dangers of, 165
  procedure, 166–67
Sensitivity analysis, 75
Serial process, 148
Service-level agreement, 215–16
Service structure, 62
Setup time, 160
Sickness, 204–5
Simulation packages, 114
Single tracing, 118–19
Staff turnover, 204
Standardization, 105
Steering group, 21
Strengths/Weaknesses/Opportunities/Threats; *see* SWOT analysis
Strategic IS/IT Planning (Hickey), 127
Strategy, definition of, 175
Strategy development, 32–36
  defining competitive position, 32–34
  impact of information systems and technology, 35
  information systems and technology strategy, 36
Substitute products, 35
Suppliers, 35
Supplies expenses, 101
Support, common, 152
Support activities, 189–90
  value of, 190–91
Support costs, increased, 4
Support response time, 42
Sustainability, 28
Sustainable advantage, 229
Sustainable improvement, 16, 19, 204
SWOT analysis, 34

T

Task forces, 21–22
Taylor, F., 237, 242
Team roles, 238

Team Roles at Work (Belbin), 238
Technology, 5–7
  added-value crisis, 6–7
  impact on organizations, 5
  shortened product life cycles, 6
A Theory of Human Motivation (Maslow), 237–39
Time allocated, 196–97
TokenRing, 170
Total acquisition cost, 207, 211–12
Total quality, 229, 243, 253–257
  attitude of mind, 257
  customer care, 257
  framework, 253–254
  program relevance, 254–55
  quality management system, 255–57
Total quality management (TQM), 159, 253
Tracing factor, 111
Transaction-dependent costs, 91
Transfer of experience, 104–5
Travel and accommodation, 101

U

Unix operating system, 168
Unnecessary movement, avoidance of, 148
Using IS/IT to Gain Competitive Advantage (Peppard), 35
Utility theory, 45

V

Value for money
  audit approach, 188
  challenge groups, 192
Value for Money Audit (Pickwell), 188
Value of the firm, 31
Videoconferencing, 174
Videophones, 174
Visual controls, 160
Voice and image, 173–74
Voice mail, 173
Volume dependencies, 202
Volume-dependent costs, 91
Volume effects, 198–202

W

Waste activities, 189–90
Wasted time, 205
Wheelwright, S., 194
Windows, 168
Working capital charges, 102
Work in progress, measuring, 157
Workload modeling
  with linear regression, 197–98
  with standard times, 195–97

Z

Zero-based budgeting, 251

Thank you for choosing Irwin Professional Publishing (formerly Business One Irwin) for your information needs. If you are part of a corporation, professional association, or government agency, consider our newest option: Custom Publishing. This service helps you create customized books, materials, manuals, and other materials from your organization's resources, select chapters of our books, or both.

Irwin Professional Publishing books are also excellent resources for training/educational programs, premiums, and incentives. For information on volume discounts or Custom Publishing, call 1–800–634–3966.

Other books of interest to you from Irwin Professional Publishing . . .

INNOVATIVE BILLING AND COLLECTION METHODS THAT WORK

Charles B. Larson

Shows accountants how to design and implement a streamlined billing and collection plan that will reduce the probability of late payments, increase revenue flow, and cut back on bureaucracy and paperwork.
ISBN: 1–55623–032–X

EVENT-DRIVEN BUSINESS SOLUTIONS

Today's Revolution in Business and Information Technology

Eric L. Denna, David P. Andros, J. Owen Cherrington, and Anita Sawyer Hollander

Revolutionizes traditional thinking about business functions, by encouraging companies to focus less on processes, and more on defining the impact of every business event.
ISBN: 1–55623–942–4

ACCOUNTING

An International Perspective

Gerhard G. Mueller, Helen Gernon, and Gary Meek

A nontechnical approach of international accounting covering key issues such as similarities and differences in accounting systems around the world, managerial accounting, and optimal forms of reporting.
ISBN: 0–7863–0007–8

MANAGING STRATEGIC AND CAPITAL INVESTMENT DECISIONS

Going Beyond the Numbers to Improve Decision Making

Thomas Klammer

Contains a collection of the ideas and experiences of the members of the work group and is based on several research projects sponsored by the CMS Program as well as providing a summary of the major findings of these research studies.
ISBN: 0–7863–0112–0

IMPLEMENTING ACTIVITY-BASED COST MANAGEMENT
Moving From Analysis to Action
Robert S. Kaplan and Robin Cooper
This research study documents key implementation issues and results, based on real-life examples and case studies of eight companies.
ISBN: 0-86641-206-9

Available at fine bookstores and libraries everywhere.